Evangelical Ecclesiology

Evangelical Ecclesiology

Reality or Illusion?

John G. Stackhouse, Jr., editor

Baker Academic

A Division of Baker Book House Co
Grand Rapids, Michigan 49516

© 2003 by Regent College

Published by Baker Academic
a division of Baker Book House Company
P.O. Box 6287, Grand Rapids, MI 49516-6287
www.bakeracademic.com

Printed in the United States of America

Library of Congress Cataloging-in-Publication Data
Regent College Theology Conference (2002)
    Evangelical ecclesiology : reality or illusion? / John G. Stackhouse, Jr., editor.
        p.   cm.
    Includes bibliographical references and indexes.
    ISBN 0-8010-2653-9 (pbk.)
    1. Church—Congresses. 2. Evangelicalism—Congresses. I. Stackhouse, John Gordon.
    II. Title
    BR1640.R44 2003
    262—dc21   2003052086

Contents

Contributors

Richard Beaton (Ph.D., University of Cambridge) is assistant professor of New Testament studies at Fuller Theological Seminary, Pasadena, California. Among his recent publications are *Isaiah's Christ in Matthew's Gospel*. He attends Church of Our Savior Episcopalian Church.

Kerry L. Dearborn (Ph.D., University of Aberdeen) is associate professor of theology at Seattle Pacific University, Seattle, Washington. She has published several scholarly articles, including "The Crucified Christ as the Motherly God: The Theology of Julian of Norwich," in *The Scottish Journal of Theology*. She is a member of University Presbyterian Church.

Bruce Hindmarsh (D.Phil., University of Oxford) is the James M. Houston Associate Professor of Spiritual Theology at Regent College, Vancouver, Canada. He is the author of *John Newton and the English Evangelical Tradition* and a member of St. John's (Shaughnessy) Anglican Church.

Edith M. Humphrey (Ph.D., McGill University) is associate professor of New Testament studies at Pittsburgh Theological Seminary, Pennsylvania. Among her recent publications are *Joseph and Aseneth* and selected articles in *Wrestling with God*. She attends the Episcopal Church of the Ascension in Oakland, Pennsylvania.

George R. Hunsberger (Ph.D., Princeton Theological Seminary) is professor of congregational mission and dean of the Center for the Continuing Education of the Church at Western Theological Seminary, Holland, Michigan. Among his publications are *Bearing the Witness of the Spirit: Lesslie Newbigin's Theology of Cultural Plurality* and the coauthored *Missional Church: The Sending of the Church in North America*. He is a minister of the Presbyterian Church (U.S.A.) and a member of the Presbytery of Lake Michigan.

Michael Jinkins (Ph.D., University of Aberdeen; D.Min., Austin Presbyterian Theological Seminary) is professor of pastoral theology
at Austin Presbyterian Theological Seminary. He came to the faculty of Austin Seminary after serving for many years as a pastor
in the Presbyterian Church (U.S.A.). His most recent books include *The Church Faces Death: Ecclesiology in a Postmodern Context; Invitation to Theology: A Guide to Study, Conversation, and
Practice;* and *Transformational Ministry: Church Leadership and
the Way of the Cross.* He is editor of *Insights: The Faculty Journal
of Austin Seminary* and associate editor of the *Journal of Religious
Leadership.*

Roger E. Olson (Ph.D., Rice University) is professor of theology at
George W. Truett Theological Seminary of Baylor University,
Waco, Texas. Among his recent publications are *The Trinity* (with
Christopher Hall) and *The Mosaic of Christian Belief: Twenty Cen-
turies of Unity and Diversity.* He attends Calvary Baptist Church.

Howard A. Snyder (Ph.D., University of Notre Dame) is professor of
the history and theology of mission in the E. Stanley Jones School
of World Mission and Evangelism, Asbury Theological Seminary,
Wilmore, Kentucky. His most recent book (with Daniel Runyon)
is *Decoding the Church: Mapping the DNA of Christ's Body.* He is
active in the Wilmore Free Methodist Church.

John G. Stackhouse, Jr. (Ph.D., University of Chicago) is the Sang-
woo Youtong Chee Professor of Theology and Culture at Regent
College, Vancouver, Canada. Among his recent publications are
Church: An Insider's Look at How We Do It and *Evangelical Land-
scapes: Facing Critical Issues of the Day.* He worships at St. Helen's
Anglican Church.

Paul F. M. Zahl (Dr.Theol., University of Tübingen) is dean of (Episcopal) Cathedral Church of the Advent in Birmingham, Alabama.
He has written six books, including *The Protestant Face of Anglicanism* and *A Short Systematic Theology.*

Preface

JOHN G. STACKHOUSE, JR.

When we, the church, are confused about who we are and whose we are, we can become anything and anyone's.

• We can become a goose-stepping, Hitler-saluting abomination, as we were in the middle of the last century in Germany.

• We can become a self-righteous, self-centered, and racist boot on the neck of our prostrate neighbors, as we were in South Africa until the end of apartheid.

• We can become a machete-wielding, genocidal horror, as we were in Rwanda just a few years ago.

• We can become a corpulent, self-important irrelevance, as we are in so much of America today.

• And we can become a sad, shrunken ghost pining for past glory and influence, as we are in Canada, Britain, and most of Europe.

When the church is confused about who it is and whose it is, it can become just another institution, just another collective, just another voluntary society. So we need ecclesiology—the doctrine of the church—to clarify our minds, motivate our hearts, and direct our hands. We need ecclesiology so that we can be who and whose we truly are.

We evangelicals have implied an ecclesiology more than we have articulated one. At least, evangelicals *as evangelicals* have done so, however industrious our theologians have been at working out ecclesiology within denominational traditions. We evangelicals have acted out our convictions about the church more than we have set them out, whether in church planting, parachurch proliferation, cooperative missionary ventures, heresy hunting and schism, liturgical innovation, varieties of pastoral education, the use of mass media, or a hundred other ways.

What we haven't much done is reflect on these evangelical ecclesial realities and try to make some theological sense of them all.

This volume presents fruit harvested from the Regent College Theology Conference of 2002, during which presenters from a variety of theological disciplines and outlooks were asked to consider carefully the very notion of an evangelical ecclesiology: Is there such a thing? Should there be such a thing? Is there an implicit ecclesiology in evangelicalism? Are some denominational ecclesiologies more consonant with evangelicalism than others? Does it even make sense to speak of an "evangelical church," or should we instead simply speak of "evangelical churches"—and interdenominational fellowships, parachurch groups, and individuals?

These individual articles were lightly edited; their idiosyncratic character remains, and no attempt was made to paper over the real tensions, and even contradictions, among them. Where these papers are strong, they offer a range of challenging assertions about the history and current state of evangelical ecclesiology. Where these papers are weak, they indicate something of what remains to be done in this crucial area of theology. This collection does not purport, of course, to offer the full range of evangelical thought: It doesn't offer the full range of thought even of each author! But on balance, this book does provide some helpful glimpses into the variety of ecclesiologies among North American evangelical theologians, glimpses that may provoke others to extend and improve on the work offered here even as, we trust, it informs and encourages church people today.

The reference to "North America" points out one of the most important limitations of this collection: its restriction to just one continent and, indeed, just one language group (albeit the dominant one) of that continent. North America does, to be sure, include a great number of evangelicals so that even a conversation so restricted can directly serve a lot of people. It is also true that the burgeoning evangelical movements elsewhere—from Latin America to Africa to South Asia—have been shaped by North American church patterns and continue in many cases to be influenced by North American leaders. So while we acknowledge that the North American church could profit greatly from an infusion of the vitality the church shows elsewhere and that our theological conversation can only be improved by hearing from theologians from around the world, we offer what we can to our brothers and sisters globally, hoping that they might find something useful in these reflections from our culture.

In convening the conference behind this book, I am glad to acknowledge the contributions of Karen Wuest, sometime conference coordinator at Regent College; Bill Reimer, manager of Regent's bookstore; Gordon Smith, sometime dean and professor of spiritual theology at Regent; Stan Grenz, formerly a colleague here and now at Baylor University; and Robert N. Hosack, editor at Baker Academic. Both Regent College and Baker Academic provided financial and logistical support to both the conference and the emergent book. Elizabeth Powell assisted me at several stages with her characteristic efficiency and grace. And Melinda Van Engen edited the book in her excellent literary ministry of discipline and healing. Throughout this process, in fellowship with these people, I have once again rejoiced to be part of the church.

Part 1
Inspiration from Our Heritage

1

Is Evangelical Ecclesiology an Oxymoron?

A Historical Perspective

Bruce Hindmarsh

When one thinks about evangelicals and what they hold dear, one would be forgiven for not thinking immediately of the church. Indeed, one might even suggest, given the history of schism among evangelicals, that "evangelical ecclesiology" is an oxymoron, like "an honest thief" or "airline food." Toward the end of this essay I will argue from the early history of evangelicalism that there is indeed something profoundly oxymoronic, or at least paradoxical, in the way evangelicals have proclaimed and appreciated the spiritual unity of all those who are truly "born again" while at the same time have so often separated from one another in practice. My main claim, however, is a historical one: Early modern evangelicalism displayed an unprecedented transdenominational and international ecclesial consciousness that was characterized by an unparalleled subordination of church order to evangelical piety. The principle of unity among evangelicals was not

15

typically spoken of as sacramental, nor did it have to do with autho-
rized orders, forms, or rites; the principle by which unity was discerned
was evangelical piety itself. The effects of this have been momentous
and lasting, not only in the enduring significance and expansion of
evangelicalism globally but also in the way in which evangelical ecclesial consciousness was from the outset uniquely bound up with modern conditions that have come to characterize life in so much of the
world today. The main body of this essay, therefore, traces the emergence of evangelicalism as an international and transdenominational
movement under unique political, material, and social conditions in
the seventeenth and eighteenth centuries, and second, expounds the
new understanding of the church evident in the writings of the early
evangelical leaders, using the evangelist George Whitefield as a chief
case study. In other words, I will first describe some unprecedented
conditions and then expound an unprecedented consciousness.[1]

But we should note at the outset that these issues were not faced only
by evangelicals 250 years ago. These same issues surfaced, for example,
in the famous confrontation of John Stott and D. Martyn Lloyd-Jones
at a meeting convened by the Evangelical Alliance in London on October 18, 1966. Lloyd-Jones caused a sensation by asking, "Are we content, as evangelicals, to go on being nothing but an evangelical wing of
a church?" and by making other remarks that were widely perceived to
be a call for evangelicals such as Stott to leave the Anglican Church to
unite visibly with other evangelicals.[2] Roger Steer claims that Lloyd-

---

1. It is true, of course, that in the process of history, every event is unique and unprecedented, on the one hand, and every event finds its genesis in prior influences and causes,
on the other. I do want to concede both these points at the outset of my essay. In particular, I do not mean to imply in any way that evangelicalism appears exceptional as the
apogee of a historical process—the so-called Whig view of history in which historical
events are seen invariably as justifying and culminating in present arrangements. But I
do want to fasten attention on the anomalous character of evangelicalism, which is
something we perhaps no longer appreciate because we do not see it against the situation
from which it emerged.

2. An indication of the decisive importance of this moment in English evangelicalism
is the way in which this confrontation between Stott and Lloyd-Jones is now being contested in the historiography of the event a generation later. For complex and contested
reconstructions of the event and the surrounding issues, see, for example, Timothy Dudley-Smith, *John Stott: A Global Ministry* (Downers Grove, Ill.: InterVarsity, 2001), 65–71;
Iain H. Murray, *David Martyn Lloyd-Jones: The Fight of Faith, 1939–1981* (Edinburgh:
Banner of Truth Trust, 1990), 522–28; Alister McGrath, *To Know and Serve God: A Biog-
raphy of James I. Packer* (London: Hodder & Stoughton, 1997), 125; and Oliver Barclay,
Evangelicalism in Britain, 1935–1995 (Leicester: Inter-Varsity, 1997), 82–84. The text of
Lloyd-Jones's address has been published under the title "Evangelical Unity: An Appeal,"
in D. Martyn Lloyd-Jones, *Knowing the Times: Addresses Delivered on Various Occasions,
1942–1977* (Edinburgh: Banner of Truth Trust, 1989).

Jones was calling for "evangelicals to leave their denominations and form a national Evangelical church."[3] In the aftermath of this debate, a number of evangelicals did indeed leave "mixed denominations," just as Lloyd-Jones took Westminster Chapel out of the Congregational Union. This standoff between Stott and Lloyd-Jones is still regarded as a watershed moment for many evangelicals in Britain today, so much so that Alister McGrath refers elliptically to "the shadow of 1966," Timothy Dudley-Smith describes it as a "defining moment," and David Bebbington claims that "the effects were catastrophic."[4] The irony here, of course, is that it was a call for evangelical *unity* that proved so divisive.

Underlying this debate was the question of whether evangelicalism constitutes the true church and, if so, whether this should be more fully realized in visible, organizational unity. This brings us to the heart of the question this book seeks to address. Is there something like a national or international "evangelical church" or at least a consciousness among evangelicals of "evangelicalism" as something ecclesial? A host of organizations certainly bear witness to evangelicalism as a religious identity that transcends or augments denominational and local ecclesial identity. National associations such as the Evangelical Alliance (1846) in the United Kingdom, the National Association of Evangelicals (1943) in the United States, and the Evangelical Fellowship of Canada (1964) and international associations such as the World Evangelical Fellowship (1951) and the Lausanne Committee for World Evangelization (1974) all point to evangelicalism as a significant bloc in the modern Christian world. But does this transdenominational evangelical identity also translate into a unique ecclesial consciousness?[5]

3. Roger Steer, *Guarding the Holy Fire: The Evangelicalism of John R. W. Stott, J. I. Packer, and Alister McGrath* (Grand Rapids: Baker, 1999), 224. Close reconstruction of the debate and analysis of the text of Lloyd-Jones's address make plain that he did not in fact make an explicit appeal on this occasion for evangelicals to secede from the Church of England and other "mixed churches" to form a united church, but the public comments of Stott on the occasion together with reports in the press and later developments clearly indicate that Lloyd-Jones's remarks were *widely perceived* as a call for immediate secession and visible evangelical union.

4. Dudley-Smith, *John Stott*, 69; and David Bebbington, "Evangelicalism in Its Settings: The British and American Movements since 1940," in *Evangelicalism*, ed. Mark Noll, David Bebbington, and George Rawlyk (New York: Oxford University Press, 1994), 370. See also David Bebbington, *Evangelicalism in Modern Britain* (London: Unwin Hyman, 1989), 267–68.

5. It is possible to see evangelicalism simply as an interesting sociological but non-ecclesial form of religion. It is a "movement" and as such is analogous to other political and social movements. In Roger Olson's essay, for example, he writes of evangelicalism as a movement defined by an ethos, but he resists any notion that this movement constitutes a church. He allows, however, that in this movement, individuals are "bound together by the Spirit of God in community." I wonder if this does not still point to what I

This is an important question for the entire church, since the character of modern evangelicalism as a religious movement is so largely unparalleled. In 1966, Stott and Lloyd-Jones were wrestling with how this movement was to be comprehended in ecclesiological terms, and this is a question that the very nature of evangelicalism invites. From the beginning of the movement in the eighteenth century, evangelicalism has been transdenominational, international, and public in a way that is unique in Christian history. This raises new, important questions about how we are to understand the church.

The uniqueness of evangelicalism as a movement may be observed if we recall that throughout the long centuries of Christendom, Christians affirmed their belief in one, holy, catholic, and apostolic church but that the visible unity of that church was publicly and decisively contested in the West by the crisis of the reformations of the sixteenth century and the wars of religion of the seventeenth century. Earlier, the division of the church between East and West was dealt with neatly by mutual anathemas in 1054. Radical movements of dissent strained the visible unity of the Catholic Church in the Middle Ages—groups such as the Waldenses first appeared in the twelfth century at Lyons—but these too were dealt with summarily by excommunication and pushed largely underground.

It was with the formation of Reformed, Lutheran, and Anglican churches in sixteenth-century Europe that the unity of the church was most visibly broken, raising acutely the question as to which communion represented the true church of Christ on earth. Notwithstanding the renewed effort to define the church in careful theological terms and the acknowledgment by some that the true church is invisible and known only to God, there was no large, visible, pan-Protestant movement uniting believers in the various churches in the sixteenth century. The Roman Catholic Church and the churches of the magisterial Reformation remained tied to a conception of the territorial church and the confessional state, however else they defined the essence of the church. Again, there were radical movements of dissent from these churches, most notably the Swiss Anabaptists and the Mennonites with their revolutionary reorganization as nonterritorial congregations of professing believers. But though the cellular structure of Anabaptism and its movemental dynamic, outside the nation state and uncoupled from territorial definition, are analogous to modern evangelicalism, Anabaptism was not transdenominational or interdenominational, nor did it achieve anything like the visibility and public presence of the later evangelical movement.

---

am describing as a unique "ecclesial consciousness." This is the question my essay seeks to explore through a reading of the early history of the movement.

Gordon Rupp, a historian and one of the leading figures in Methodism in the twentieth century, recognized the pressing theological questions posed by modern evangelicalism. He identified in the Evangelical Revival "the evident fruit of the Spirit in times and places which make nonsense of the older rigid categories of orthodoxy." He also drew attention to the need for an ecclesiology to make sense of this, arguing that "if . . . there is in this story indeed the record of a work of God, then the full implications of this must be brought to bear in the theology of the Church about its own nature and destiny."[6] Rupp was himself an influential participant in the ecumenical movement, and he wrote this in 1965, the year of the Second Vatican Council, during which the pope and the ecumenical patriarch of the Eastern Orthodox Church nullified the mutual anathemas that had been in force since 1054. Rupp recognized that the appearance of evangelicalism as a historical fact posed a central question that was in his own day being asked by those who were active in the World Council of Churches: How do we account for true believers in other communions, those in whom we recognize the regenerate life of the Spirit of God? The evangelical debates about unity in 1966, symbolized by the confrontation between Stott and Lloyd-Jones, were held against the background of this wider ecumenical movement in the 1960s and addressed the same question. Rupp reminds us, then, that the early history of the Evangelical Revival is of great relevance to these debates.

Ecclesiology after Armageddon: The Political Conditions of Modern Church Life

For the sake of a beguiling clarity, let us assume that the conditions for this sort of evangelical ecclesial consciousness first appeared on October 24, 1648—three and a half centuries ago, give or take a few years. That was the date of the Peace of Westphalia, which ended the savage Thirty Years' War in Europe. And that was the day the ideal of Christendom—one people, under one ruler, observing one religion—died. After the Thirty Years' War, the Holy Roman Empire was divided into roughly three hundred principalities, bishoprics, and free cities, and the great dream of a medieval, Christian kingdom was in tatters. The loss of life during the war had been staggering, and economic decline and plague had taken an additional toll. The morale of Europe had been shattered.

6. Gordon Rupp, "Introductory Essay," in *A History of the Methodist Church in Great Britain*, vol. 1, ed. Rupert Davies and Gordon Rupp (London: Epworth, 1965), xvi.

What was so appalling was that ecclesiology was one of the causes of the war. As Reginald Ward has observed, this war and its aftermath were the closest Europe ever came to confessional Armageddon.[7] How did this situation arise? In the aftermath of the Protestant Reformation, a sort of détente had been achieved in 1555 by the Peace of Augsburg, which allowed princes to determine the religion (Catholic or Protestant) of their own regions and permitted subjects free passage if they wanted to emigrate to a region more sympathetic to their beliefs. In 1618, a group of Protestants from Bohemia broke up a meeting of Catholic rulers in Prague and threw two councilors out a high window. With that aggravation, a war began that gradually drew most of Europe into its circle, pitting Protestant against Catholic, Lutheran against Calvinist, Christian against Christian. There seemed no hope of outright victory and no hope of peace. The ideal of Christendom went up in flames all across Europe. After years of fighting, sheer exhaustion finally led to a negotiated settlement, the Peace of Westphalia in 1648.

The treaties that made up the Westphalia settlement declared that toleration be shown to certain religious minorities, even if members of these groups lived under a ruler who professed differently. In other words, if you were Lutheran but your prince was Catholic, you no longer had to pack your bags and move somewhere else. After the Peace of Westphalia, some churches were even divided in half between Catholics and Protestants or used at different hours by different congregations. The Westphalia settlement did not cover all regions, and the peace it was supposed to secure would be tested at many points. But the settlement was still an apt symbol of the death of Christendom and the beginning of a new world with new ecclesiastical ideals. Moreover, although ancien régime states continued and the ideal of the confessional state and the territorial church persisted in various forms, the tumult and violence of religious war had led to a number of new departures.[8] Not only were there experiments in radical religion both within

7. W. R. Ward, *Christianity under the Ancien Régime, 1648–1789* (Cambridge: Cambridge University Press, 1999), 2–4.

8. The Westphalia settlement was limited in a number of ways, and political tensions certainly continued after 1648. For example, in the Archbishopric of Salzburg, which was outside the Westphalia agreement, religious intolerance resurfaced dramatically when thirty thousand Protestants suddenly found themselves expelled from the region and on the move as religious refugees in 1731–32. Other Protestant minorities in Bohemia, Austria, Hungary, Silesia, and Poland also found themselves without protection under Westphalia. The continued insecurity and religious experimentation of these minorities created an important background for the rise of a pan-Protestant evangelical awakening. See W. R. Ward, *The Protestant Evangelical Awakening* (Cambridge: Cambridge University Press, 1992), 15–36.

and without the established churches, but there were also new constru-als in politics and political philosophy that would have far-ranging im-plications—not least for ecclesiology.

The situation in Britain during the seventeenth century was parallel to the Continent in important ways. Britain also had its war of religion; the English Civil War was in large part a confessional conflict. Through-out the entire interregnum, there were apocalyptic hopes and fears for the church. Ecclesial experimentation was at its height during the Commonwealth and early years of Cromwell's Protectorate. Then came the Restoration of the Monarchy in 1660, the Act of Uniformity in 1662, and the repressive penal legislation of the Clarendon Code—all of which represented an attempt to turn back the clock and restore abso-lute conformity in religious observance. It was too late. Two thousand ministers in the Church of England followed their consciences and left the established church, swelling the ranks of the Nonconformists. Not-withstanding the waves of religious emigration to the New World, reli-gious minorities were now a permanent feature in English society. They could not simply be destroyed or assimilated by state bureau-cracy. After a benign constitutional revolution, the English Parliament finally recognized and embraced this reality in the Act of Toleration of 1689, which secured liberty for trinitarian Protestants outside the Church of England. For the rest of the so-called long eighteenth cen-tury, the English were proud of their constitutional liberty and looked with pity and contempt across the Channel to those papists who still la-bored under the religious tyranny of the ancien régime in France or under the Hapsburgs. In Britain too, then, Christendom died a sort of death in the seventeenth century.

The Peace of Westphalia in 1648 and the Act of Toleration in Britain in 1689 each represented a new political arrangement for religion that can be called modern. The recognition of minority religious rights in these legislative programs was limited and was described paternalisti-cally at the time as "toleration," but we can see the cloud the size of a man's fist on the horizon and call it "pluralism." This was the beginning of the establishment of a state of affairs that is taken for granted in all Western democracies and that provides constitutional guarantees of freedom of religion. These new arrangements were embodied in legis-lative programs and written about in works of political philosophy, such as John Locke's *Letters Concerning Toleration* (1689–93). Again, it should be stressed that this was just a beginning and that religious ten-sions remained. The Peace of Westphalia recognized only Roman Cath-olic, Lutheran, and Reformed churches. The Act of Toleration provided guarantees only for trinitarian Protestants. Many minorities remained outside the protection of these agreements. Even under the advanced liberties of the English constitution, legally tolerated Dissenters still suffered significant political and social disabilities. Yet notwithstanding these limitations, an enormously important sea change had occurred. To come to maturity in John Locke's world of relative constitutional liberty, as the early evangelicals did, was to do ecclesiology under new conditions of possibility.

This history is important for us to appreciate as we examine the relationship between evangelicalism and the church in theological terms, since there is a real danger that we may overlook how profoundly our own attitudes are formed by historical conditions. The authors of the essays in this book originally gathered together in the autumn of 2002 as observant Christians from a variety of church communions to discuss ecclesiological questions in the genial setting of a transdenominational theological college, and we enjoyed both lively debate and a convivial dinner. This taken-for-granted condition of our scholarship is itself the consequence of significant historical events in the early modern period not unrelated to the rise of evangelicalism. During most of church history, this sort of gathering would have been unthinkable. This was, for example, a situation the sixteenth-century Anabaptists could hardly have imagined.

Modern evangelicalism arose in a new world with an appreciation for political liberty and a strong folk memory of religious intolerance, violence, and war in the recent past. And its understanding of the church very much reflected these new conditions. Just as European theology after the Second World War was profoundly chastened by the experience of war and the ineradicable memory of the compromises the church had made with National Socialism, so evangelical ecclesiology in the seventeenth and eighteenth centuries retained a vivid consciousness of an earlier religious holocaust. Thus, John Wesley looked back on the history of religious conflict in the previous century and saw it as a sad confirmation of innate human sinfulness. "There is a . . . horrid reproach to the Christian name, yea, to the name of man, to all reason and humanity," he lamented. "There is war in the world! War between men! War between Christians! I mean, between those that bear the name of Christ, and profess to 'walk as he also walked.'"[9] Wesley deplored this religious violence associated with confessional politics. He urged instead a "catholic spirit," saying, "I ask not therefore of him with whom I would unite in love, 'Are you of my Church?'" Instead, he asked one question only: "Is thine heart right, as my heart is with thy

9. John Wesley, "The Doctrine of Original Sin," in *The Works of the Reverend John Wesley,* vol. 9, ed. Thomas Jackson (1872; reprint, Grand Rapids: Baker, 1984), 221.

heart?"[10] Thus, seventeenth-century warfare and politics offer the first clue that the evangelical attitude toward the church, arising in the aftermath of these momentous events, would be unprecedented. It would be more possible now to conceive of the church as being among all the visible churches and to realize this ideal in public contexts and new forms alongside the formal, institutional church. As Ward argues, there was a "separation of religious from ecclesiastical life," and the religious mood involved "the longing to go behind the present confessional division of Europe into a larger religious unity."[11]

This raises serious questions when we think about the theology of the church today. Did evangelicalism represent a separation of religion from traditional ecclesiastical life? Is there a theology of the church that can explain this enduring phenomenon? Is it still possible to say with Cyprian that "he cannot have God for his Father who has not the church for his mother" or with Augustine that "outside the church there is no salvation"?[12]

Before examining the rise of modern evangelicalism in the revivals and religious movements of the early to mid eighteenth century, we should note briefly three ecclesiastical experiments that emerged from the tumult of the seventeenth century, since they anticipated developments in later evangelical ecclesiology. First, some of the radical sects in England and elsewhere began to require from candidates a personal testimony of their experience of grace and to use this as a standard for admission.[13] Unlike the earlier Anabaptist and separatist churches, these radicals required not just a profession of faith and evidence of moral probity but also testimony of an experience of God's grace that could be expressed in narrative and that allowed other believers to discern the true, mystical body of Christ. When evangelicalism arose in the next century, many of the elements of this radical ecclesiology reemerged. The idea that the true church consists of those who have personally experienced the grace of God and who can narrate this experience reappeared in the context of evangelical preaching and small group meetings.

10. John Wesley, "Catholic Spirit," in *John Wesley's Sermons: An Anthology,* ed. Albert Outler and Richard Heitzenrater (Nashville: Abingdon, 1991), 304. Wesley certainly goes on to explain that he means by this "catholic spirit" no easy latitudinarianism, and his sermon raises all the questions about the paradoxical nature of evangelical ideals of union in Christ that I return to at the conclusion of this essay.

11. Ward, *Protestant Evangelical Awakening,* 51.

12. Cyprian, *De Cath. Eccl. Unitate* 6; Augustine, *On Baptism* 4.17.

13. See, for example, the ecclesiology of John Rogers (1627–65?), a Fifth Monarchist in Dublin who published his views in *Ohel or Beth-shemeth, or, A Tabernacle for the Sun, or Irenicum Evangelicum. An Idea of Church Discipline, in the Theoretick and Practick Parts* (1653).

The second significant ecclesiastical experiment is associated with Philip Jakob Spener (1635–1705), whose *Pia Desideria* (1675) was the catalyst for the renewal movement known today as Pietism. At the heart of Spener's ministry was a fresh ecclesiological proposal. He envisaged regenerate believers not as a separate church but as a *collegia pietatis,* a college of piety, that might help renew the Lutheran Church. Groups of believers were to be small churches within the church, *ecclesiola in ecclesia.* There was a parallel in England about the same time in the religious society movement, written about by Josiah Woodward in his *Account of the Rise and Progress of the Religious Societies in the City of London* (1698). Such groups formed the matrix for the early revival in London and elsewhere, the most famous example being Wesley's "Holy Club" in Oxford.[14] From the Methodist band meetings to the small group Bible studies and Alpha Courses of evangelicalism today, the original Pietist ideal of the *ecclesiola* has remained a vital expression of evangelical ecclesiology.

The third experiment represented an expansion of Spener's original Pietist vision. A revival in 1727 at Herrnhut on the estate of Count Nikolaus von Zinzendorf (1700–1760) in Upper Lusatia led to the formation of the Renewed Moravian Brethren, or simply the Moravians, as John Wesley and the English evangelicals would come to know them. Zinzendorf gave leadership to the Moravian community, which he first envisaged as an *ecclesiola* within Lutheranism. Over time, however, and with the growth of the movement, he came to view Moravianism as an international *Brüdergemeine* ("brotherhood") that would serve to foster local piety and regenerate the established churches: Lutheran, Reformed, Anglican, and even Roman Catholic. Each of these churches represented a *tropus*, a distinctive *paideia* or cure of souls within the church universal. Colin Podmore expounds Zinzendorf's ecclesiastical ideals, saying, "The *Brüdergemeine* would be a place of experiment, a temporary making visible of the unity of the children of God which already existed in the one nameless true Religion of Christ."[15] Zinzendorf's program was creative and eclectic, and it was predicated on and unthinkable apart from the new religio-political conditions of the Peace of Westphalia.[16] The Moravians would be a key catalyst for evan-

---

14. John Walsh, "Religious Societies: Methodist and Evangelical, 1738–1800," in *Voluntary Religion*, ed. W. J. Sheils and Dianna Wood, Studies in Church History (Oxford: Blackwell, 1986), 279–302.

15. Colin Podmore, *The Moravian Church in England, 1728–1760* (Oxford: Clarendon Press, 1998), 162. See also Howard Snyder, *Signs of the Spirit* (Grand Rapids: Zondervan, 1989), 123–80.

16. The eclectic nature of Zinzendorf's ecclesiology is well presented in W. R. Ward, "The Renewed Unity of the Brethren: Ancient Church, New Sect, or Interconfessional Movement?" in *Faith and Faction* (London: Epworth, 1993), 112–29.

gelical revival among English Protestants in the middle third of the eighteenth century, and their ecclesiastical ideals would be carried over into modern evangelicalism and extended.[17] The rapid expansion of evangelical revival in the English-speaking world would in fact turn these ecclesiastical ideals into something unprecedented.

Thus, these three ecclesial experiments anticipated the evangelical movement. The ideal of the narrative community (radical congregationalism), the small church within the "mixed church" (Pietism), and the interconfessional and international brotherhood (Moravianism) would be taken up into the modern evangelical movement.

The Transatlantic Evangelical Revival: A New Departure in Ecclesiology under Modern Conditions?

While various movements anticipated the evangelical experience in the eighteenth century, none of them evolved into an international, transdenominational phenomenon of the scope of the Evangelical Revival. The early evangelical movement was characterized by both the revitalization of individual ministers who began to preach with more power and conviction and, in Jonathan Edwards's words, "the conversion of many hundred souls."[18] The movement progressed not like a chain reaction, beginning with John Wesley's conversion in London and spreading out from there, but more like popcorn popping all at once in different places once the conditions were right and the heat was high enough. The surprising work of God in the Connecticut Valley revival of 1734–35, the spectacular outdoor crowds and emotional scenes in London and Bristol in 1739, the Cambuslang revival in Scotland in 1741–42, and the spectacular descent of George Whitefield on the American colonies signaled the beginning of revival on a new scale. Through such activities large numbers of women and men were provoked to serious spiritual concern and led through the travail of conversion.

What was the ecclesiastical configuration of this movement? The local organization was the small group. Seekers and converts were

17. Frederick Dreyer, *The Genesis of Methodism* (Bethlehem, Pa.: Lehigh University Press, 1999) argues that Methodism itself is best explained as a form of the Moravian diaspora. This fails to account for the wider genesis of English evangelicalism outside the Wesleyan movement, but it indicates something of the importance of Moravianism as a catalyst for the Evangelical Revival and the rise of Methodism. See also John Walsh, "Origins of the Evangelical Revival," in *Essays in Modern English Church History in Memory of Norman Sykes,* ed. Gareth V. Bennett and John D. Walsh (Oxford: Oxford University Press, 1966), 157.

18. Jonathan Edwards, *A Faithful Narrative of the Surprising Work of God in the Conversion of Many Hundred Souls in Northampton* (London: printed for John Oswald, 1737).

typically gathered into small cells by evangelical pastors or lay leaders, groups that recalled the Pietist and Moravian use of religious societies and class meetings. As the single mother Margaret Austin wrote, after evangelical preaching touched her conscience, "I had a strong Desire to get into the Bands: I went to the Reverend Mr John Wesley and he admitted me. And the first night we met, hearing the others tell the State of their Souls—it was of much strength to me to speak of the State of mine."[19] The evangelical minister John Newton explained likewise to a Scottish correspondent that in his parish "we are Ecclesia intra Ecclesium. I preach to many, but those whose hearts the Lord touches are the people of my peculiar charge."[20] He gathered these believers into a society within the parish. These intimate gatherings of spiritually earnest souls were at the heart of the revival.

The larger movement was understood as an international "work." It is called the Evangelical Revival in Britain and the Great Awakening in America. Together they are seen as the beginning of the evangelical "movement," but at the time this movement was generally referred to as a "work" or a "work of God." What seemed most remarkable to contemporary observers was the concentration in time and the extension in space.[21] In 1745, Wesley asked his opposers, "In what age has such a work been wrought, considering the *swiftness* as well as the *extent* of it?"[22] A few years later he wrote, "Many sinners are saved from their sins at this day, in London, . . . in many other parts of England; in Wales, in Ireland, in Scotland; upon the continent of Europe; in Asia and in America. This I term a *great work of God;* so great as I have not

19. Margaret Austin to Charles Wesley, 19 May 1740, Early Methodist Volume, John Rylands Library, Manchester.

20. *Original Letters from the Reverend John Newton to the Rev. W. Barlass* (New York: n.p., 1819), 52.

21. Cf. Michael Crawford, *Seasons of Grace* (New York: Oxford University Press, 1991), 13–14.

22. John Wesley, *The Appeals to Men of Reason and Religion and Certain Related Open Letters*, ed. Gerald R. Cragg, vol. 11 of *The Works of John Wesley*, ed. Richard P. Heitzenrater and Frank Baker (Nashville: Abingdon, 1989), 276. Likewise, in 1742, Whitefield wrote, "I believe there is such a work begun, as neither we nor our fathers have heard of. The beginnings are amazing; how unspeakably glorious will the end be!" (Luke Tyerman, *The Life of the Rev. George Whitefield*, vol. 1 [London: Hodder & Stoughton, 1877], 553, quoting a letter written by Whitefield from London, 6 April 1742.) And Jonathan Edwards wrote to William McCulloch in Scotland in 1743, saying, "We live in a day wherein God is doing marvelous things; in that respect we are distinguished from former generations," and he expected this to only increase: "What has now been doing is the forerunner of something vastly greater, more pure, and more extensive" (C. C. Goen, ed., *The Great Awakening*, vol. 4, *The Works of Jonathan Edwards* [New Haven: Yale University Press, 1972], 539–40).

read of for several ages."[23] Again, the description of this as a "work" (singular) bears witness to the perception that the myriad local experiences of evangelical activity in different nations and churches were still one and undivided. It is not merely an act of historical imagination or postmodern construction to see this activity as comprehending a larger spiritual solidarity.[24] Here then in the consciousness of a rapid, global, and singular divine work is another factor that will lead to a unique rethinking of the meaning of the church by evangelicals.

This is not the place to analyze the origin and sources of this transatlantic quickening of religious concern, but we should outline further some of the cultural conditions under which the transatlantic revival took place. We have already noted the way in which the Act of Toleration in 1689 provided a profoundly altered political landscape for the

23. Wesley, *Appeals to Men of Reason,* 374. One of the places we can see this swiftness and extent is in the periodical press. By the early 1740s, there were four major evangelical magazines in the English-speaking world that were regularly reporting on the progress of the gospel at home and abroad. London had the *Weekly History,* Glasgow had the *Glasgow Weekly History,* Edinburgh had the *Christian Monthly History,* and Boston had the *Christian History.* The word *history* in the title of each of these periodicals was not used in the sense of ancient history but in the sense of current affairs—the weekly and monthly history of the gospel in the world. On February 20, 1742, the London magazine included a letter in which the writer said, "If Conversion-work is a Miracle, being a thing done above Nature, what must such Numbers of such Conversions be? When a little one becomes a Thousand, and a small one a mighty Nation, who will doubt, it is the Lord that hastens it?" On May 14, 1743, the Boston magazine reported, "How astonishing are the Dispensations of a provoked holy God in our Day! That, in the midst of Backslidings and Provocations from his Churches, he should *come suddenly into his Temple,* by a glorious Ministration of his Spirit with the Word, first in *America,* through the *British* Colonies there; then in *Britain* itself, and particularly in several Parts of the West of *Scotland;* whereby many are awakned [*sic*] and converted from Sin to God."

24. Jon Butler, "Enthusiasm Described and Decried: The Great Awakening as Interpretative Fiction," *Journal of American History* 69 (1982): 305–25, argued controversially that the Great Awakening was the invention of the nineteenth-century historian Joseph Tracy. It seems clear to me, on the contrary, that there is overwhelming evidence from both sides of the Atlantic that contemporaries recognized from earliest days that myriad local revivals were evidence of one "work" of God. As John Wesley commented on the American awakening, "Evidently one work with what we have here" (John Walsh, "'Methodism' and the Origins of English-Speaking Evangelicalism," in *Evangelicalism,* ed. Mark Noll, David Bebbington, and George Rawlyk [New York: Oxford University Press, 1994], 19). Superb evidence for early recognition of a united, global revival may be found in the hymn in twelve stanzas by the layman Joseph Humphreys, "Of Intercession and Thanksgiving for the Progress of the Gospel in Various Parts of the World," in *Sacred Hymns for the Use of Religious Societies,* ed. John Cennick (Bristol: Felix Farley, 1743), 89–92. The interpretation of Frank Lambert that the Great Awakening was "invented" or constituted in language through the emerging eighteenth-century print culture is parallel to what I am seeking to identify as a larger ecclesial consciousness (Frank Lambert, *Inventing the "Great Awakening"* [Princeton, N.J.: Princeton University Press, 1999]).

practice of religion in the eighteenth century. But a number of other changes in society acted to create an environment for the practice of faith that we recognize as strikingly modern. It was in part these very conditions that allowed the revival to spread and become a general phenomenon and that fostered a unique ecclesial self-consciousness among those within this new religious bloc.

What were some of these changes in society? Improvements in shipping, roads, and communication and the related growth in the efficiency of postal service were key factors in stimulating a larger traffic of ideas, people, and goods in the North Atlantic, and evangelicals were at the forefront of the flux and excitement this created. It was simply more efficient to travel and move goods as the century progressed. For example, transatlantic shipping doubled in volume by the middle of the century, and evangelicals shared in this increase. In fact, few people used the merchant marine more than George Whitefield.[25] Again, there was an extraordinary boom in road building and improvements, achieved in part through turnpike trusts, and no one tested these more than John Wesley, who traveled more than a quarter million miles in his lifetime.[26] The speed and volume of postal correspondence rose steadily, and evangelicals taxed this system to its utmost. The Pietist August Hermann Francke had roughly five thousand correspondents during this period, and John Wesley was not far behind.[27]

These developments in turn led to greater mobility and increased communication for the population generally. Arthur Young celebrated "the general impetus given to circulation; new people—new ideas—new exertions—fresh activity in every branch of industry."[28] A visitor to England commented, "Nobody is a provincial in this country. You meet nowhere with those persons who were never out of their native place, and whose habits are wholly local."[29] The sense, then, among evangelicals of a general work of God that extended across national and ecclesiastical boundaries was predicated in part on new travel and communication patterns. It were as though the rails on which the movement rode had been laid down in advance. Just as Roman roads were impor-

25. Whitefield's extensive travel and the growth of transatlantic commerce are described in Frank Lambert, *"Pedlar in Divinity": George Whitefield and the Transatlantic Revivals, 1737–1770* (Princeton, N.J.: Princeton University Press, 1994).

26. W. R. Ward, "John Wesley, Traveller," in *Faith and Faction*, 249–63.

27. Ward, *Protestant Evangelical Awakening*, 2; Frank Baker, ed., *Letters I, 1721–1739*, vol. 25 of *The Bicentennial Edition of the Works of John Wesley* (Oxford: Clarendon Press, 1980), 28–30.

28. Quoted in Roy Porter, *English Society in the Eighteenth Century* (London: Penguin, 1990), 193.

29. Ibid., 39.

tant for the expansion of the early church, and the printing press was crucial to the extension of the Reformation, so many of the material conditions of life in the eighteenth century were an infrastructure for a general North Atlantic religious awakening and for the representation of it as such in the periodical press and in evangelical correspondence and literature.[30]

Moreover, because of the religious toleration achieved through law in the previous century, the world in which evangelicals grew up in eighteenth-century England included Anglicans, Baptists, Presbyterians, and Independents (Congregationalists) as legally recognized parts of the social landscape, and evangelicalism moved along the interstices of all these groups.[31] For those who lived in or visited the American colonies, the givenness of religious diversity was even greater.

We are accustomed to describe such conditions of life—material, political, and religious—as modern and to refer to these arrangements as modernity, though these conditions were present in the eighteenth century only in embryo. We so often take these arrangements for granted, but in the eighteenth century, when the evangelical movement took its rise, such conditions put people on the move as never before and exposed them to changes that were both liberating and unsettling. Traditional ties to the family and the land, the squire and the parson, were broken, and religion increasingly operated in a world in which people understood themselves as mobile, free moral agents. The consciousness of what it is to be a person and part of a community was, in this context, very different from what existed under the ancien régime or at the height of Christendom. Commu-

30. To these material conditions we could add many more, including the development of hundreds of miles of navigable inland waterways that contributed to economic expansion, manufacturing, and demographic change. Agricultural reform accelerated the movement of people from country to town, and the proportion of those living in urban centers approximately doubled during the century. Improvements in health and medicine contributed to rapid population growth generally. The popular press churned out more and more newspapers, book production rose sharply, and more people could read. The marketplace itself expanded such that historians have coined the phrase "consumer revolution" to describe the new levels of disposable income and availability of retail goods during the period. The keynote of all these changes was that people were placed on the move and traditional roles were increasingly supplanted by a keener sense of individual agency.

31. This is different from the situation on the Continent, where in most countries the three religions—Roman Catholic, Lutheran, and Reformed—were the only ones licensed by the state. Moreover, there was no legal basis for conversion between religions, and there was no legal recognition of Dissenters or Nonconformists, as in Britain. The terms *Sekt* ("sect") and *Sektierer* implied much more opprobrium than the English equivalents. See Hans Otte, "The Pietist Laity in Germany, 1675–1750: Knowledge, Gender, Leadership," in *The Rise of the Laity in Evangelical Protestantism*, ed. Deryck Lovegrove (London: Routledge, 2002), 50–51.

nity in the evangelical revival was not a religious monopoly controlled by traditional ecclesiastical authority and backed by legal sanction; it had much more to do with free association. This does not mean, however, that the evangelical revival represented rank voluntaryism, individualism, and constructivism. Women and men in the revival still had a keen sense that their identity in Christ and in the church was given, not merely constructed, but it was given through the "means of grace" and by participation in a narrative community rather than through law, custom, and political authority. The Christian's task was to "wait upon God in the means of grace," that is, to look for the appearing of God in preaching, holy communion, the reading of Scripture, prayer, Christian conversation, friendship, and so on.[32] Thus, John Valton wrote to John Wesley after receiving holy communion on Easter in 1766 that he had a "gracious season . . . for the Lord was in the means" but that another man had lost his "good impressions" since "leaving the means of grace."[33] So although evangelicals gathered together as an act of free association, they also understood this to be because of a prior "calling out" and "calling together" of the Holy Spirit through the means God ordained. If these early evangelicals acquired a new sense of individual agency under the modern conditions of life that emerged in this period, they could still be described as deeply communitarian in their common life.

Should it be any surprise though that this was a movement that consistently overflowed the banks of traditional, established church order? Evangelicals could be decidedly mischievous when it came to church order, or "irregular," as they called it. As the experience of evangelical awakening persistently crisscrossed the boundaries of nations and churches, men and women increasingly identified less with their churches and more with their local evangelical fellowships and with the international evangelical community. In this vein, the Anglican John Newton wrote to a non-Anglican Scottish correspondent, saying, "My heart is . . . more especially with those who, like you, can look over the pales of an enclosure, and rejoice in the Lord's work where he is pleased to carry it on, under some difference of forms."[34] Clearly, the character of this work led to renewed reflection on the meaning of the church altogether—in fact, a new ecclesial consciousness.

32. Wesley and the Moravians clashed in 1740 over the question of "means," and this was one cause of their schism. Wesley regarded the Moravians as quietist for their alleged rejection of "means," but in this the Moravians were even less "constructivist" in their approach to religious identity than the Wesleyans. See Podmore, *Moravian Church*, 57–71; cf. Dreyer, *Genesis of Methodism*, 31–54. See also Wesley's sermon "The Means of Grace" (1746), in *John Wesley's Sermons*, 157–71.

33. John Telford, ed., *Wesley's Veterans*, vol. 6 (London: Robert Culley, 1913), 28, 30.

34. *Original Letters*, 49.

This historical phenomenon leaves us with a theological problem. How do we understand "what God hath wrought"? If we believe that the Spirit of God did indeed call out and grant new birth to large numbers of people from among the divided churches, that these people experienced communion with one another not only in local fellowship but also increasingly through international communication and travel, and that many Christians identified with this movement in a church-like way, then we have something unprecedented to think about. This was not an issue in the undivided early church, and it was not an issue during the long centuries of Christendom. It became an issue during the Reformation but then ended in near confessional holocaust. It was only in the aftermath of this, under the conditions of the modern era, that such a new religious consciousness was really possible.

Unprecedented Ecclesial Consciousness: Observations on the Ecclesiology of Evangelicalism

Thus far we have observed some of the unprecedented conditions under which an international evangelical movement appeared and progressed, and we have seen how the early evangelicals had both a local consciousness of immediate fellowship in the small group or band meeting and an international consciousness of a transdenominational fellowship in the wider work of God in the world. I would like to expound this consciousness of the church further by examining the testimony of some of the participants of the early evangelical movement. George Whitefield was perhaps the most representative figure in the evangelical movement as a whole in the eighteenth century because he was a catalyst for significant revival among Anglicans in England, Presbyterians in Scotland, Congregationalists in New England, and many others. In his own person as the "Grand Itinerant," he experienced the movement as no one else, and his letters provide a vivid sense of the way in which this caused him to rethink the church and to subordinate church order to evangelical piety. From his correspondence, together with the remarks of a few other evangelical leaders, we are able to reconstruct some of the ways in which the early evangelicals reconceived their theology of the church. Three features stand out as distinctive.

1. *There is no distinctively evangelical doctrine of church order.*

Church order may be defined as "a stated form of divine service, or administration of a rite or ceremony, prescribed by an ecclesiastical authority."[35] And, of course, authority was precisely the issue that was called into question by historical developments in church and society

---

35. *Oxford English Dictionary* (1933), s. v. "order," no. 17.

in the seventeenth and eighteenth centuries. Conceived widely, church order refers to any visible form or organization of the church, but the issues in the eighteenth century included, at the very least, church-state constitutionality, the ordering of the ministry and governance of the church, and the mode and administration of the sacraments. Evangelicals united in mission and spiritual friendship, but they did not unite under one visible church order.

Yet while evangelicals were divided by these issues, they did not generally regard them as constituting the essence of the church. In 1739, Whitefield wrote from Philadelphia to Phillip Doddridge's academy in Northampton, England. Doddridge was an Independent, one of the leading Nonconformists of his generation. He and Whitefield would certainly have differed over issues of church order, just as John Stott and Martyn Lloyd-Jones would later. Yet Whitefield wrote, "Though you are not of the church of England, yet if you are persuaded in your own minds of the truth of the way wherein you now walk, I leave it. However, whether Conformists, or Nonconformists, our main concern should be, to be assured that we are called and taught of GOD, for none but such are fit to minister in holy things."[36] Thus, neither Anglican nor Congregationalist church order was understood as being the essence of the church or its ministry. The essence of the church lay rather in what we might call the convocation of the Spirit, the awareness that "we are called and taught of God." In this sense, Whitefield viewed the church as essentially pneumatic.

Whitefield recognized at an early date that one could regard church order as essential, as the Protestant Orthodox did, or one could regard regeneration by the Holy Spirit as essential, as evangelicals did, but one could not do both.[37] If, for example, one argued that the essence of the church includes a divine-right episcopacy of apostolic succession, then one necessarily unchurched everyone else. Clearly, Congregationalist evangelicals, such as Doddridge, would then belong only to a religious organization, not to the one, holy, catholic, and apostolic church. This Whitefield could not say, since he recognized Doddridge as manifestly "called and taught of God." He recognized that insofar as one elevates church order, precisely thus far does one draw away from the evangel-

36. John Gillies, ed., *The Works of . . . the Revd. George Whitefield*, vol. 1 (London: n.p., 1771), 81.

37. "The men who ushered in new ways of christianising their world, Spener and Francke, Baxter and Watts, Doddridge and Wesley, all appeared as middle men of one kind or another. Someone needed to mediate between the world of ecclesiastical precision, and the world of spiritual nutriment. . . . [T]he mediators were going to have to go behind the scholastic Orthodoxies of recent generations to do it" (Ward, *Protestant Evangelical Awakening*, 49).

ical affirmation that all those who are discernibly regenerate by the Holy Spirit are necessarily members of Christ and members of his church. This problem remained whether one was a high-church Anglican or a divine-right Baptist, since any form of polity could in principle be regarded as essential. Evangelical ecclesiology was therefore articulated around the local fellowship of true believers and the consciousness of the universal church, but all the ecclesiastical constructions in between (e.g., church order) were radically reduced to adiaphora. Insofar as they were not, they caused friction among evangelicals.

✗ (2) *The mystical church is discernible among the divided visible churches.*

To a Presbyterian minister Whitefield wrote:

> What a divine sympathy and attraction is there between all those who by one spirit are made members of that mystical body, whereof JESUS CHRIST is the head! . . . Blessed be GOD that his love is so far shed abroad in our hearts, as to cause us to love one another, though we a little differ as to externals: For my part, I hate to mention them. My one sole question is, Are you a christian? . . . If so, you are my brother, my sister, and mother. . . . Yet a little while, and we shall sit down together in the kingdom of our Father.[38]

Here the crucial seventeenth-century question of what constitutes a true church was exchanged for the question of what constitutes a true Christian (again, dropping from mid-range ecclesiology about church order to local ecclesiology about "where two or three are gathered," or rising to mystical ecclesiology about the eschatological kingdom). While eschewing visible forms as unmentionable "externals," Whitefield clearly believed that the secret work of the Holy Spirit in constituting men and women as members of Christ's mystical body was discernible in a certain "divine sympathy and attraction" among them. True believers recognize in one another a mystical bond, as God's own love causes them to love one another. Whitefield took Jonathan Edwards's concept of the "religious affections" and made it an ecclesiological principle.[39] The church is not constituted by stated ecclesiastical authority but by elective affinity of a spiritual sort. This is not unlike the view of seventeenth-century radicals that the church is a narrative community of the manifestly regenerate, except that for Whitefield this nar-

---

38. Gillies, *Works of . . . the Revd. George Whitefield,* 126.

39. Edwards defined "religious affections" as "the more vigorous and sensible exercises of the inclination and will of the soul" and insisted that "true religion, in great part, consists in the affections" (Jonathan Edwards, *Religious Affections,* ed. John Smith, vol. 2 of *The Works of Jonathan Edwards* [New Haven: Yale University Press, 1959], 96, 99).

rative community manifested itself within the mixed visible church and drew members from different visible communions together in a trans-denominational experience of solidarity.

✗ (3.)*The oxymoron of evangelical ecclesiology is that while celebrating the spiritual union of all the truly regenerate, the movement itself was dogged by separatism.*

Whitefield wrote from America to his own followers at the Tabernacle in London, reminding them that no truths are of any value unless they find their way into one's heart and issue in holiness and love. This he hoped the Tabernacle preachers and people would remember.

> Let us not dispute, but love. . . . You must remember what I have often told you about Calvin. He was turned out of Geneva for several years; but in less than twelve years time they wished for Calvin again. But what is Calvin, or what is Luther? Let us look above names and parties; let Jesus, the ever-loving, the ever-lovely Jesus, be our all in all. So that he be preached, and his divine image stamped more and more upon people's souls, I care not who is uppermost.[40]

He thus eschewed confessional partisanship in favor of piety ("the ever-loving, the ever-lovely Jesus"). But in this there was an enormous and culpable naïveté and sentimentalism. Here was a movement that was founded on a vision of local intimacy and international fellowship. Here was a movement that recognized in the proclamation of the gospel a parallel convocation of the Holy Spirit. Here was a movement that sought to move among the visible churches to realize in time and space the underlying unity of all the children of God. And yet here was a movement that was dogged by separatism and internal schism. Wesley and Whitefield split in the free grace controversy in 1739 over Calvinism. Wesley, Whitefield, and the Moravians split in 1740 over quietism. Lady Huntingdon went through evangelical chaplains like serial lovers. Wesley gave up on the evangelical clergy within the Anglican Church in the 1760s, seeing them as a "rope of sand." And the Anglican evangelicals and the Nonconformist evangelicals divided over "regularity." These early evangelicals proclaimed unity, but so often they experienced schism.

If one rejects visible order, one will sooner or later simply fill the vacuum with another form of visible organization. When something is to be said among Christians, a choice must be made between words, and this places one in the realm of discursive theology. When something is to be done among Christians, a choice must be made between actions,

40. Gillies, *Works of . . . the Revd. George Whitefield*, vol. 2, 428–29.

and this places one in the realm of church order and liturgy. The underlying emphasis in Reformation theology that the Christian life is an affair of the spirit was elevated among evangelicals in their understanding of the church. For example, while Calvin distinguished between the invisible church and the visible church, he was still concerned in page after page of the *Institutes* to uphold strongly the divinely ordered authority of the visible church. Evangelicals, in contrast, were preoccupied almost wholly with the invisible church. As John Newton argued, Christ's kingdom was not of this world and did not consist in "meats and drinks" or "forms and parties."[41] It did not consist in forms? For most evangelicals, the distinction in the magisterial Reformation between the visible church and the mystical church gave way and was elided into a different distinction *within* the visible church: the distinction between nominal and true believers. Here is where they focused their proselytizing zeal in nations in which almost all the people were formally Christian through baptism. Nominal profession of Christian faith was linked to the merely physical aspects of church life and discipline ("going to church and sacrament"), but true belief was equated with a wholly inward and spiritual experience of regeneration.

But visible forms did inevitably emerge among the partisans of the revival. The most distinctive and widespread form (at least in England) was associational, or to use the contemporary term, "connexional." The evangelical societies, the *ecclesiolae*, were articulated around the leaders themselves. Wesley's connexion was the most well oiled; Whitefield's, the worst. Lady Huntingdon had a connexion, as did other lesser figures such as John Cennick and Benjamin Ingham (both of whom took their connexions into Moravianism). Even Zinzendorf's organization can be understood in part as his own personal connexion. At one level of analysis, the connexional form was an extension of the understanding of the church as an aggregation, from the bottom up, of believers. Small groups of local converts became linked to other groups through the itinerant messenger of the gospel. And the fact that the movement divided into different phalanxes could be regarded benignly as the parting of friends who divided over secondary matters but did not unchurch one another. Indeed, there are many examples of continued fellowship between divided evangelical partisans throughout the century. Thus, notwithstanding the division between Whitefield and Wesley, Whitefield insisted that his longtime friend be the one to preach his funeral sermon—Wesley, and Wesley alone.[42] An inability to cooperate organizationally did not end spiritual fellowship. At another level,

41. *The Works of John Newton*, vol. 5 (London: n.p., 1808–9), 41.
42. Tyerman, *Life of the Rev. George Whitefield*, vol. 2, 614.

however, connexionalism was especially vulnerable to a popular cult of personality and rhetorical suasion. Does this show up in the movement's early schisms, which could be construed in part as personality conflicts between strong leaders? The ecclesial authority of political rulers in church and state had been decisively rejected or subordinated to other spiritual ideals, but authority could not be rejected forever.

This, then, was the central paradox of evangelical ecclesiology. It represented a new ecclesial consciousness in the modern world, one that seemed, as Zinzendorf dreamed, to manifest temporarily the underlying unity of the children of God and to express this in various extra-ecclesiastical settings. Evangelicals witnessed to this ideal and partially realized it. But at the same time, the movement was always a restless "movement," iconoclastic of all forms of order, often guilty of schism, and in danger of turning the proclamation of the eternal gospel into matters of popular suasion and the politics of public personalities. These issues in many cases remain a part of the paradoxical relationship between evangelicalism and ecclesiology today.

I have been seeking to speak in this essay as a historian in order that, in Gordon Rupp's words, the full implications of "what God hath wrought" in the rise of evangelicalism might be "brought to bear in the theology of the Church about its own nature and destiny." The historical phenomenon of evangelicalism leaves us all with a theological nut to crack. We need not, of course, understand the phenomenon in the way that Whitefield or other early evangelicals did. When John Newton and John Wesley disagreed over election, Newton wryly offered that he would give Wesley the credit for *being* elect even though he did not believe in election. Edith Humphrey's essay in this volume points to a Catholic reading of the evangelical phenomenon that might allow that what the union evangelicals experienced was ultimately sacramental, even if they did not all highly value the sacraments or agree on matters of sacramental theology and practice. At the other end of the spectrum, Roger Olson's essay suggests that we regard the evangelical phenomenon not as something fundamentally ecclesial but as a renewal movement with a distinctive ethos, an ethos uniquely compatible with free church ecclesiology. In addition to these helpful proposals and the other contributions to this volume, we need further careful theological attention paid to the sheer anomaly of evangelicalism as it has appeared in the midst of the modern world.

At the very least, we need to see the paradoxes in evangelical ecclesiology in terms of a deeper, more theological sort of irony. Whether in 1740 or in 1966, the evangelical experience of schism in the midst of spiritual ideals was not just oxymoronic; it was tragic. It was tragic in the old sense of the word, in which a situation is recognized as especially sad because a fatal flaw brings calamity upon an otherwise noble character. John Newton captured the tragic sense when he once saw the decayed remains of a nobleman's great house in the country and described it in Milton's language as "majestic though in ruins." I think the early evangelicals really did glimpse something of grandeur in their spiritual discernment of the mystical body of Christ among the nations and indeed among the churches. The extent of this movement and its unique appearance under the conditions of the early modern world represented something unprecedented. That these ideals were ever only partly realized, that these ideals were frustrated time and again by the cussedness and perversity of the human heart—well, this tragedy drives us, as it drove them, back to the deeper evangelical paradox of the cross, under which the whole church continues to dwell "till with the vision glorious her longing eyes are blest, and the great church victorious shall be the church at rest."

2

Recovering a Trinitarian and Sacramental Ecclesiology

Kerry L. Dearborn

Grace of love be thine . . .
The guard of the God of life be thine,
The guard of the loving Christ be thine,
The guard of the Holy Spirit be thine,
To cherish thee,
To aid thee,
To enfold thee.
The Three be about thy head,
The Three be about thy breast,
The Three be about thy body
Each night and each day,
In the encompassment of the Three
Throughout thy life long.[1]

The glory of the gospel of Jesus Christ is the revelation of God's Triune nature and the outpouring of God's healing love into our world. Jesus promises the very presence of God—Father, Son, and Spirit—to

1. Alexander Carmichael, ed., *Carmina Gadelica: Hymns and Incantations*, III (London: Oliver & Boyd, 1928), 229.

his people: "Those who love me will keep my word, and my Father will love them, and we will come to them and make our home with them" (John 14:23 NRSV). Indeed, Father, Son, and Spirit have come to make us God's own dwelling place, to build a church that is so shaped by the presence and nature of the Triune God that it is able to show forth God's nature and purposes "in Jerusalem, in all Judea and Samaria, and to the ends of the earth" (Acts 1:8 NRSV). One would surmise that this foundational reality would be so central to evangelicals that the Trinity could no longer be dismissed as an abstract mathematical enigma.

However, when asked to respond to the question, What would you like evangelical theologians to consider regarding ecclesiology? my immediate question was, Why doesn't our ecclesiology more fully reflect our belief in the Triune nature of God? The trinity with which I was raised in my own branch of evangelicalism was Father, Son, and Bible, but even that trinity did not seem to shape the way we thought about church. It is both curious and grievous that as Lesslie Newbigin contended, "When the average Christian in this country hears the name of God, he or she does not think of the Trinity."[2] Weakened understandings of the nature of the Trinity and of the nature of God's presence by the Spirit impoverish our ecclesiology and our sense of the sacramental nature of the church and of all of life. Rather than reflecting the Triune God whom we worship, we more often reflect the culture around us. Dallas Willard likens our non-discipleship to the elephant in the living room that everyone recognizes but no one will discuss.[3] We have fallen prey to the sacred/secular dichotomy, ignoring the ever present reality of God with us. Bereft of an awareness of God's presence, we are driven by fear. As Jürgen Moltmann states, "Out of fear of life and fear of death we fall short of what our lives could be."[4] Forgetting that God is for us and in us, the one who created and owns all things, we struggle to offer an alternative to the greed and acquisitiveness of our culture. Rather than overflowing with God's Triune love, we as North American white evangelicals are wary of the stranger, wary of those who are in our midst from different races and ethnicities.[5] Though we believe in Christ, who did not hold on to his entitlements but emptied himself and went into

2. As cited in James Torrance, *Worship, Community, and the Triune God of Grace* (Downers Grove, Ill.: InterVarsity, 1996), 20.

3. Dallas Willard, *The Divine Conspiracy* (San Francisco: HarperSanFrancisco, 1998), 301–2.

4. Jürgen Moltmann, *The Source of Life: The Holy Spirit and the Theology of Life*, trans. Margaret Kohl (Minneapolis: Fortress, 1997), 20.

5. For a helpful perspective on the segregated state of North American evangelicalism, see Michael O. Emerson and Christian Smith, *Divided by Faith: Evangelical Religion and the Problem of Race in America* (Oxford: Oxford University Press, 2000).

the far country in the form of a servant, we tend to be as eager to dominate and cling to our rights as those who do not call Jesus "Lord."

What would an ecclesiology look like that was more fully shaped by the Trinity and thus helped to shape its members accordingly? One tradition in the Western church's heritage that expresses a trinitarian ecclesiology is the Celtic Christian church. This paper explores Celtic Christian ecclesiology, which was shaped by this tradition's central affirmation of God as Father, Son, and Spirit, and seeks relevant wisdom that can inform contemporary evangelical approaches to the church.[6] Miroslav Volf contends that "the way one thinks about God will decisively shape not only ecclesiology, but the entirety of Christian thought." Volf also suggests that the need for ecclesial communion to correspond with trinitarian communion has become an almost "self-evident proposition," though one that has not been fully developed or explored.[7] I would like to offer some glimpses of a Celtic tradition in which the correspondences between God's Triune nature and the shape of the church and Christian life seem more obvious and pervasive than in our own day.[8] Because of its trinitarian sensibilities, Celtic Christianity can offer evangelicals four significant ecclesial gifts. The first is a sense of identity that derives from the wonder of who God is as Father, Son, and Spirit and trust in God's presence with and for us. The second is a sacramental vision flowing from God's presence that perceives the miraculous nature of all of life. The third is a liturgical rhythm through which the church brings to bear the rich resources of faith to impact every aspect of life. And the fourth gift is an approach to mission that reflects such an identity, sacramental vision, and liturgical rhythm.

This ancient tradition warrants serious exploration, though not because of a naïve idea that we can return to such a way of life or because all things Celtic have become somewhat trendy. Rather, it is because the Celtic tradition offers a window into actual expressions of trinitarian-shaped faith over a period of many centuries. It is also important to acknowledge that Celtic expressions of Christian faith did not comprise an ideal reality, though there has been much hagiography of such traditions throughout the years. There was no Celtic golden age. Neither is there one monolithic expression of Celtic Christianity to which one

---

6. Remnant expressions of a Celtic Christian tradition are evident, for example, in the Iona community of Scotland. However, I will be examining this tradition when it was at its height during the Middle Ages.

7. Miroslav Volf, *After Our Likeness: The Church as the Image of the Trinity* (Grand Rapids: Eerdmans, 1998), 191.

8. I offer this perspective knowing, as Volf suggests, that one must be willing to qualify the nature of correspondences between the Triune Creator and the faltering creatures that we are.

can point. However, within the varieties and frailties of its manifestations, recurring themes shaped its development while its center held to the Triune God and its missionary fervor spread that love outward.[9]

Admittedly, all discussions of history are selective. Because this is a paper on the correspondences between Celtic ecclesiology/spirituality and the Trinity, more emphasis will be placed on positive correlations than on negative aspects of Celtic traditions.[10] Belief in God's presence throughout all of life fostered an openness to draw wisdom from a variety of sources, including pagan Celtic traditions as well as Eastern Orthodox understandings.[11] Through Celtic Christianity one can glimpse community life flowing from an encounter with and a response to the Triune God. We can begin to visualize the dynamic interrelation of the divine persons and all aspects of faith communities' lives. We can also explore the way in which this fostered a sacramental vision of the church and of all of creation. David Ford contends against those who would dismiss the value of seeking wisdom from the past by arguing, "We are free in a new way to recognize what is of value in premodernity, modernity, and postmodernity."[12] Communities can emerge and have emerged from being profoundly gripped by the wonder of God's life in Triune communion. If such trinitarian-centered life was possible for Celtic Christians throughout much of the Middle Ages, then perhaps an adapted form of it can help evangelicals reflect the wonder of God more effectively in our time. As one Celtic scholar explains, "Celtic Christianity speaks to our own hearts and needs today, for perhaps no other Christian spirituality has shown such a deep yet simple sense of God's presence in the world. The Celtic Christians seldom left the spiritual behind in the living of their lives, nor the world behind in their prayers."[13]

The first section of this chapter explores Celtic ecclesial identity. To convey Celtic identity accurately, this section offers a brief overview of

9. For more in-depth overviews of Celtic history, traditions, and perspectives, see, for example, Peter Berresford Ellis, *The Ancient World of the Celts* (New York: Barnes and Noble, 1999); Oliver Davies, trans., with the collaboration of Thomas O'Loughlin, *Celtic Spirituality* (New York: Paulist Press, 1999); Graydon Snyder, *Irish Jesus, Roman Jesus* (Harrisburg, Pa.: Trinity Press International, 2002); and Timothy J. Joyce, OSB, *Celtic Christianity* (New York: Maryknoll, 1998).

10. For a more skeptical look at Celtic Christianity, see Ian Bradley, *Celtic Christianity: Making Myths and Chasing Dreams* (New York: St. Martin's Press, 1999).

11. As Volf points out in *After Our Likeness*, Catholic and Orthodox voices can greatly enrich Protestant ecclesiological perspectives, all of which must be grounded in "an appropriate understanding of the Trinity" (xi).

12. David F. Ford, *The Shape of Living: Spiritual Directions for Everyday Life* (Grand Rapids: Baker, 1997), 21.

13. Avery Brooke, preface to *Celtic Invocations*, ed. Alexander Carmichael, selections from vol. 1 of *Carmina Gadelica* (Noroton, Conn.: Vineyard, 1972), 8.

Celtic history and influences and Celtic Christians' sense of the nature of God, in whose image the Celtic church sought to be formed. From this identity flowed the sacramental vision of the Celts, which is discussed in the second section. Their vision impacted the way they viewed their role as a church and their responses as God's people to the world around them. Viewing life sacramentally encouraged the creation of liturgies that brought their faith to bear on all aspects of life. This is the subject of the third section. The fourth section explores the ways in which the mission of the church enfleshed the identity, sacramental vision, and liturgical orientation of Celtic Christians as they communicated trinitarian faith to those both within and beyond their ecclesial walls. The final section draws out insight for contemporary evangelicals for the shaping of our identity, sacramental vision, liturgy, and mission around the affirmation that God is Father, Son, and Spirit.

Identity of the Celtic Church

Celtic ecclesiological identity emerged from the blending of Celtic pagan faith with the desert tradition of the ancient Coptic Church. Celtic pagan faith was oriented toward strong bonds of kinship, ideas of divinity that affirmed both masculine and feminine nature, an openness to divine immanence, and the tendency to think naturally in terms of threes. Three "was considered a powerful symbol of spiritual strength and intimacy with God, and it represented spiritual synthesis, the reconciliation of apparent opposites."[14] These orientations harmonized well with the vibrant trinitarian theology of Eastern Orthodoxy, its emphasis on the relational nature of personhood, and its attentiveness to the presence of God through the Spirit. The pneumatological richness of Eastern Orthodox theology led Celtic Christians toward an ecclesial identity that was both trinitarian and sacramental. Before describing that identity in more detail, a description of the way in which these influences came to bear on Celtic peoples is warranted.

Historians trace Celtic peoples to central Eastern Europe around 1200 B.C.E. These peoples migrated first to Western Europe and by roughly 100 B.C. had spread as far north as Ireland. As Celtic scholar Timothy Joyce points out, today the Celts "are recognized as the 'European Aborigines,' like Native American tribes already on the land with their own developed culture prior to being conquered, driven out, or as-

14. Edward C. Sellner, *Wisdom of the Celtic Saints* (Notre Dame, Ind.: Ave Maria Press, 1993), 40. Sellner describes the ongoing affinity of Celtic Christians for the number three, stating that in "the stories of the Celtic saints there are literally hundreds of references to three—from the three angels who appear at Brigit's baptism to the three gifts God gives to Columcille" (40).

similated by more powerful invaders."[15] Celtic cultures survived predominantly in regions that escaped the rule of Rome, thus in northern
Scotland, Wales, Ireland, and parts of England. Celtic forms of Christianity are usually associated with particular traditions in these parts
of the British Isles, evident between the fifth and twelfth centuries.

Eastern Orthodoxy penetrated Celtic life through a variety of means.
Eastern Christian churches of Asia Minor and leaders such as Irenaeus
and St. Anthony were early influences on Celtic Christians.[16] Trade
routes provided direct connections with the East, from whence the
Celts had migrated, having carried with them Eastern types of music
and myth.[17] One can see the influence of Egyptian desert monasticism
in shaping Celtic theology and in the great love and respect conveyed
toward the Eastern desert. As an example of the Celtic affinity with
desert monasticism, Joyce points out that though Ireland is clearly not
a desert, the word for desert is found forty times in Irish place names.[18]
In fact, Celtic monasteries had a cell for prayer and retreat that was
called a *dysert*.[19] The high crosses in Ireland contain scriptural scenes
plus the figures of St. Paul of Thebes and St. Anthony of Egypt.[20]

Eastern Orthodox and Celtic pagan influences shaped an ecclesial
identity that was first and foremost trinitarian. Joyce points to the Trinity as an example of a doctrine that would have seemed "very natural"
to the Celts, such that he writes, "Christianity was a peaceful and almost
natural development in Ireland."[21] Because of a rich appreciation for relationships, Celts were able to move from modalistic understandings,
for example, of their goddess Bridget (believed to have appeared in
three forms: fire, poetry, and fertility), to the Christian understandings
of the tri-personal nature of God, who exists as a communion of love. As
Celtic scholar Esther de Waal writes, "In a society in which household,
family, and kin were central realities perhaps men and women felt
themselves at home with a Godhead whose very essence was a harmonious relationship of persons."[22] Celtic Christians embraced the Trinity

15. Joyce, *Celtic Christianity*, 1. Snyder traces them back even earlier than 1200 B.C.E.
in *Irish Jesus, Roman Jesus*, 3–4.

16. Joyce, *Celtic Christianity*, 23–24.

17. Ibid., 23.

18. Timothy J. Joyce, "The Celtic Spiritual Tradition and the Religious Imagination"
(plenary address for "Creative Imagination: Embodying Time, Space, and Form," Point
Loma Nazarene, San Diego, Calif., 8 February 2002). Esther de Waal states, "In Wales
and in Ireland there are still as many as five hundred place names, *disserth* or *dysart*" (*The
Celtic Way of Prayer* [New York: Doubleday, 1997], 95).

19. Sellner, *Wisdom of the Celtic Saints*, 24.

20. de Waal, *Celtic Way of Prayer*, 94.

21. Joyce, *Celtic Christianity*, 19.

22. Esther De Waal, ed., *The Celtic Vision* (Liguori, Mo.: Liguori, 1988), xxix.

at the very heart of their spirituality, where "the Triune [God] of [their] strength"[23] profoundly shaped their prayers and daily life. As John Miriam Jones points out, "Love for the Trinity was preeminent among Celtic Christians."[24] Portrayal of the Trinity as a circle of three, as in Andrei Rublev's well-known icon titled "The Holy Trinity," would have been very harmonious with Celtic ways of thinking, in which the circle was more central to Celtic life than the straight line. Celtic prayers speak of being enfolded and protected in the love of the Three.

> I am lying down to-night with God,
> And God to-night will lie down with me,
> I will not lie down to-night with sin, nor shall
> Sin or sin's shadow lie down with me. . . .
>
> I will lie down this night with the Three of my love,
> And the Three of my love will lie down with me.[25]

To understand Celtic ecclesial identity, it is important to explore more fully Celtic Christian beliefs about God. Who is the God in whose image Celtic churches found their identity and to whom they turned to shape their community life and practice? What aspects of their beliefs about the Trinity then impacted their view of church? And how did this develop into such a profound sense of the sacramental nature of the church and of all of life?

First, Celtic egalitarian ideas about the Trinity allowed for differentiation within the Trinity without hierarchy. One encounters this as a pervasive understanding when reading Celtic prayers, blessings, and songs in the *Carmina Gadelica*, five volumes of material collected and edited by Alexander Carmichael. Differentiation is evident in a number of ways. The Father is the "one who created me,"[26] "the eternal Father of the world,"[27] the one "who gavest Thy loved Son in covenant for me, . . . purchased my soul with the precious blood of Thy Son," the "Lord of Life,"[28] and the "Being of life."[29] The Father is often viewed as the one who protects[30] and the one who is all-powerful.[31] But the power of the

---

23. Carmichael, *Celtic Invocations*, 90.
24. John Miriam Jones, *With an Eagle's Eye* (Notre Dame, Ind.: Ave Maria Press, 1998), 56–57. Cf. Michael Mitton, *Soul of Celtic Spirituality* (Mystic, Conn.: Twenty-Third Publications, 1996), 36–37.
25. Carmichael, *Carmina Gadelica*, I, 67.
26. Ibid., I, 3.
27. Ibid., III, 41–47.
28. Ibid.
29. Ibid., I, 105.
30. Ibid., I, 5.
31. Ibid., I, 339.

Father is not described as it is in some other traditions of Christianity in which God is distant, wrathful, and retributive. Invocations call on "God the Father all-powerful, benign."[32] It is the Father who is "kind and just,"[33] whose "mild grace" is available in blessing,[34] and who would "take you in His own generous clasp / In His own generous arm."[35] The Father's power is expressed as a "fragrant clasp of love" to take you "when you go across the flooding streams and the black river of death."[36]

The Son, or Christ, is recognized as the "one who purchased me"[37] and who is "with me directing."[38] He is "Jesu the Son of tears and of sorrow,"[39] the "Son, who didst overcome death,"[40] for he is the "Christ of love."[41]

And the Spirit is the one "who cleansed me,"[42] who is "with me strengthening"[43] with "thy co-assistance, O! Holy Spirit."[44] The Spirit is also described as "the Holy Spirit of power."[45]

Often the Father is distinguished as "the God of life" and the one who "formed all flesh," the Son as "the Christ of love" who "suffered scorn and pain," and the Spirit as the "Spirit of Grace" who "will heal my wound."[46]

Along with the emphasis on differentiation, Celtic prayers and writings maintain close continuity between Father, Son, and Spirit in character, action, and presence. All three persons "cherish me" and "make me holy."[47] One does not gain the sense in reading Celtic writings that the Father and the Son are dwelling remotely in the heavens, with the Spirit alone left to do the work of God on earth. It is a different perspective than that of many contemporary evangelicals, which one can hear popularly expressed, for example, in Melody Green's song "There Is a Redeemer": "Thank you, O my Father, for giving us your Son and leav-

32. Ibid., I, 329.
33. Ibid., III, 337.
34. Ibid., III, 243.
35. Ibid., III, 903.
36. Ibid., III, 203.
37. Ibid., III, 297.
38. Ibid., I, 5.
39. Ibid., I, 339.
40. Ibid., III, 337.
41. Ibid., I, 105.
42. Ibid., I, 3.
43. Ibid., I, 5.
44. Ibid., I, 339.
45. Ibid., III, 337.
46. Ibid., III, 255 and III, 137.
47. Ibid., III, 63.

ing your Spirit till the work on earth is done." Celtic Christians maintained more of a sense of that which Jesus promised in John 14:23: "Those who love me will keep my word, and my Father will love them, and we will come to them and make our home with them" (NRSV). The sense of dwelling in the presence of the Triune God and being enfolded by the persons of the Trinity also bears relation to Jesus' prayer in John 17:21: "that they may all be one. As you, Father, are in me and I am in you, may they also be in us, so that the world may believe that you have sent me" (NRSV).[48] Celtic invocations to the Trinity powerfully convey the pervasive presence of the three persons.

> The Three Who are over me,
> The Three Who are below me,
> The Three Who are above me here,
> The Three Who are above me yonder;
> The Three Who are in the earth,
> The Three Who are in the air,
> The Three Who are in the heaven,
> The Three Who are in the great pouring sea.[49]

The Trinity is "the Three that seek my heart,"[50] the "Three who would justify me,"[51] and the Three who dwell with us eternally.[52] Grace was not viewed so much as a commodity created by God as the very presence of God with us.[53] Egalitarian understandings of the Triune persons are apparent in Celtic affirmations of all three persons "at work to make God's world whole."[54] There is a sense of the "Three-One" mutually serving and loving in all contexts. Jones points out that we learn more about the immanence of God from the Celts than about his transcendence.[55] But I would qualify that Celtic belief in the character of God's immanence flowed from their more relational view of God's eternal nature, and it shaped their understanding of the meaning of such words

---

48. Cf. Volf's development of the theological foundation from which he asserts that "such participation in the communion of the triune God, however, is not only an object of hope for the church, but also its present experience" (*After Our Likeness*, 129).

49. Carmichael, *Carmina Gadelica*, III, 93.

50. Ibid., III, 33.

51. Ibid., I, 73.

52. Ibid., I, 333–35.

53. Cf. "For grace in essence is a way of talking about God's creative, life-giving, beneficent presence to and within all, both personal and impersonal entities, spiritual and material. And that is the comprehensive impression conveyed by Celtic Christianity at its best and most characteristic" (James P. Mackey, ed., *An Introduction to Celtic Christianity* [Edinburgh: T & T Clark, 1995], 13).

54. de Waal, *Celtic Vision*, xxx.

55. Jones, *With an Eagle's Eye*, 23.

as *sovereign, ruling,* and *Lord.* True, they would perhaps be less likely to sing the third verse from the popular trinitarian hymn "Holy, Holy, Holy," which proclaims, "Holy, Holy, Holy! Though the darkness hide Thee, though the eye of sinful man Thy glory may not see." For them, God's nature as a communion of loving, self-revealing persons is the way in which the Godhead is eternally sovereign, ruling, and Lord.[56] One can see consistency between their understanding and that of Orthodox faith as described by Constantine Tsirpanlis: "The three Persons, in the Holy Trinity, share in the activity of each of them. The Father and the Son are included in every action of the Spirit."[57]

It is not surprising that the shape the Celtic church assumed reflected its embrace of God as a loving communion of persons who is both Creator of all and dynamically present in this world. Celtic ecclesial identity expressed three priorities in light of its theology: (1) to be a community of believers who were drawn into the loving communion of the Triune God; (2) to experience and embody that kind of communion in their own relationships in the church; (3) to participate with God in extending the invitation of such union with God and with others to the world (to be discussed in this chapter's section on Celtic missiology).

Communion with God

Union with God was the fundamental way Celtic believers understood the gift of salvation in Christ. Humans were created for relationship with God, and Christ's coming as the second Adam was the way in which fractured God-human relationships could experience reconciliation. God was seen as the initiator of the relationship, creating all things out of the overflow of Triune love, redeeming and healing in Christ what had become distorted and broken, and cleansing and empowering God's creation through the Holy Spirit. God's initiating love works to awaken in humans a response of wholehearted commitment and devotion.

Because of Celtic Christians' desire to respond to and enter into a life of intimacy with God, Celtic communities were shaped less like parish churches and more like monastic communities. Rigorous disciplines were observed to aid all believers in following Christ and serving him more intimately. The Christian life was seen as a call to holiness, which was considered an integral part of salvation in which one participated by the Spirit's help in God's Triune life. The emphasis was not on "sin

---

56. de Waal, *Celtic Vision,* xxix. Cf. N. D. O'Donoghue, who describes "one of the constants of Celtic piety: the Triune God with his heavenly Host and his marvelous creation of earth and sky and ocean is a living intimate presence," in "St. Patrick's Breastplate," in Mackey, *Introduction to Celtic Christianity,* 50.

57. Constantine N. Tsirpanlis, *Introduction to Eastern Patristic Thought and Orthodox Theology* (Collegeville, Minn.: Liturgical Press, 1991), 85.

management," so common in the Western church, but on essential transformation to become more like Christ.[58] Thus, the call to live the life of a monk extended to all, even those who were married with children.[59] Celtic Christians abided in a continual rhythm of prayer (which will be discussed in the third section on liturgies), and fasts and pilgrimages helped them to identify with Christ in his own *kenōsis*, as described by Paul in Philippians 2. These disciplines were also ways to live in greater harmony with God's eternal self-giving nature.

Three points need to be clarified in relation to Celtic ascetic approaches to faith. First, such disciplines were not developed as a way of managing or assuaging guilt. Theological anthropology reveals that Celts were not encumbered by the dark shadow of guilt as a part of their religious outlook. Rather, they focused on humanity in terms of the image of God, seeing it as something that Father, Son, and Spirit had created, redeemed, and continue to heal and sustain. In this they took a different track than mainstream Western theology, which under Augustine's and Tertullian's influences emphasized original sin and legal approaches to theology.[60] Rather than being based on notions of the fall, with sin at the core of our being, Celtic Christianity understood the image of God to be that which is deepest in us. Sin was viewed as having distorted but not erased the image of God. According to J. Philip Newell, in contrast to the Mediterranean tradition, Celts saw people more in light of the "beauty of our origins" than of the "ugliness of our failings."[61] In accordance with Eastern perspectives, God's work in the world was to bring healing and wholeness and release from bondage through his "all sustaining, all permeating" presence.[62]

Second, such rigorous effort was not viewed as a way to earn merit or to diminish the wonder of God's grace. Grace was understood as God's very presence with believers to equip and empower them to live as God's own sons and daughters. Disciplines were ways to receive the gifts of God's beatitudes, such as purity of heart and meekness. Celtic believers reflected a more Eastern Orthodox view, described by Veli-Matti Kärkkäinen as freedom through "cooperation, . . . a synergy of the two wills, divine and human."[63]

58. For a helpful discussion of "sin management," see Willard, *Divine Conspiracy*, 35–59.

59. Ibid., 33.

60. Joyce, *Celtic Christianity*, 23.

61. J. Philip Newell, *Celtic Benediction* (Grand Rapids: Eerdmans, 2000), vii.

62. Mackey, *Introduction to Celtic Christianity*, 15–16; and N. D. O'Donoghue, "St. Patrick's Breastplate," 50.

63. Veli-Matti Kärkkäinen, *An Introduction to Ecclesiology* (Downers Grove, Ill.: InterVarsity, 2002), 19.

Third, such spiritual rigor was seen as being consistent not only with Christ's self-giving but also with the heritage of Christ's church. Celts were deeply influenced by stories of the desert fathers and mothers, particularly St. Anthony (251–356), as noted previously. Thus, as Edward Sellner points out, "The Celtic church was characterized by . . . leaders who ate sparsely and spent long hours in prayer, sometime immersed nightly in the ocean's frigid waters."[64] Though influenced by Eastern monasticism, Celtic forms of monastic life tended to include a greater emphasis on community and care of the common people, along with intense missionary evangelism. In those ways Celtic Christians veered away from the more isolated approaches of the East.[65] The dangers of Celtic asceticism were found in the extreme demands it made on people or in the self-righteous attitudes it could produce.[66] In any case, such rigor in Celtic life challenges postmodern thinkers tempted to romanticize Celtic faith and to use it as a rather dilettante addition to their own spiritual eclecticism.

The desire to be one with the Triune God included being willing to give up that which was most precious, as the Father gave up his own Son, and the Son emptied himself of his divine prerogatives. A common ascetic practice that allowed one to join with Christ in self-giving was leaving home and hearth to wander or going on a pilgrimage. Celtic heroes such as St. Patrick, St. Columcille, and St. Ninian were people of pilgrimage, called *peregrini*, who left the land they loved to carry the love of God to a new region.[67] Thus, in his *Confession*, Patrick expresses relinquishment of his "native country and kin," vowing never to return or to leave Ireland, the place to which he had been called. "Today I can offer . . . confidently my life as a living victim to Christ my God."[68] Where close relationships were so highly treasured, the relinquishment of home, family, and land was considered the hardest form of martyrdom to endure. It was referred to as "white martyrdom" in contrast to "red martyrdom," sacrificing one's life for Christ, and "green martyrdom," participating in severe ascetic practices.[69] In this way the church could reveal its identity as an image of the Triune God, so

64. Sellner, *Wisdom of the Celtic Saints*, 18.

65. G. L. Bray, "Asceticism and Monasticism," in *New Dictionary of Theology*, ed. Sinclair B. Ferguson and David F. Wright (Downers Grove, Ill.: InterVarsity, 2000), 48.

66. Joyce, *Celtic Christianity*, 33–35.

67. According to Jones, the phenomenon of Celtic pilgrimage abroad was curtailed by the late eighth century, after which the emphasis became more the "pilgrimage of the heart" (Jones, *With an Eagle's Eye*, 83).

68. St. Patrick, *Confession*, in R. P. C. Hanson, "The Mission of Saint Patrick," in Mackey, *Introduction to Celtic Christianity*, 43.

69. Sellner, *Wisdom of the Celtic Saints*, 23; cf. Joyce, *Celtic Christianity*, 36.

united with God that it could share in a kind of giving that, however small and feeble in comparison, could point to the Father's giving of the Son and the Son's self-emptying.

Communion with One Another

The central conviction that God exists as a communion of loving persons shaped approaches toward relationships within Celtic Christian communities that have been fairly uncommon throughout the history of the Western church. Embracing the wonder of a God who exists in mutual, self-giving relationships fostered community life that was based on mutuality and unity with diversity. Church leaders worked alongside laypeople to serve one another in a "mutual sharing of gifts."[70] Bishops were active members of the community, ministering directly to the people without the leverage of hierarchical structures. Jones asserts that "it was a community of equals."[71] Education, pastoral care, and liturgical leadership were provided by both men and women, and both men and women in turn helped the leaders "to grow their crops, manage their farms, fish, plant trees and keep their bees."[72] As Edward Sellner explains, "The early founders of the Celtic church 'did not reject,' according to a ninth-century manuscript, *Catalogue of the Saints in Ireland*, 'the service and society of women.'"[73] Women were given leadership opportunities and legal rights similar to those of men. Thus, women could hold "powerful ecclesial positions in communities consisting of both women and men."[74] In fact, Joyce points out that "the earliest known Irish monastic foundations had women as their heads."[75] The most famous abbesses of double monasteries were St. Brigit in Kildare, Ireland, and St. Hild of Whitby, in Northumbria.[76] The rights afforded women were consistent with Celtic pre-Christian culture according to many scholars and confirmed in a recent study by Celtic scholar Peter Berresford Ellis.[77] They were also consistent with Celtic Christian egalitarian views of the Trinity and the conviction that God was dynamically present in and through all things. No person was too low and no work too menial to be a vehicle of God's love and truth. (This idea will be developed more fully in the section on Celtic Christian sacramental approaches to life.)

70. Sellner, *Wisdom of the Celtic Saints*, 18.
71. Jones, *With an Eagle's Eye*, 57.
72. Sellner, *Wisdom of the Celtic Saints*, 18.
73. Ibid., 19.
74. Ibid.
75. Joyce, *Celtic Christianity*, 47.
76. Sellner, *Wisdom of the Celtic Saints*, 19.
77. Peter Berresford Ellis, *Celtic Women: Women in Celtic Society and Literature* (Grand Rapids: Eerdmans, 1996).

Celtic belief in the Trinity and the corresponding desire to participate in relationships of intimacy with God and with one another also
affected the size and character of Celtic ecclesiastical structures. Along
with the early desert Christians, Celtic Christians "valued simplicity
and equality of all in the eyes of God."[78] This propensity was also consistent with traditional Celtic social structures, called clans, which re
mained localized and only loosely connected to other tribes and clans.[79]
Thus, rather than moving toward the more complex and intercon-
nected institutional hierarchy of the Roman Church, Celtic communities remained small monastic villages.[80] "There is no indication that
any large church buildings were ever built."[81] Instead, they tended to
build smaller and more numerous circular church buildings. Rather
than seeking power through expansive politically charged networks,
Celtic believers sought to find strength in closer and more intimate relationships. So vital were relationships for the life of faith that believers
were urged to find an *anamchara,* Gaelic for "friend of the soul" or simply "soul friend."[82] Such a friend and mentor was a person with whom
one could be completely honest, sharing both one's failures and visions
and dreams. Sellner, who researched the ministry of soul friendship for
his doctoral dissertation at Notre Dame, cites the medieval *Book of
Leinster* to demonstrate the pervasive nature of soul friendships in the
Celtic church: "St. Brigit . . . is quoted as telling a cleric who visited her
regularly that 'anyone without a soul friend is like a body without a
head.'" Soul friends were not necessarily male, older, or ordained.
Rather, they were sought for their holiness of life and wisdom in learning, such that both males and females comprised the best-known soul
friends of early Celtic Christians.[83]

The way Celtic believers sought to develop relationships that reflected the self-giving mutuality of the Trinity also affected their approach to possessions. Striving to maintain an egalitarian approach to
community life and respecting God's provision of all things, they eschewed the idea that one could possess and own things. Communities
held things in common, for as John O'Riordain notes:

> There is no word in the Irish language for "private property" and there is
> no verb "to possess." The term for one's property is *mo chuid*—my por-
> tion; the underlying social and legal position being that the wealth of the

78. Sellner, *Wisdom of the Celtic Saints,* 17.
79. Joyce, *Celtic Christianity,* 16.
80. Ibid., 36.
81. Ibid., 37.
82. Sellner, *Wisdom of the Celtic Saints,* 8–9.
83. Ibid., 26.

community was owned by the community and out of that resource each got enough to live on.[84]

A common prayer expresses this concern for charity and justice: "God forbid that we should keep anything belonging to our neighbours."[85] This attitude toward possessions, along with Celtic associations of horses with nobility and prestige, created a challenge for St. Aidan of Lindesfarne in terms of having his own horse. Giving his horse away became an "important symbolic act of renunciation and humility."[86] Celtic Christians seemed to understand what Moltmann so powerfully articulates in *The Source of Life:* "The opposite of poverty isn't property. The opposite of both poverty and property is community. For in community we become rich: rich in friends, in neighbours, in colleagues, in comrades, in brothers and sisters."[87] A common Irish saying reflects this priority: "May your home always be too small to hold all your friends."

Celtic Christian approaches to friendship were not always as "rich" as one might have wished. One major weakness in their community life was that their emphasis on developing intimacy within clans was not accompanied by a continual effort to live at peace with those of other clans. Celts are known for their interclan battles, both before and after becoming Christianized.[88] Celtic monastic communities, in reflecting a commitment to unity in diversity, were like Eastern Orthodox churches that were "made up of a number of independent, yet related autocephalous churches. . . . Just as in the Trinity the persons are equal, so in the church no one bishop can claim to wield absolute power over all the rest."[89] Unfortunately, unlike Eastern Christians, Celtic believers did not tend to organize church councils to resolve differences between clans but instead took up the sword and entered into blood feuds.

Though relationships with other clan members could at times erupt into feuds, Celtic communities were not parochial or forgetful of the larger scope of reality. In fact, the community in which Celtic Christians saw themselves participating included those who had gone before

84. John J. O'Riordain, CSSR, *The Music of What Happens* (Winona, Minn.: St. Mary's Press, 1996), 69.

85. Diarmuid O'Laoghaire, "Prayers and Hymns in the Vernacular," in Mackey, *Introduction to Celtic Christianity*, 302.

86. Sellner, *Wisdom of the Celtic Saints*, 34.

87. Moltmann, *Source of Life*, 109.

88. However, Graydon Snyder asserts, "The Jesus revolution brought an end to warrior ferocity. . . . The Jesus tradition, with its rejection of violence, filtered out Celtic ferocity. This is not to say that fighting departed from the Irish soil. Surely there continued to be quarrels among the tuath. But the *Vitae* and the traditions do not reflect Irish ferocity. Tenacity, yes, ferocity, no" (Snyder, *Irish Jesus, Roman Jesus*, 206).

89. Kärkkäinen, *Introduction to Ecclesiology*, 20.

them. Being united with God involved being joined to others who shared in this Triune communion.[90] As Father, Son, and Spirit came to make their home with them, time opened up to eternity. This world and the next were closely intertwined, like the interweaving lines in Celtic art. This was also consistent with their pre-Christian under-standing.[91] Without a Western dualism of time and eternity and the spiritual and material realms, these believers lived the reality of He-brews 12:1, sensing that they were "surrounded by so great a cloud of witnesses." Prayer was envisioned as joining with a great company of spiritual beings, centered in the Trinity and extending to hosts of an-gels and saints. The most well-known Celtic prayer, *St. Patrick's Breastplate*,[92] conveys this vision of life powerfully. It begins by calling on the Trinity:

> For my shield this day I call:
>   A mighty power:
>   The Holy Trinity!
>   Affirming threeness,
>   Confessing oneness,
>   In the making of all
>   Through love.

The second stanza is a call for Christ's power. The third extends to the power of the seraphim, angels, archangels, the "glorious company of the holy and risen ones, . . . visions prophetic, commands apostolic." Even creation is included in this mighty host of protecting goodness, as evident in the fourth stanza:

> For my shield this day I call:
>   Heaven's might,
>   Sun's brightness,
>   Moon's whiteness,
>   Fire's glory,
>   Lightning's swiftness,
>   Wind's wildness,
>   Ocean's depth,
>   Earth's solidity,
>   Rock's immobility.

90. James P. Mackey refers to these "others" as "extended family" (preface to Davies, *Celtic Spirituality*, xvii).

91. Maria Buckley, *Celtic Spirituality* (Dublin: Mercier Press, 2001), 14.

92. This ancient hymn is also known as *Lorica Sancti Patritii* and "The Deer's Cry." Though it has been attributed at times to St. Patrick, who lived in the fifth century, "the Breastplate in its extant form cannot be traced further back than the eighth century" (O'Donoghue, "St. Patrick's Breastplate," 45).

The prayer continues, inviting God to surround the one praying, to protect him or her from all things (both supernatural and natural destructive powers). Again, it calls on Christ to be "my strong protector" and leads to the most familiar part of the prayer:

> Christ beside me, Christ before me,
> Christ behind me, Christ within me;
> Christ beneath me, Christ above me;
> Christ to right of me, Christ to left of me;
> Christ in my lying, my sitting, my rising;
> Christ in heart of all who know me,
> Christ on tongue of all who meet me,
> Christ in eye of all who see me,
> Christ in ear of all who hear me.

The eighth stanza repeats the words of the first, and the final stanza rises as a crescendo of praise:

> For to the Lord belongs salvation,
>   and to the Lord belongs salvation,
>   and to Christ belongs salvation.
>   May your salvation, Lord, be
>   With us always.[93]

One can see that though Christ is central in this highly revered poem, Celtic believers envisioned a glorious company of beings as their protectors. One Celtic scholar argues that "if one does not understand the nearness and apprehensibility of this 'other world' of the angels and saints, there is no hope at all of understanding Celtic Christianity."[94] In the presence of this heavenly community, one could live:

> Without malice, without jealousy, without envy,
>   Without fear, without terror of any one under the sun,
>   But the Holy Son of God to shield me.[95]

As part of God's beloved creation, animals also could be included in the fellowship of the saints, even "in nibbling, in chewing, in munching."[96] Thus, they too were commended to the protection and love of God and God's emissaries and saints:

93. Ibid., 46–49.
94. Ibid., 51.
95. Carmichael, *Carmina Gadelica*, I, 231.
96. Ibid., I, 247.

Encompass each goat, sheep and lamb,
Each cow and horse, and store,
Surround Thou the flocks and herds,
And tend them to a kindly fold,
Tend them to a kindly fold.[97]

One can see that having embraced the reality of God's presence with them, Celtic Christians developed an ecclesiology that was cosmic in nature. Celtic communities understood themselves as being connected with all of life. Again, this parallels Eastern conceptions: "At the very core of Orthodox theology in general and ecclesiology in particular is the relation of humanity to creation as [a] whole, the cosmos. The church is described in cosmological terms."[98] This perspective also deeply shaped the way in which Celtic Christians approached the stranger and those who had not heard the gospel, as will be explored later.

The conviction of God's Triune presence with Celtic Christians fostered an identity that was trinitarian, one that drew them into intimate and mutual relationality while extending to them relationships of a cosmic scope. It also created an identity of the church as God's sacrament. The church was called both to reflect the image of the Trinity and to be a sacrament of the Trinity to the world.

Sacramental Vision

Celtic people, who viewed themselves as enfolded by God's presence and filled with God's renewing life, understood their lives and the church as incarnational and sacramental. According to Oliver Davies, "Christianity that developed in the Celtic countries during the early Middle Ages is characterized by a strongly incarnational theology, with an emphasis in diverse ways on physicality and materiality that supports both asceticism and sacramentality."[99] We have already looked at Celtic ascetic practices. This section explores the Celtic sacramental vision that led them to develop particular liturgical expressions that touched every aspect of their lives.

Celtic Christians received the sacraments of the church as God's presence, given to them through, though not reduced to, tangible expressions. Having received God's presence through God's gracious means and being thus united with God in Christ, they themselves participated in becoming means of God's grace to the world. They shared in God's sacramental self-offering or "sacred oath" *(sacramentum)*, in-

97. Ibid.
98. Kärkkäinen, *Introduction to Ecclesiology*, 20.
99. Davies, *Celtic Spirituality*, 11.

viting the world into the Triune communion of love.[100] The ways in which they related to one another and to the created order were meant to incarnate the presence of God.

Sacramental Vision of Others

We have already touched on the trinitarian shape of Celtic Christians' intra-church relationships and the idea that they understood the image of God, rather than sin, to be that which is deepest in all people. The priority given to the reality of God's image in all people and the belief that humanity could and did host the divine help to explain why Celtic churches extended a view of sacramentality to women and to people outside their communities (at least those with whom they were not warring). Their sacramental vision created a relative inclusivity of both people and perspectives. Such inclusivity flowed from the trinitarian center of their faith rather than contravening or diminishing their core beliefs. If the Spirit of God could bring the reality of God to bear on a person's life, surely God could also speak through that person, regardless of background, ethnicity, or gender.[101] Thus, women as well as men could be harbingers of God's good news to the community of faithful and to those yet to hear of the evangel.[102] This is redolent of Moltmann's perspective, which he articulates in *The Source of Life:* "In the fellowship of the Holy Spirit, men and women are charismatically commissioned and endowed to preach the gospel. . . . The ordination of women is not a matter of adaptation to changed social conditions. It has to do with new life from the beginnings of the Christian church: life out of the fellowship of the Holy Spirit."[103] Thus, it is not anomalous to discover a Celtic prayer titled "The Baptism by the Knee-Woman."[104] Celtic Christians lived out the conviction that the fellowship of the Triune God is a sacramental presence in the lives of both men and women, who are thus anointed to convey Christ to those around them.[105]

With such a sacramental vision, it is not surprising that Celtic Christian communities were also places of great learning. God was viewed as the source of all truth. Though God's wisdom was evident most pro-

---

100. For information on the Latin term *sacramentum* and its varied uses, see Hans Schwarz, *Divine Communication* (Philadelphia: Fortress, 1985), 53–56.

101. Mackey, *Introduction to Celtic Christianity,* 15–16; and O'Donoghue, "St. Patrick's Breastplate," 50.

102. As mentioned previously, egalitarian views of men and women were also part of the legacy of pre-Christian Celtic culture and were sustained by the Celts' later nonhierarchical understanding of the Trinity. Cf. Joyce, *Celtic Christianity,* 17.

103. Moltmann, *Source of Life,* 101–2.

104. Carmichael, *Carmina Gadelica,* III, 17–19.

105. Jones, *With an Eagle's Eye,* 29.

foundly in the Scriptures and in the baptized community of those in communion with God, one could discover wisdom in a wide range of sources. Celts were eager to learn from others as they went abroad and to draw others into their learning communities. Bede the Venerable (c. 672–735) describes scholars on pilgrimage going to Irish Celtic monasteries to study:

> In the course of time some of these devoted themselves faithfully to the monastic life, while others preferred to travel round to the cells of various teachers and apply themselves to study. The Irish welcomed them all gladly, gave them their daily food, and also provided them with books to read and with instruction, without asking for any payment.[106]

Celtic monasteries preserved intellectual and artistic treasures and became the schools, "even the universities of their time, with thousands of students from all over Europe."[107] The importance of the Bible is evident in the central place it was given to guide the communities' understanding, prayers, and life.[108] Celtic copies and illuminations of the Scriptures are renowned for their beauty and intricacy. Two examples of prominent Celtic theologians whose learning extends to us today are John Scotus Eriugena and St. Columban.[109]

Sacramental Vision of the Created Order and the Arts

The sacramental vision of Celtic peoples also fostered a holistic spirituality in which the material world, nature, and the arts were viewed as means through which God could speak to people.

> There is no plant in the ground
> But is full of His virtue,
> There is no form in the stand
> But is full of His blessings. . . .
>
> There is no bird on the wing,
> There is no star in the sky,
> There is nothing beneath the sun,
> But proclaims His goodness.
> Jesu! Jesu! Jesu!
> Jesu! Meet it were to praise Him.[110]

106. Quoted in Sellner, *Wisdom of the Celtic Saints*, 22.

107. Joyce, *Celtic Christianity*, 157.

108. Cf. Tomás Ó Fiaich, "Irish Monks on the Continent," in Mackey, *Introduction to Celtic Christianity*, 107.

109. Joyce, *Celtic Christianity*, 157.

110. Anonymous woman in Harris afflicted with leprosy, "Jesu Who Ought to Be Praised," in Carmichael, *Celtic Invocations*, 56–57.

Such a comprehensive sacramental approach to life flowed from a particular way of understanding creation and Creator. The relationship between creation and the Creator, nature and grace, has been a point of contention throughout the history of the church. Those whose theology places more emphasis on the fall tend to minimize the correlation between creation and Creator, nature and grace. Celtic believers would stand alongside those who see a closer connection between nature and grace, between God's creation and God's presence in and through creation. One sees obvious harmony between Irenaeus's view of the goodness of creation and wholeness and Celtic perspectives.[111] This is not because Celtic believers denied the fall or were naïve about sin. Their ascetic practices and lifestyles reflect great attentiveness to the battle with sin and the consequences of the fall. Rather, it is because their emphasis was fundamentally centered on the goodness of God, who in grace creates, sustains, liberates, and empowers. As previously mentioned, Celtic sensibility to the nature of God as Triune was at the heart of their sacramental approach to creation. Creation was viewed as part of God's "sacred oath" of love to the world.[112] Nature could convey the truth and goodness of God because Celtic Christians understood the "Three-One" to be at the heart of all things, continually moving outward in self-giving love in order to permeate all of life and to draw all of life into divine healing love. Creation was ennobled first by having been created by a loving Father, who proclaimed it good. Second, creation was seen as blessed in being able to host the divine. The reality of the incarnation as God with us, the eternal Word made flesh, was understood as God's affirmation of the material world, which was drawn with humanity into the process of re-creation in Jesus' life and death. Third, the presence of the Triune God through the Holy Spirit in Christ and through Christ to the world was seen as the way in which God continues to penetrate and consecrate the earthly domain to bring God's healing and restoration.

It is important to clarify that Celtic sacramentalism did not devolve into pantheism or romanticism, which is more common in postmodern Celtic thought.[113] As Jones explains, "The hills, the sky, the sea, the forests were not God, but their spiritual qualities revealed God and were connected to God. All the world was a theophany, a marvelous revelation of God's good-

---

111. Joyce, *Celtic Christianity*, 24.

112. For further reading on Celtic sacramental belief, see Jones, *With an Eagle's Eye*, 21–22; Mackey, *Introduction to Celtic Christianity*, viii, 18, 50; de Waal, *Celtic Vision*, xxx–xxxii; and Sellner, *Wisdom of the Celtic Saints*, 21–22.

113. Cf. "This is no sentimental or romantic pantheism. It is a recognition that everything good comes from God, to be enjoyed for itself and as a reflection of its creator and giver" (de Waal, *Celtic Vision*, xxv).

ness, wonder, and inventiveness."[114] The Celts loved nature, though they recognized the "dark side, the menace of nature's mighty powers as well as its beauty."[115] The message of the *Carmina Gadelica* was not that the world was an idyllic pastoral paradise for the Celts. There was a harshness and rigor to life, "particularly for those engaged in crofting."[116] Rather, the message was that the breath of God's presence touched everything, so that everything could reflect God's mercy and goodness. Creation's goodness was not equated with comfort or ease but rather with its ability to reflect God's own goodness and to aid in sharpening one's own character toward such goodness. Celtic believers saw creation as equipped by God to point beyond itself to the deeper mysteries and meanings of life, which Joyce refers to as a "symbolic consciousness" and which he connects to the sacraments of bread and wine for the way in which through them truth is made tangible to us. Thus, for example, Celts cherished the truth conveyed to them by the eagle. They observed the eagle's soaring freedom to gain a clear vision of that which was remote and distant. The eagle became a reminder to them to rise with God's Spirit and to yearn for an ever more penetrating vision into the wonders of life.

The arts, like God's creation, could be a fount from which truth could flow to refresh and challenge both seekers and believers. Again, one can see the difference between this approach to the aesthetic realm and the way the mainstream Western theological tradition viewed this aspect of life. Whereas Augustine distrusted the visual sense and the use of the imagination, Celtic Christians saw the senses and the imagination as included in the good, creative, and redeeming work of God.[117] Celtic monastic life shared Augustine's view that one could experience God in moments of withdrawal and times of solitude, but their theology was at odds with Augustine's perspective from the *Confessions,* in which he states:

> But what do I love when I love you? Not the beauty of any body or the rhythm of time in its movement; not the radiance of light, so dear to our eyes; not the sweet melodies in the world of manifold sounds; not the perfume of flowers, ointments and spices; not manna and not honey.[118]

114. Jones, *With an Eagle's Eye,* 21.
115. Joyce, *Celtic Christianity,* 17.
116. de Waal, *Celtic Vision,* xxx.
117. This perspective is evident, for example, in Augustine's statement, "The true appropriation of beauty comes only when sense and imagination have resolutely been left behind" (in R. O'Connell, *Art and the Christian Intelligence in St. Augustine* [Oxford: Basil Blackwell, 1978], 37–38. On the other hand, Augustine seemed to appreciate the rich symbolism of Scripture and to allow for a poetic nature in God (Paul Avis, *God and the Creative Imagination* [London: Routledge, 1999], 61).
118. Augustine, *Confessions* X.6.8.

Augustine argued that love of God meant turning away from the sensory realm and looking inward to love what is in the inner self. In contrast, Celtic Christians were what Joyce calls "God-intoxicated people" who relished all of life and who believed that the incarnation gave value to what is sensual, human, and of the material order.[119]

Celtic art, like every other aspect of Celtic Christian life, instantiated Celtic theology. The lines of Celtic drawings had no beginning and no end but as mentioned before interpenetrated one another, like time and eternity. Joyce describes "La Téne Art" as follows:

> Full of swirls, circles and geometric figures, it is a form of abstract art unique for the time, especially in the West. These designs are playful, with a sense of the unending and eternal, showing some relation to or influence from the East. Visually, the Celts liked color, brightness, movement, and human and animal shapes in abstract forms.[120]

Dreams, stories, and song were treated as vehicles of spiritual wisdom. Musicians and storytellers were honored in Celtic society.[121] The people were "full of hymns and prayers, full of music and songs . . . however wild the weather, however miry the road, however dark the night going homeward."[122] Even the language of the Celts, according to poet John O'Donohue, was "a language of lyrical and reverential observation rather than a discursive one."[123] Stories were an esteemed way of educating both women and men and conveyed the creativity and courage of both male and female leaders. Though significant theologians such as John Scotus Eriugena emerged from within Celtic traditions, their number was limited, for theology was generally not conveyed in the more conventional conceptual-analytic and prosaic manner.[124] It was expressed rather as an integration of faith, experience, intellect, and imagination. Leaders, such as St. Columcille of Iona, were poets as well as scholars and writers. Initially, poetry of both a serious and a hu-

119. Furthermore, as de Waal points out, the corporate nature of Celtic spirituality emphasized belonging and relationships, which tended to prevent "any inward journey from becoming one of interior self-exploration" (*Celtic Way of Prayer*, 26).

120. Joyce, *Celtic Christianity*, 6. For a more extensive description of Celtic art, see Hilary Richardson, "Celtic Art," in Mackey, *Introduction to Celtic Christianity*, 359–85.

121. Joyce, *Celtic Christianity*, 16.

122. Carmichael, *Carmina Gadelica*, III, 351.

123. Quoted in Buckley, *Celtic Spirituality*, 77.

124. Mackey, *Introduction to Celtic Christianity*, 16. Edwin Muir, in his poem "The Incarnate One," warns of the "logical hook / On which the Mystery is impaled and bent / Into an ideological argument" (quoted in Malcolm Guite, "Through Literature: Christ and the Redemption of Language," in *Beholding the Glory*, ed. Jeremy Begbie [Grand Rapids: Baker, 2000], 29).

morous nature emerged as doodling on the margins of their copies of Scripture. This did not express a devaluation of Scripture but rather a joy in the biblical evangel and a greater emphasis on the religious imagination. Poetry eventually flourished in Celtic culture and dealt with themes of "God and nature, flora and fauna, the year's turning."[125] Dance was fundamental to heroism such that one ancient saying, attributed to the Irish, cautions, "Never give a sword to a person who can't dance."[126] One could not entrust a weapon to a warrior who was not a dancer, musician, poet, or artist.

Aesthetics enriched worship, and worship shaped Celtic aesthetics, as evident in Celtic prayers, blessings, and visual creativity. High crosses dotted the countryside and offered a kind of "pictorial Bible," which made Scripture accessible to all.[127] One of the most magnificent expressions of the integration of art and faith is found in *The Book of Kells*. This illumination of Scripture was made in Iona and transported to Meath to protect it from destruction by Norse invaders.[128]

The trinitarian, cosmic, and sacramental vision of Celtic Christians kept them from compartmentalizing life dualistically in sacred and secular realms. Spiritual and material, heaven and earth were so interrelated that Celts embraced a unique sense of time. Past and present intertwined in a nonlinear way. Eternity was always present rather than remote. Because time itself was seen as one of God's good creations, the ordinary and the routine could participate as rhythms of God's reign.[129] Thus, time itself was viewed sacramentally, which led Celtic Christians to infuse their days with prayer.

Liturgies of Holistic Spirituality

To remind themselves of the presence of God and God's kingdom realities, Celtic Christians developed an extensive range of liturgies. These poetic rhythms pertained to all of life and helped them to experience every day as God's gift through which "The Gospel of the God of Grace / [would] Be from thy summit to thy sole."[130] A contemporary Welsh poet offers a vision of "keeping house among a cloud of witnesses."[131] Celtic believers lived by such a vision and inculcated rhyth-

125. Buckley, *Celtic Spirituality*, 30.
126. Joyce, *Celtic Christianity*, 7.
127. Ibid., 25.
128. Buckley, *Celtic Spirituality*, 32.
129. Sellner, *Wisdom of the Celtic Saints*, 25.
130. Carmichael, *Carmina Gadelica*, III, 193.
131. Waldo Williams, "Pa Beth Yw Dyn?" in *Dail Pren* (Llandysul: Gomer Press, 1956), 67.

mic liturgies into their lives to sustain heightened awareness amid the mundane challenges of daily living.[132] Frequent expressions of awe and respect for the wonder of God and God's kingdom sustained freedom from feeling tyrannized by time. Celtic sacramental vision evoked a desire to let the chronology of the day become a rhythm of praise, prayer, and gratitude to the one who in grace would draw so near. Bell towers sounded calls to prayer that reached for miles across the countryside. "The spirituality of ordinary lay people was a monastic spirituality . . . which means . . . essentially to follow a liturgical life shaped by a regular, ordered rhythm—yearly, seasonal, daily."[133]

All of life was integrated with worship of the Triune God through prayers, invocations, and praise. When a child was born, three drops were immediately placed on the child's forehead in the name of the Father, Son, and Holy Spirit.[134] When the day began, morning invocations were offered to the "King of moon and sun," to "the King of hosts Who loved us."[135] Prayers were offered at dressing, at the kindling or smooring of the fire, and when partaking of the first food of the day. Each event became an opportunity to rejoice in the wonder of God's good gifts and provision and to be reminded of who God is. Thus, for example, lighting the fire and smooring the fire became ways to reflect on the miracle of divine power, the need for constant renewal, and the Triune encompassment of God around them. Esther de Waal describes the smooring of the fire in the following way:

> The ceremony of smooring the fire at night would also be performed symbolically and with loving care. The embers would be spread evenly on the hearth in the middle of the floor, and formed into a circle which would then be divided into three equal sections around a boss in the center. A peat was laid between each section, the fire laid down in the name of the God of life, the second the God of peace, and third the God of grace. The circle would then be covered over with ashes sufficient to subdue but not extinguish the fire in the name of the three of light. When this was done the woman stretched out her hand and quietly intoned a smooring prayer.[136]

132. Though the scope of this chapter does not allow the inclusion of many examples, interested readers may discover an extensive range of Celtic liturgies in the following works: *Carmina Gadelica*; de Waal, *Celtic Vision*; de Waal, *Celtic Way of Prayer*; Jones, *With an Eagle's Eye*; Buckley, *Celtic Spirituality*; Newell, *Celtic Benediction*, etc.

133. de Waal, *Celtic Way of Prayer*, 52–53.

134. In a ceremony that would precede baptism, the aid-woman would sprinkle three drops of water on the newborn's head in the name of the Trinity and the mother would whisper, "The blessing of the Holy Three / Little love, be dower to thee / Wisdom, Peace and Purity" (de Waal, *Celtic Vision*, xxviii and 61–62).

135. Carmichael, *Carmina Gadelica*, III, 29.

136. de Waal, *Celtic Vision*, 36.

Celtic prayers dedicated "the whole person and every activity to God."[137] A sacramental view of time encouraged them to view fishing, nursing a baby, herding, and farming as ways to give glory to God. Prayers were created to honor God while entering into these daily vocations so that all work could be experienced as a place of God's visitation and a way of testifying to God's goodness. Liturgies developed around seed, water, and food to ensure that material things were not treated as ends in themselves but as prisms through which one could encounter the beauty of God and God's wisdom. Attention was continually drawn back to the Triune God, whether through sprinkling seed with water in the name of the Trinity three days before it was sown or through blessing water to be used for healing "in honor of the three members of the Trinity, whom they addressed as 'everlasting, kindly, wise.'"[138] This made Celtic believers both celebrative and playful, for their lives were permeated with awareness of God's goodness and God's presence. Such heightened attentiveness to God's presence also made them mindful of those who were struggling so that celebration days such as Christmas were days on which, for example, an entire fishing catch was distributed to widows, orphans, and the poor.[139] Death also was not beyond prayers of blessing but was seen as a time for all who loved the dying person to surround her as she embarked on her pilgrimage of "crossing the black river of death." Her soul friend would bless her with a prayer called a "soul leading" or "soul peace," and all present would commend her into the care of the "three persons of the Godhead and all the saints of Heaven."[140] All could be trusted into the care of God, every detail and every monumental aspect of life.

> As it was
> As it is,
> As it shall be
> Evermore,
> O Thou Triune
> Of grace!
> With the ebb,
> With the flow
> O Thou Triune
> Of grace!
> With the ebb,
> With the flow.[141]

137. Ibid., 85.
138. Ibid., 21, 95.
139. Ibid., 22.
140. Ibid., 62.
141. Carmichael, *Carmina Gadelica*, II, 217.

Celtic Missiology

Celtic Christians enfleshed their trinitarian, sacramental, and liturgical ecclesiology when sharing their faith with others. This is evident in both the way people were welcomed into their communities and the way people were sent to distant lands. Hospitality was highly valued. Celtic views of humanity encouraged believers to approach strangers with warmth and generosity.[142] Celtic runes of hospitality to strangers flowed from the belief that in each person the sacramental presence of Christ waited to be discovered.[143] As David Adam writes, "The Celtic Christians did not so much seek to bring Christ as to discover him; not to possess him, but to see him in 'friend and stranger'; to liberate the Christ who is already there in all his riches."[144] The way one treated a stranger was correlated with the way one treated Christ. Thus, it was with an attitude of hospitality that the church was both propelled outward to extend God's love and mercy to the world and also structured to welcome all people in. *Peregrini* were not sent out so much to conquer as to invite people into the glorious feast of faith that God has provided for all people.[145] Since they viewed mission as the work of the Holy Spirit, Celtic Christians approached their participation in that work with both passion and humility.[146]

From its beginnings, Celtic mission reflected a kind of openness and respect wherever Celtic missionaries went. Since Celtic Christians did not claim possession of all truth, they sought to honor truth wherever they discovered it. One of the earliest missionaries to the Celts, St. Patrick, inspired this understanding of missiology. In the midst of rejecting certain customs and condemning violent practices, St. Patrick demonstrated respect for aspects of indigenous Celtic culture, which he assimilated into the Christian faith.[147] This was one reason that "Irish Celts made the transition to Christianity quite readily, accompanied by neither martyrdom nor persecution."[148] Jones comments that Celtic Christians "were ideal missionaries, respecting the culture of those they

---

142. For a rich understanding of the role of hospitality in Christian tradition, see Christine Pohl, *Making Room: Recovering Hospitality as a Christian Tradition* (Grand Rapids: Eerdmans, 1999).

143. Jones, *With an Eagle's Eye*, 29.

144. David Adam, *The Cry of the Deer* (London: SPCK, Triangle Books, 1987), 28.

145. Cf. "Celtic monks had a compulsion to share the joy of their consciousness of the Holy Three and of God's creation" (Jones, *With an Eagle's Eye*, 58).

146. Ibid., 59.

147. For example, St. Patrick rejected the pagan ritual of seeking protection by the sucking of breasts, and he condemned Celts for murdering and enslaving people (Ludwig Bieler, trans., *The Works of St. Patrick* [New York: Paulist Press, 1953], 26, 42, 83).

148. Jones, *With an Eagle's Eye*, 12.

served."[149] Celtic missionaries sought to find bridges of commonality between pagan and Christian faith. While being committed to cast out practices and beliefs that contradicted the gospel, they were yet willing to include perspectives that were harmonious. One example involves Celtic pre-Christian views of God's maternal as well as paternal nature and of women as heroines alongside male heroes. Rather than seeing women in a subordinate light, Celtic converts to Christianity were readily able to accept the scriptural affirmation that women also were created in the image of God, redeemed by Christ, filled with the Holy Spirit, and gifted for leadership in the church. Thus, women were not saddled with ongoing castigations that they were seductive daughters of Eve but were able to be witnesses to the glory of God. Letters as old as the sixth century describe men and women traveling together as missionaries, with women assisting with the celebration of the eucharist. One letter from a bishop in Gaul to Irish missionaries conveys both the reality of the phenomenon and the horror the bishop felt about the inclusion of women in these practices.

> Through a report made by the venerable Sparatus, we have learned that you continually carry around from one of your fellow-countrymen's huts to another, certain tables upon which you celebrate the divine sacrifice of the Mass, assisted by women whom you call *conhospitae;* and while you distribute the eucharist, they take the chalice and administer the blood of Christ to the people. This is an innovation, and unheard-of-superstition. . . . For the love of Christ, and in the name of the Church United . . . we beg you to renounce immediately upon receipt of this letter, these abuses of the table. . . . We appeal to your charity, not only to restrain these little women from staining the holy sacraments by administering them illicitly, but also not to admit to live under your roof any woman who is not your grandmother, your mother, your sister, or your niece.[150]

Contrary to this bishop's view, Celtic believers understood mission to include all people and all places. Celtic churches saw themselves as participating with God in extending healing love to the world through all that believers did in every aspect of their lives, both at home and in pilgrimage abroad. With God "as the most immediate reality of their lives," every place offered the opportunity to invite others into this shared communion.[151] As prayers were offered for the morning kindling of the fire, believers also prayed:

149. Ibid., 58.
150. Sellner, *Wisdom of the Celtic Saints*, 20. Cf. Ellis, *Celtic Women*, 142.
151. de Waal, *Celtic Vision*, xviii–xix.

> God, kindle Thou in my heart within
> A flame of love to my neighbour,
> To my foe, to my friend, to my kindred all,
> To the brave, to the knave, to the thrall.[152]

Even so, as mentioned previously, the Celtic Christian sense of joy in God was so great that leaving home and hearth to share that joy with others was honored as the greatest form of self-giving.

Conclusion

These Celtic "cloud of witnesses" can enrich our lives with their ecclesial gifts of trinitarian identity, sacramental vision, liturgical rhythm, and missiological boldness and humility. With such gifts Celtic Christians were able to unite what is often seen in contemporary life as mutually exclusive. They integrated deep centeredness in the Triune God with respect for those who believed differently. They combined joy in creativity and beauty with a rigorous and disciplined approach to faith and learning. They combined whimsy and playfulness with lives of poverty and sacrifice. They combined rich humor about the little things with deep seriousness about the kingdom reality in their midst. With all that could be said, I would like to conclude with three ways in which Celtic Christianity is profoundly relevant for contemporary evangelicals.

Living in Light of the Triune Nature of God

First, the Celtic Christian tradition offers guidance in our quest to reflect more faithfully the nature of the Triune God whom we serve and adore. We need not leave the implications of God's Triune nature to theological discussions. Nor should we relegate the significance of the Trinity to a prosaic emphasis on unity and diversity or unrealistic pleas to love one another with the "completely selfless love of God."[153] The Celtic tradition reveals specific ways to live our faith in a more integrated and holistic manner so that our identity is more fully rooted in the living God.

This would require that we become more fully convinced that God is indeed at home with us. Like Celtic Christians, we can learn from others, such as our Pentecostal and Wesleyan brothers and sisters, the meaning of having been anointed, filled, and gifted with the Holy Spirit.[154] With Eastern Orthodox believers we can embrace the truth that where the

152. *Carmina Gadelica,* I, 232–33, in de Waal, *Celtic Way of Prayer,* 30–31.

153. Volf, *After Our Likeness,* 191.

154. Howard Snyder has pointed out the following parallels between Celtic and Wesleyan spirituality and ecclesiology: toleration for paradox, accent on grace, salvation as healing, diversity of gifts, call to holiness, positive asceticism, discipline, small Celtic buildings and Methodist chapels, male-female soul friends and Methodist male and fe-

Spirit is, there the Father and the Son are also. Living with greater expectation and openness for God to speak and act in the midst of our ecclesial gatherings would reflect our belief that God is present. This would mean resisting the pressure to create highly structured performances as worship services, after the model of a television or radio show. It would also mean valuing smaller and less formal gatherings.[155]

Furthermore, having our ecclesial identity in the Triune God would aid us in becoming more affirming of our differences in gifting and backgrounds. Rather than using these differences as excuses to lord it over one another, we would be free to serve one another as Jesus commanded and exemplified. Perhaps this trinitarian identity would even lead us to be less mono-ethnic in our congregations and more ecumenical. Diversity exists in the very being of God as Father, Son, and Spirit. Jesus said that the world will believe by the love we have for one another. We can learn negatively from the Celts that feuding with those close at hand while going to far countries to preach the love of Christ inhibits a compelling witness. This is especially pertinent in our time. The body of Christ is becoming increasingly more diverse, for as Philip Jenkins and others have identified, we are in the midst of a major shift in global Christianity from a predominance of northern Christians to that of Christians from the Southern Hemisphere.[156] The evangelical movement is spreading both nationally and globally.[157] Evangelical churches would be able to offer great hope in the midst of the world's many fractured communities and reflect their identity in Christ more effectively by manifesting unity in the midst of diversity in local gatherings. Celtic Christians demonstrated that such unity is best built through relational and personal bridges rather than through imposed impersonal structures. If our own identity is firmly anchored to our Triune God, then we can approach others humbly and with respect, expecting to learn from them. Much of this would depend on our willingness to view those with whom we differ in a sacramental way, as bearers

---

male class leaders, joy and celebration, positive appreciation for nature, Celtic communities and Methodist class meetings (response to the reading of this paper at "The Evangelical Church: Reality or Illusion?" theology conference, Regent College, Vancouver, B.C., 5 October 2002).

155. The Alpha Course is one example of an effective small, more informal gathering that extends hospitality and education to help people grow in Christian faith and relationships.

156. Philip Jenkins, *The Next Christendom: The Rise of Global Christianity* (Oxford: Oxford University Press, 2002).

157. David Cho, "Evangelical and Charismatic Congregations Fill More Pews," *Seattle Times*, 17 September 2002, citing a study titled "Religious Congregations and Membership: 2000."

of Christ's presence. Modeling a commitment to reflect the image of the Trinity could begin with church leadership teams comprised of both men and women from a range of ethnic traditions.

Celtic Christians show us that living in the light of the Triune nature of God can also impact our approach to time and space. Our churches generally reflect the approach to time and space of the culture around us rather than that which is dynamically responsive to the Triune God. We struggle to keep everything balanced in our lives, often in a wild juggling act. We come up with strategies to achieve time management, as if time is primarily something over which we can assert control. Celtic Christianity shows us ways to approach time in which each moment and all moments are centered in the dynamic presence of God. What would this look like for evangelical ecclesiology? First, it would call for the church to teach and model the reality that time itself is a gift from God. As a gift, time is best approached with gratitude rather than as a threat. The church could lead the way in providing a sense of Sabbath shalom and a "broad place" (Ps. 18:19) as people gather to worship the giver of time. Rather than structuring worship as one more tightly filled and programmed element of the week, the church could allow time and space for people to breathe in the life-giving and renewing power of the Spirit of God and to breathe out their anxieties about their often harried existence.

Second, under Celtic influence, churches could help believers respond more faithfully to issues of time as they are sent out into the week. As Celtic believers opened themselves to the creative life of God, they developed psalms and songs to provide continual reminders that the moments and the days belong to God, such that the most menial tasks of the week became altars of self-offering and gratitude to God. Churches could encourage the creation of liturgies that offer people a celebrative rhythm that gives shape to their daily lives. Offering Celtic-like prayers for daily work and routine could help believers expand their imaginations and envision the kingdom of God in their midst. Such prayers could also provide ongoing means through which God could continually draw one's attention back to his purposes and presence. A contemporary example is a web site called "Sacred Space" developed by Irish Jesuits. The site aids Christians from fourteen language groups to open up to God and the Scriptures in order to dwell in God's presence in the midst of the day, even while working at the computer.[158] Celtic approaches would also call for churches to equip their people to go into

---

158. See www.jesuit.ie/prayer. Also, Christine Aroney-Sine, *Listen to the Beat* (Grand Rapids: Baker, 2003) offers numerous ways to experience God's presence and express God's ways through the rhythms of life.

the world and into their jobs as "ministers" of the gospel rather than primarily honoring people's volunteer time spent in and for the church.

What would it mean for people to approach their vocations as the *perigrini*, who modeled their leaving of home and hearth after Christ's *kenōsis* in the incarnation and crucifixion? What would it look like to approach one's normal chores with the mind-set of being "cruciform" and grateful to be so united with Christ? Celtic-informed churches could see part of their mandate as equipping parishioners to engage in this transformation. Rather than living a dichotomization of sacred and secular, God's people could be free to live with less fragmentation. The Celtic cloud of witnesses can remind us today that the gospel is something we can experience from our "summit to our sole."

Equipping church members to live with this integrated and cruciform orientation would demand of the church greater attentiveness to spiritual disciplines. As Dietrich Bonhoeffer points out in *The Cost of Discipleship*, one of the outcomes of the Reformation is a misunderstanding of grace coupled with a paralyzing fear of legalism. "The upshot of it all is that my only duty as a Christian is to leave the world for an hour or so on a Sunday morning and go to church to be assured that my sins are all forgiven. I need no longer try to follow Christ, for cheap grace, the bitterest foe of discipleship, which true discipleship must loathe and detest, has freed me from that."[159] Training and nurturing people more fully in the spiritual disciplines, as was normal for Celtic Christians, would be ways of challenging such a false view of grace. Such training could provide ways for us to grow in spiritual fitness such that grace could have a transforming power both in and through our lives. Admittedly, spiritual disciplines and formation have become fashionable topics in recent years. Celtic Christianity can encourage us to persevere in the disciplines as a response to God's Triune love rather than to dabble in them as techniques for success. It can encourage us to overcome the dichotomies between our faith and our lives through the gift of an "undivided heart" (Ps. 86:11) as we recenter all of life around God's presence with and for us.

Living with a Sacramental Vision

Second, Celtic Christianity offers ecclesial wisdom regarding orientation toward others, the created order, and the arts. Approaching the world more sacramentally means believing with Kallistos Ware that "creation is not an event in the past, but a relationship in the present."[160]

159. Dietrich Bonhoeffer, *The Cost of Discipleship* (London: SCM, 1984), 42.
160. Kallistos Ware, *The Orthodox Way* (Crestwood, N.Y.: St. Vladimir's Seminary Press, 1999), 45.

God's creative and renewing presence could come to bear on all we see and do. Churches that grasp and convey this sacramental vision could help their people recognize that "there are only two ways to live your life—one is as if everything is a miracle, the other is as though nothing is a miracle."[161] Rather than stifling creativity in the church with the mind-sets of "We've never done it that way" or "We've always done it this way," churches could foster an openness to creativity, the arts, and the miraculous in our midst.[162] Artistic emphases are part of our most ancient traditions, dating as far back as the catacombs, which "bear witness that wherever Christians prayed, they sought to create a visual environment that reminded them of the Kingdom of God and helped them to pray."[163]

Such a sacramental vision would also help evangelical churches take stewardship of the environment more seriously. Evangelical churches can learn from those who cherish creation without even knowing the Creator. Disembodied and dematerialized spirituality is a denial of the incarnation and of God's repeated demonstrations that creation can host the divine. Churches that manifest God's presence in caring for creation would be able to offer freedom from the idolatry of things and from the denigration of things.

Dorothy Sayers has argued that the church tends to be rather soft on and almost encouraging of the hard-hearted sins of greed and covetousness.[164] Viewing the material world sacramentally would offer liberation for both the rich, who are stimulated toward ever increasing appetites, and the poor, who see with increasing frustration and hopelessness the widening gap between their lives and those of the affluent. With Celtic Christians we can seek to develop churches resembling generous families rather than businesses. Knowing that God is present in our space and is breathing life and renewal into creation could liberate us from greed and provoke generosity. It could free us to see God's work in the seemingly small and marginal and help us to resist the pull toward the grandiose and powerful. A sacramental vision could increase our confidence and commitment to the reality that the church itself is

161. Attributed to Albert Einstein in Alice Calaprice, ed., *The Expanded Quotable Einstein* (Princeton, N.J.: Princeton University Press, 2000), 319.

162. Centers for evangelicals to pursue interests in theology and the arts exist at Regent College, Vancouver, B.C.; Fuller Seminary, Pasadena, Calif.; and St. Andrews University, Scotland. People who emerge from these centers seek evangelical churches that are open to changes in worship forms and leadership.

163. Jim Forest, "Through Icons: Word and Image Together," in *Beholding the Glory*, 86.

164. Dorothy L. Sayers, "The Other Six Deadly Sins," in *Creed or Chaos* (Manchester, N.H.: Sophia Institute Press, 1974), 85–113.

a sacrament that can participate with God in conveying the enfolding and liberating presence of the "Three-One" to the world.[165]

Living with Missiological Boldness and Humility

Finally, Celtic Christianity could help us recognize ways in which other cultures exhibit marks of the gospel neglected by our own culture. Celtic Christian life may not be as remote as we think. Many two-thirds world cultures share values in common with Celtic Christianity and trinitarian faith—prizing community and relationships over tasks and efficiency, focusing more on a *kairos* than a *chronos* approach to time, honoring relationships of both a temporal and an eternal nature, delighting in nature and in imaginative creativity, refusing to dichotomize the material and the spiritual realms, and sensing deeply the presence of the divine in their midst. Diarmuid O'Laoghaire's description of Celtic Christians could be a description of people in many parts of the two-thirds world: "They were poor, very poor, living in close community."[166] Yet celebration and gratitude are often more integral to their lives, as they were to those of the Celts, than these qualities are to our own. In humility, we as evangelicals could seek to appreciate these differences and to learn from them. We could also be wary lest we contribute to squelching these ways of life, as the Greco-Roman culture came to dominate and smother much of Celtic Christian tradition. Greater faithfulness to God in this area will come as we are freed to see Christ in the stranger, the alien, and those in other cultures.

Celtic Christianity reminds us to celebrate what God is doing in others' lives and to remember that it is God's power that transforms rather than our own human-centered programs. It calls us back to an ecclesiology rooted in Scripture and rich in community life, celebration, and gratitude. Enfolded by the love of God, we can embrace the beauty of our world with less possessiveness, the wonder of God's work with less exclusiveness, and the self-giving call of God's nature in us with less fear. The world has skidded long enough toward ruin through the greed and individualism of dominant cultures. As evangelicals participating in God's purposes, we can join with those of faith throughout the world and throughout time to help seekers move in an entirely different direction—on a journey with God and the host of heaven sing-

---

165. Cf. Clark Pinnock, who remarks that "in the early centuries, the churches were sacramental and charismatic" (*Flame of Love: A Theology of the Holy Spirit* [Downers Grove, Ill.: InterVarsity, 1996], 119).

166. Diarmuid O'Laoghaire, "Prayers and Hymns in the Vernacular," in *Introduction to Celtic Christianity*, 302.

ing, "Blessed be God our Father, the Lord Jesus Christ, and the Holy Spirit."

> May we arise today
> Through a mighty strength, the invocation of the Trinity
> Through belief in the threeness,
> Through confession of the oneness
> Of the Creator of Creation.[167]

> O Sun behind all suns
> O Soul within all souls
> Grant [us] the grace of the day's glory
> Grant [us] the strength of the sun's rays
> That [we] may be well in [our] own souls
> And part of the world's healing this day
> That [we] may be well in [our] own souls
> And part of the world's healing this day.[168]

---

167. Adapted from Kuno Meyer, trans., *Selections from Ancient Irish* (London: Constable, 1911), quoted in de Waal, *Celtic Vision,* xxiii.

168. Newell, *Celtic Benediction,* 41.

Part 2
Programmatic Proposals

3

The Marks
of Evangelical Ecclesiology

HOWARD A. SNYDER

What Is Going On Here?

Visit an evangelical church in almost any North American city—
Tacoma, Washington, or London, Ontario, or Dayton, Ohio. For that
matter, visit an evangelical church in virtually any city in the world that
is tied into our increasingly globalized society. What do you find?

You will likely find certain recognizable public worship patterns that
are telltale signs of the varied history of evangelicalism and of evangelical ecclesiology. More than likely, one of four fairly distinct liturgical
patterns, or a blend of these patterns, will be evident. This chapter
briefly describes these patterns and then digs into the deeper questions
they raise. In particular, this essay addresses two interrelated questions: How can evangelical ecclesiology best be described? And what
are its principal sources? In the process, I will argue that while there *is*
such a thing as evangelical ecclesiology, we might more appropriately
speak of evangelical *ecclesiologies,* in the plural, and ask what each variety might contribute to the whole.

The genres of most evangelical worship can be classified as Anglo-

Catholic, revivalist, Pentecostal-charismatic, rock concert, or some combination of these four. Let's consider them in turn.

The *Anglo-Catholic* pattern (average time: 60 minutes[1]) is marked by a traditional liturgy dating back many centuries. It includes readings from both the Old and New Testaments, often based on a lectionary; read prayers; and hymns in predictable meter, often based on the Psalms and biblical imagery, accompanied (if not overwhelmed) by organ music (preferably a pipe organ). The hymns are more doctrinal than experiential in tone and often trinitarian in form. There is no hand clapping. This pattern includes a relatively brief homily and quite possibly communion. More than likely, the architecture, like the liturgy, can be traced back to medieval Europe. The congregation is mostly well educated and economically secure.

The *revivalist* pattern (average time: 60–75 minutes) is distinctly different. Anyone who knows the history of revivalism will recognize that this type of worship service is an adaptation of a revival meeting. Gospel songs from nineteenth- and early twentieth-century America or England—several verses plus a chorus with repeated phrases—are often used.[2] The worship style is informal, and the tone of the music is experiential, with much of the language focusing on "my" experience of God, conversion, and Christ's atonement, with little trinitarian accent. There is effective use of emotive biblical imagery. The singing is accompanied by a piano or electric organ (unless it is a church in the noninstrumental tradition), with possibly a guitar or other instrument added. More than likely, just one Scripture passage is read, relating to the sermon; no lectionary is followed. Though singing is highly important, the sermon is the apex of the service and probably ends in some type of appeal for commitment. The architecture is a hybrid—essentially an adaptation of the plain meeting-house style combined with elements from older, traditional styles. There probably are no stained-glass windows, except perhaps at the front. The most visible religious symbols are a cross and an open Bible. A demographic profile of the congregation would reveal that the people generally rank somewhat lower than those of the previous model in terms of education, income, and employment, and the average age may be somewhat lower. A sig-

1. Obviously, the time frames indicated for each pattern are imprecise and suggestive. They represent general averages from my own experience in the United States and abroad.

2. About a dozen years ago I visited a public Christian worship service in Shenzhen, China, that still used a pre-1949 hymnal. Though I did not understand the language, I recognized gospel songs such as "Savior, Like a Shepherd Lead Us" from my own church background.

nificant proportion of the congregation is employed as school teachers, nurses, small entrepreneurs, and office workers.[3]

Most traditional African-American worship follows this pattern, though with distinctive cultural elements, a greater use of choirs, and longer, more interactive preaching. The service typically lasts longer (two hours or so), but there is some coming and going of people throughout the service, unlike in predominantly Anglo-American services. Depending on the locale and history of the congregation, some elements of the Pentecostal-charismatic pattern may also be included.

The *Pentecostal-charismatic* pattern (75–105 minutes) also has identifiable elements, though it covers a range from classical Pentecostalism to more recent charismatic styles. Overall this pattern resembles the revivalist more than the Anglo-Catholic genre. The service, however, is more emotive and high energy, with an accent on the Holy Spirit and the present experience of the Spirit more than on Jesus Christ and conversion. Music consists largely of praise songs that came out of the twentieth-century charismatic renewal and the Jesus Movement, with some folk elements. The singing is accompanied by guitars and possibly other instruments, including a piano or electronic keyboard, and several onstage singers or a praise choir. During many of the songs, people clap rhythmically and enthusiastically. A traditional hymn may be sung with an upbeat tempo. There are fairly long periods of singing and praise, interspersed with spontaneous (more or less) brief prayers and possibly "singing in the Spirit." Speaking in tongues may take place within the congregation and perhaps from the platform. The worship space is a large auditorium (possibly a converted theater or warehouse) with little or no liturgical symbols, unless banners have been added. The sermon focuses on daily Christian living and practical life problems, how to live in the Spirit in the everyday world. Many in the congregation are young professionals, though this may vary, and a considerable socioeconomic range may be evident. If the congregation is more classically Pentecostal, other Pentecostal elements such as words of prophecy (perhaps spoken in tongues), healings, and earlier Pentecostal songs are present.

The *rock concert* pattern (90–120 minutes) blends elements of the above styles (particularly revivalist and charismatic). The underlying

3. In my own tradition (growing up Free Methodist in Michigan), these first two patterns were blended. However, the morning service more recognizably followed the Anglo-Catholic style, and the evening "evangelistic service" (as it was often called) was almost pure revival-meeting style. Communion was celebrated quarterly and was even more Anglo-Catholic, with a liturgy dating back (in some elements) a thousand years before the Reformation.

rock concert structure is dominant, however, even though the service may at first appear to be Pentecostal or charismatic. The important point here is not just that the music has been influenced by rock 'n' roll but that the *structure* of the rock concert has become a liturgical form. The entire service is high energy and electronically empowered, with an ensemble of electric guitars, keyboards, and drums and a noticeably higher volume. There are extended sets of music during which most people remain standing, possibly with hands raised but more likely with fingers pointing upward or other gestures rather than the typical receptive, open-palm gesture of charismatic worship. (A more recent gesture is an arms-raised, open-palmed, pushing-upward motion.) The music consists of short phrases repeated many times. The content includes biblical expressions or phrases relating to feeling God's presence, often with a focus on commitment or recommitment and on the present and future coming of the Spirit. Syncopated or irregular rhythms are underscored by a strong, pulsing beat. The congregation often claps after each song or set of songs. There may be no Scripture reading and little prayer, except perhaps for a brief prayer toward the beginning of the service and a few moments of quiet meditation before the teaching. The sermon is usually a Bible teaching relating in some way to personal experience and perhaps delivered in the form of a personal testimony. It may be reinforced by a brief dramatic presentation. The congregation tends to be fairly young.

This fourfold typology may not exhaust the range of possibilities, but it does capture the main varieties of evangelical worship today. Like all typologies, it is an oversimplification. I have often encountered these four patterns just as I have described them, but I have also experienced blendings and mutations of these types—though the distinctive elements were still recognizable. We might think of these four patterns as partially overlapping circles.

One influential blending of these styles is the Willow Creek model (Willow Creek Community Church is in upscale Barrington, Illinois, northwest of Chicago). The Willow Creek model is a "soft" blend of the charismatic and rock concert models with some elements of a nightclub (it is comfortable and nonthreatening). Yet it is carefully time limited with an emphasis on planned excellence. It can also be seen as an adaptation of the revivalist pattern in that the primary focus is evangelism and communicating the essential gospel message.

My point in highlighting these four patterns is not to make a sociological or generational analysis nor to evaluate the strengths and weaknesses of each. My point rather is to ask, What is going on here? What if anything does this diversity of worship patterns say about evangelical conceptions of the church—their nature and their derivation? Do these patterns represent distinctly different ecclesiologies or variations of an identifiable (largely Western) evangelical ecclesiology—or perhaps the absence of an ecclesiology?

It may be helpful to observe, however, that whether there is an "evangelical ecclesiology" is partly a matter of definition. Some might argue that no ecclesiology exists where a doctrine of the church is not explicitly articulated and/or officially (creedally or otherwise) owned. I take a more functional approach and argue that every ecclesial group (i.e., every group that in fact functions as "church") has an actual ecclesiology, whether implicit or explicit, articulated or unarticulated. Further, there is no theological or biblical reason to assume that an articulated ecclesiology is necessarily more coherent than or superior to an implicit one.

So let us inquire into the varieties and sources of evangelical ecclesiologies, viewing them theologically, historically, and sociologically.

The Traditional Marks of the Church

One approach to evangelical ecclesiology is to ask about the "marks" or "notes" of the church as traditionally understood.[4] One could evaluate contemporary evangelical ecclesiologies in terms of the traditional marks, or one could ask whether evangelical ecclesiologies clarify, nuance, or challenge the traditional marks in any way. The approach I have chosen involves commenting briefly on the marks as traditionally understood; raising questions about the classical understanding, particularly on the basis of Scripture (an evangelical thing to do!); and then inquiring into the marks of evangelical ecclesiology. This brief inquiry is thus itself an exercise in *evangelical* ecclesiology: Rather than accepting the four traditional marks as givens, I ask, as evangelicals at their best have always done, Are we really being faithful to the Good News in our ecclesial life and thought?

The classical marks or notes *(notae)* of the church are four: unity, holiness, catholicity, and apostolicity *(ecclesia una, sancta, catholica, et*

---

4. "Are there some signs *(semeion, signa, criteria)*, or marks *(stigma)*, or characteristics *(proprietates)*, or notes *(notae)*, or predicates that signal clearly where the *ekklesia* is to be found? Are certain attributes of communities able to be tested to distinguish between authentic and counterfeit claims, between orthodoxy and heterodoxy, truth and falsity? If not we are left with no way to identify the *ekklesia* even if it should be there," writes Thomas Oden. He adds, "The classic, consensual answer is that the church is recognizable by means of distinguishing marks that differentiate it from other social processes" (Thomas C. Oden, *Life in the Spirit*, vol. 3, *Systematic Theology* [Peabody, Mass.: Prince Press/Hendrickson, 1998], 298). Oden sees the various expositions of such marks and signs in the Christian tradition as "complementary, not contradictory" (299).

apostolica). Based on the Nicene Creed, Christian theology confesses one, holy, catholic, and apostolic church.[5] These four attributes are understood to be essential characteristics of the church, though not a definition of the church—that is, whatever else may be claimed about the church, it is essentially one, holy, catholic, and apostolic, or it is not the true church of Jesus Christ.[6]

Since these marks or notes are enshrined in one of the earliest great creeds, they have been almost universally accepted through the centuries. Other marks may also have been lifted up—for instance, that the church is constituted by the Word and the Spirit—but these four have largely remained unquestioned among Protestants, Catholics, and Orthodox.[7]

There have, of course, been debates about the number and meaning of the marks.[8] Lists of marks have ranged from three to as many as a hundred. The Reformed tradition has often identified unity, holiness, indefectibility, universality, imperishability, and sometimes charity as essential attributes. As Thomas Oden notes, "Various other attributes and criteria have been applied at various times as descriptive criteria of the true church, among them antiquity, efficaciousness of teaching, union of members under one visible head, holiness of the lives of members, validated miracles, prophetic vision, the unhappy end of the church's enemies."[9] Some of these have been especially prominent in evangelical traditions.

The "most widely received, traditional, consensual Protestant definition" of the church, Oden notes, has focused on three essential elements: Word, sacrament, and discipline. Oden sees these as linking with the four classical notes to form what he calls "the Centrist Ecu-

5. I discuss these marks and their adequacy in Howard A. Snyder with Daniel V. Runyon, *Decoding the Church: Mapping the DNA of Christ's Body* (Grand Rapids: Baker, 2002), chap. 1. Some of what follows summarizes pages 17–18 and 21–26 of that book.

6. See Jaroslav Pelikan, *The Emergence of the Catholic Tradition (100–600),* vol. 1 of *The Christian Tradition: A History of the Development of Doctrine* (Chicago: University of Chicago Press, 1971), 156.

7. G. C. Berkouwer, *The Church,* trans. James E. Davison (Grand Rapids: Eerdmans, 1976), 14. Berkouwer organizes his dogmatic exposition of the church around the four classical marks. Craig Van Gelder notes that the communion of saints element from the Apostles' Creed has sometimes been seen as a fifth classic mark describing "the social reality of the church," so that these "five attributes came to be the common way of describing the church over the next centuries" (Craig Van Gelder, *The Essence of the Church: A Community Created by the Spirit* [Grand Rapids: Baker, 2000], 50).

8. See, for example, H. F. Woodhouse, *The Doctrine of the Church in Anglican Theology, 1547–1603* (London: SPCK, 1954), 59–74.

9. Oden, *Life in the Spirit,* 298. Oden notes that Luther listed seven signs: preaching, baptism, the Lord's Supper, the power of the keys, ordination, prayer, and suffering under persecution.

menical Tradition" regarding the church's essence. He proposes a "consolidating thesis": "That *ekklesia* in which the Word is rightly preached and sacraments rightly administered and discipline rightly ordered will be one, holy, catholic, and apostolic."[10]

In short, the four classical marks have generally been accepted by Protestants (and by evangelicals if they have engaged the question), though other marks or elements or criteria have been added. C. Berkouwer says that the "striking thing" is that "the general question about whether the Church is truly one and catholic, apostolic and holy, is not asked; rather, a number of [additional] marks are mentioned, viz., the pure preaching of the gospel, the pure administration of the sacraments, and the exercise of church discipline."[11]

Oden summarizes the four marks in a trinitarian, christological, and to some degree missional sense:

> The *ekklesia* is *one* because it shares in a single body, *corpus Christi,* the risen Lord. It is being made *holy* by participating by faith in the perfect holiness of the Son through the power of the Spirit. It is universal or *catholic* because it offers the whole counsel of God to the whole world. It is *apostolic* because it is sent into the world even as the Son was sent. These are reliable marks of the church.[12]

Two things are immediately clear, however, when we examine the four marks in light of the actual faithfulness, unfaithfulness, and renewal of the church throughout history. First, this formulation of the essential, defining character of the church arose in a particular context and was in fact used as a test to exclude Christians who understood the church differently. Second, at various points in history, earnest, fully orthodox Christians have argued plausibly that *other* marks more truly define the essence of the church's being and faithfulness. This raises the question of the functional adequacy of the classical marks, particularly as they relate to issues of revival, renewal, and the institutional failings of the church—matters often of central concern within evangelical movements.

Questioning the Traditional Marks

Is there a fundamental inadequacy in the classical fourfold delineation of the marks that needs addressing? The very diversity of discus-

10. Ibid., 299.

11. Berkouwer, *Church,* 14f. Berkouwer is speaking here specifically of the Belgic Confession, but the point applies more generally.

12. Oden, *Life in the Spirit,* 297. See the somewhat parallel summary statement on 303.

sions about marks, notes, qualities, and criteria provides ample witness that the dynamic mystery that is the church cannot be captured by a set of specific marks. But beyond these limitations, is there a more fundamental flaw? I suggest two inherent limitations: the ambiguity of the traditional marks and, more seriously, their inadequate biblical grounding.

In the first place, the four classical marks are highly ambiguous. Through the centuries theologians have debated just what they mean and how to interpret them. The marks can be understood in nearly opposite ways. Using sociological categories, one might posit contrasting "church" and "sect" interpretations. Unity and apostolicity, for example, mean very different things to a *church* (which will tend to define them of the institution) and to a *sect* (which will tend to define them charismatically and movementally). One early Anglican writer noted that unity and some other purportedly essential marks could be characteristics of evil as well as of good; there is unity and antiquity, for instance, "in the devil's Church equally as in God's."[13]

Frequently, the marks have been interpreted, or reinterpreted, so as to harmonize with some other schema. For example, someone concerned about the spiritual vitality and evangelistic vigor of the church will interpret these marks in a way consistent with that concern—as John Wesley did.[14] Someone concerned with authority in the church might emphasize unity in doctrinal teaching and apostolic authority and succession, as in classical Roman Catholic ecclesiology. Someone concerned primarily with church growth may reinterpret the marks so as to undergird a church-growth theology, as does Charles Van Engen in *God's Missionary People*.[15] Oden treats the four marks dynamically, bridging the gap between what the church is called to be in Jesus Christ and its frequent failure to be faithful to its calling. When the church as the body of Christ functions optimally, all Christians "are guided by Christ as the body by its head," organically and healthily manifesting unity, holiness, catholicity, and apostolicity. "When bodily passions tyrannize over mind, when conscience is diminished by lust, the whole body malfunctions," and the marks are distorted or obscured.[16]

The ambiguity of the marks makes it clear that they cannot stand alone; they must be held in tandem with other ecclesial affirmations. The traditional marks seem to have little direct relevance for most

13. Woodhouse, *Doctrine of the Church*, 61, citing Anglican preacher and martyr John Bradford (c. 1510–55).

14. Howard A. Snyder, *The Radical Wesley and Patterns of Church Renewal* (1980; reprint, Eugene, Ore.: Wipf & Stock, 1996), 76.

15. Charles Van Engen, *God's Missionary People* (Grand Rapids: Baker, 1991). Though Van Engen's treatment is creative, he simply accepts the four classical marks as givens.

16. Oden, *Life in the Spirit*, 291.

evangelical ecclesiology, which generally either has said little about the traditional marks or has interpreted them in evangelistic, missionary, or movemental terms.

Perhaps evangelicals have felt little allegiance toward the four traditional marks in part because they are not very explicitly biblical. This suggests a more serious limitation to the traditional marks: They have an inadequate biblical basis.

The New Testament passage that most clearly emphasizes the unity of the church, for instance, is Ephesians 4:3–6: "Make every effort to keep the unity of the Spirit through the bond of peace. There is one body and one Spirit—just as you were called to one hope when you were called—one Lord, one faith, one baptism; one God and Father of all, who is over all and through all and in all" (NIV). This passage is no doubt highly ecclesiological, stressing particularly the unity (and by implication the catholicity) of the church. Other passages in Ephesians point to the church's holiness (especially 5:26–27) and apostolicity (especially 2:20, "built on the foundation of the apostles and prophets," and 3:5, "revealed by the Spirit to God's holy apostles and prophets"). If one takes in view the entire New Testament, a number of other passages may be cited—for example, John 17 on the unity of the church.

If we approach Scripture more inductively, however, we find that the four traditional marks tell only part of the story and thus bias ecclesiology in a particular direction. In a sense, the four marks give only a half picture; they highlight only one side of the church's spiritual genetic inheritance.[17] Ephesians 4 is a good example. Verse 7, immediately following the passage quoted above, says, "But to each one of us grace has been given as Christ apportioned it" (NIV). Here the apostle introduces the accent of charismatic diversity in contrast to the unity stressed at the beginning of the chapter.

This is not the place for extended biblical exegesis. However, if we go to the Bible with the hunch that the four traditional marks may tell only part of the story, we quickly find evidence of the "missing half." New Testament passages show, for example:

1. The church is *many* as well as *one*. It is manifold and diverse. This is evident both in the diversity of the first Christian congregations and also in those passages that celebrate the ethnic, socioeconomic, and class diversity of the church (e.g., 1 Cor. 12:13; Gal. 3:23–29; Col. 3:11). Surely the apostle Paul's point in these passages is not only the unity we have in Christ but also the diversity, whose sociological evidence in the

---

17. This is elaborated on in Snyder and Runyon, *Decoding the Church*, in which the genetic model of DNA is used heuristically to explore aspects of the church's life and mission.

church is what makes the unity so miraculous.[18] The "one body, many members" theme in the New Testament is also relevant. The church both locally and globally is *both* one and many.

2. The church is *charismatic* as well as *holy*. The same Holy Spirit who sanctifies the church invests it with gifts. The church functions best with *both* the fruit and the gifts of the Spirit, incarnating both the character and the charisma of Jesus. Because of the Holy Spirit, the church is inherently charismatic. Several Scripture passages link the holiness of the church with its being a gift-endowed community of the Spirit (e.g., Acts 1:8; 2:4–38; Heb. 2:4; 1 Peter 2:9).

Church history shows the difficulty of holding holiness and charisma together, both in theology and in practice. Charismatic gifts often prove controversial. The Spirit gives gifts to whom he pleases, not always to whom official leaders would prefer (1 Cor. 12:4–11). Leaders tend to focus on holy or sacred doctrine, tradition, or office and to deny or limit charisma, while newly gifted believers may rely on charisma and be lax in ethical holiness (1 Cor. 3:1–3; 13:3). Among many examples of this dynamic is the early twentieth-century split in the Holiness Movement that birthed modern-day Pentecostalism.[19]

3. The church is both *universal* and *local*. The New Testament uses the word *church* in both the local and the universal or catholic sense. The actual history of the early Christian communities and the apostolic teaching about adapting to local customs of food and dress underscore the same point. The New Testament puts at least as much stress on the local character of the church as it does on its universality. The church exists both as the worldwide body of Christ (in this world and beyond) and as very diverse, particular, local communities, each with its own flavor, style, and culture. The church both transcends culture and is contextualized or incarnated in particular cultures.[20]

Here also the church finds it difficult to keep the biblical balance. Often as denominations grow and bureaucratize, they increasingly

18. One can trace similar themes in the Old Testament. Israel, though one, was twelve tribes; she was to have particular concern for aliens and sojourners who acknowledged God and became part of God's people; and God repeatedly reminded Israel that his people would eventually incorporate people from many nations.

19. See Vinson Synan, *The Holiness-Pentecostal Tradition: Charismatic Movements in the Twentieth Century* (Grand Rapids: Eerdmans, 1997).

20. Classical expositions of the church's unity and catholicity often acknowledge that these marks do not deny and may in some sense incorporate diversity and "localness" or contextualization. But since local contextual diversity is not given equal weight with unity and catholicity, the bias is in favor of the more general qualities over the more particular ones. This has its parallel in the tendency of Western trinitarian theology to posit first and put more stress on the oneness of God than on God's threeness.

value uniformity: doing things "our way" in every place, with a kind of franchise mentality. Yet in local contexts, churches tend to adapt to local realities and take on local character. This often then plays out theologically as a tension or conflict between unity at the broader level and freedom, independence, or autonomy at the local level. Both sides can and often do make their appeal to Scripture.[21]

4. The church is as truly *prophetic* as it is *apostolic*, "built on the foundation of the apostles and prophets" (Eph. 2:20). Jesus is both the apostle and the prophet who establishes the church (Acts 3:22; Heb. 3:1). The biblical pairing of "apostles and prophets" is a sign that two emphases here must be held together. Biblically, there is a certain priority of apostles over prophets, as suggested in 1 Corinthians 12:28 and Ephesians 4:11. Apostles establish the church on the basis of and under the authority of Jesus Christ and have initial oversight responsibility, while prophets subsequently stir up, inspire, invigorate, and when necessary pronounce judgment on the church.

The church is apostolic in the sense that it is sent into the world as the Father sent Jesus, sent to continue the works Jesus began (John 14:12; 20:21). Jesus first sent out his twelve apostles, then Paul and an expanding corps of apostolic witnesses (Rom. 16:7; Eph. 4:11). Faithfulness to both the words and the works of Jesus Christ is involved with true apostolicity.

But the church is also prophetic. If its apostolicity is really empowered by the Holy Spirit, then it *will* be prophetic. Biblically, it seems the church is prophetic primarily in two senses: first, in being a community that visibly incarnates the prophetic message of justice, mercy, and truth found in the Old Testament as well as in the life of Jesus, and second, in proclaiming the good news of God's reign. This means different things in different historical contexts, but it always means being salt and light in the present world (Matt. 5:14; John 8:12; Phil. 2:15).

In sum, if we consult the full range of Scripture, we see that the church is *both* one and diverse; *both* holy and charismatic; *both* univer-

---

21. Many churches, as they become large denominations, tend to value uniformity over particularity, universality over locality, transcultural transcendence over cultural incarnation, and predictability over innovation. In sectarian (including many evangelical) movements, the tendency is often in the opposite direction. Yet in the familiar sect-to-church pattern, such movements (evangelical or not) with time also often tend to accent the universal over the local. This is not strictly a sect-to-church phenomenon, however; some sectarian movements initially place high value on their universal appeal ("This is the new, unique thing God is now doing!"), but as they lose their zeal, they become less cohesive or "connectional" and more locally focused. Both these patterns can be traced in the history of numerous North American denominations, especially in the nineteenth and twentieth centuries.

sal and local; *both* apostolic and prophetic. Scripture shows that this complementary "missing half" of the church's genetic code is as firmly grounded in divine revelation as are the more traditional and familiar marks. These contrasting qualities are not the *opposites* of the four classical marks, though at some level they are in tension with them. The complement of unity is not division but *diversity*. The complement of holiness is not sinfulness but *charisma*. Catholic pairs not with locally limited but with *contextual* or locally incarnated. The complement of apostolic is not heretical but *prophetic*—focused on justice as well as on truth, on being a contrast society as well as a winsome evangelistic community.[22]

Though Christian theology has spoken of one, holy, catholic, and apostolic church, less frequently has it affirmed the church as *diverse, charismatic, local,* and *prophetic.* Yet if we take our ecclesiological cues from the New Testament, we see that it is precisely this second set of qualities that is particularly prominent. In Acts, the *diversity* of the church is clear when one compares the different early Christian communities, such as those at Jerusalem, Antioch, Philippi, and Corinth. The *charismatic* nature of the early church is obvious in the "signs and wonders" accent in Scripture. The *locality* or localness of the church is evident precisely in the fact that the church had to be planted and contextualized in specific local social environments. The *prophetic* character of the early church is seen in its formation of a contrast society (Acts 2:42–47) whose values and worldview clashed with those of the dominant society (Acts 19).

These two sets of qualities can yield contrasting models of the church if the complementarity is not maintained. Correlating these qualities to a movement/institution (or organism/organization) frame-

---

22. I am not arguing that there is a "binary" or strict parallel relationship between these two sets of marks but merely that the second set points to limitations of the first. Interestingly, the British Methodist theologian William Pope (1822–1903) in his *Compendium of Christian Theology* similarly suggested "correlative qualities of the one Church of Christ" that connect "each attribute with its seeming counterpart." He paired unity with diversity and variety, sanctity with imperfection, catholicity with "localisation," and apostolicity with confessionalism, adding also the pairs invisible/visible, indefectible/mutable, and triumphal/militant or glory/militant weakness (which Oden relabels meekness). Pope argued that "the true church of Christ is a body in which these opposite attributes unite." However, he prioritized the first set in this pairing over the second, speaking of "higher and lower" attributes rather than making them truly correlative, using with some caution the analogy of the two natures of Jesus Christ. "The higher and Divine church is in the visible and human as a temple: distinct from it" (William Burt Pope, *A Compendium of Christian Theology,* 2d ed., 3 vols. [New York: Hunt and Eaton, 1889], 3:266–87). See Oden, *Life in the Spirit,* 291. Oden agrees that within the "unified organism" that is the body of Christ, "many complementary attributes are associated."

work suggests a dynamic in which one set of qualities tends to predominate during some stages of the church's life and the other set during other stages:

Organic Movement	Organized Institution
Diverse, varied	One, uniform
Charismatic	Holy (sacred)
Local, contextualized	Catholic, universal
Prophetic Word	Apostolic authority

When the church is a dynamic movement, it tends to be prophetic, charismatically empowered, diverse (perhaps contrasting with the larger church), and more contextualized to its immediate social environment.[23] But when the church transitions into a more settled institution or organization, it tends to celebrate (and enforce) its oneness, holiness (especially sacredness as institution), universality, and apostolic authority.[24] This is true historically and sociologically but also theologically. That is, these contrasting models tend to emerge historically in different social contexts, but they also testify to a deep theological truth about the church—namely, that faithful churches live in dynamic tension with these pairs of character traits (or genetic predispositions).

It might be tempting at this point to resort to the visible/invisible distinction, as ecclesiology (evangelical and otherwise) often does. Or one could make a distinction between the actual and the ideal church, or between the church as theologically understood and the church as sociologically understood (which can be another form of the invisible/visible distinction).

Biblically, however, such dualism is not permissible. Though clearly the church transcends its visible, earthly embodiment, nowhere does the New Testament use the visible/invisible distinction as a way of explaining or justifying the frequent unfaithfulness or imperfection of the earthly visible church. The New Testament does distinguish between the *calling* of the church and the church's *actual behavior*, but this does not amount to the visible/invisible distinction. Quite the opposite: The

23. Typically, much of the dynamic of a new social movement springs from its immersion in its immediate social context.

24. We can recognize that even in its institutional phase the church may stress unity, holiness, etc., as spiritual-organic qualities and that it may in fact be to some degree diverse, charismatic, local, and prophetic—though the accent tends to fall more on the institutional aspects of these qualities. It is also true that the church in its movement stage often aims to be one, holy, catholic, and apostolic in a dynamic, functional sense, no doubt with varying levels of success.

calling/actual-behavior distinction warns that the church must not resort to invisible or ideal categories to evade its responsibility to be, in
social visibility, fully the body of Christ. "I urge you to live a life worthy
of the calling you have received" (Eph. 4:1 NIV); "live lives worthy of
God, who calls you into his kingdom and glory" (1 Thess. 2:12 NIV).[25]

Biblically, the church legitimately manifests and is called to visibly
show forth equally both sets of marks as an expression of its genetic en-
dowment. It would be misleading to set these two pairs of marks in
opposition to each other. Given the mystery of the church as the multi-
faceted emblem of God's kingdom, it is clear that these contrasting qualities must be taken not as opposites but as correlatives—as complementary, corollary truths about the one mystery that is the body of Christ,
equally important to the church both theologically and sociologically.
An accent only or primarily on the four traditional marks reduces the
mystery of the church and may be biased against the repeated renewing
work of the Holy Spirit. It packages ecclesiology too neatly, setting the
stage for splits and new movements that sense intuitively that something is missing in the church's essential self-understanding. A more
biblically normative and holistic ecclesiology affirms that the true
church is always, at one and the same time, one and many, holy and
charismatic, apostolic and prophetic, catholic and contextual—and that
the church is called always in every context to visibly embody these
qualities, even if it often does so imperfectly. This, it seems to me, is a
truly evangelical ecclesiology, even though this (or any) delineation of
marks does not embody a full theology of the church.[26]

If we base ecclesiology on the full range of biblical revelation rather
than only on the Bible as "normed" (and perhaps "de-radicalized") by
particular creeds, we have a fuller, more potent, and fundamentally truer
image of the mystery that is the body of Christ than if we accept uncrit-

25. Paul's description of the church in 1 Corinthians 3 as "carnal" or "worldly" or "in
the flesh" is similar. He said the church was "God's temple" in which "God's Spirit lives"
(3:16), but the Corinthian church was not living consistently with this reality. He expected them to be *both* holy and charismatic. From this perspective the letters to the
seven churches in Revelation 2–3 are also important ecclesiologically.

26. Most ecclesiological discussions rightly do not limit themselves to a treatment of
"marks" or "notes" but include other aspects of the church's life and witness. The church
as "image" or "reflection" or "echo" of the Trinity should be considered in this connection. Would not a proper trinitarian ecclesiology stress both these sets of marks in mutual interdependence—a sort of ecclesiological *perichōrēsis*—rather than stressing one to
the exclusion or eclipsing of the other? See Snyder and Runyon, *Decoding the Church*,
54–56; Miroslav Volf, *After Our Likeness: The Church as the Image of the Trinity* (Grand
Rapids: Eerdmans, 1998); and Colin Gunton, *The Promise of Trinitarian Theology*, 2d ed.
(Edinburgh: T & T Clark, 1997), chap. 4, "The Community: The Trinity and the Being of
the Church."

ically the classical marks, making them fundamentally definitional. We need this more complete picture of the church's being and calling: Not only one, holy, catholic, apostolic church but also many, particular, charismatic, prophetic churches. These two sets of qualities *together* make up the complex reality of the church, each pair synergistically representing or constituting complementary qualities or facets of the church's life.

It is just at this point that the question of the *sociology* of the church deserves some attention. I suggested above that it would be biblically and theologically illegitimate to affirm that *theologically* the church is one, holy, catholic, and apostolic but that *sociologically* it might (less perfectly or ideally) be many, charismatic, local, and prophetic. The church is called to be visibly, in society and in its social form, just what it is called to be theologically. A healthy evangelical church will exhibit all eight of these character qualities in its actual social form as well as in its theological self-description.

Here we might ponder the "religious economy" model advanced by sociologists Rodney Stark and Roger Finke. This approach gives ecclesiology a helpful dose of sociological realism.[27] Consider the following propositions that Stark and Finke claim apply to religious groups or "firms":

> The higher a group's level of tension with its surroundings, the higher its average level of member commitment.
>
> Congregational size is inversely related to the average level of member commitment.
>
> Growth (especially at the congregational level) and the professionalization of their ecclesiastics will tend to shift religious organizations from higher to lower tension—from sects to churches.
>
> To the extent that tendencies toward greater tension are suppressed, the average level of commitment of a religious group will be reduced by the departure or expulsion of the most highly committed members.

27. See, among other works, Roger Finke and Rodney Stark, *The Churching of America, 1776–1990: Winners and Losers in Our Religious Economy* (New Brunswick, N.J.: Rutgers University Press, 1992); Rodney Stark, *The Rise of Christianity: A Sociologist Reconsiders History* (Princeton, N.J.: Princeton University Press, 1996); and Rodney Stark and Roger Finke, *Acts of Faith: Explaining the Human Side of Religion* (Berkeley: University of California Press, 2000). While the "religious economy" model is controversial and has been criticized as having limited applicability, it does highlight the degree to which churches function as social organisms. Stark and Finke's essential contribution is not the claim that "the contemporary religious marketplace is thronged with seekers looking for something importantly different" (John Stackhouse), which may or may not be true, depending on context, but rather the recognition that factors such as commitment level, congregational size, professionalization, and relative tension with the surrounding culture do in fact affect the ecclesial behaviors and beliefs of Christians. In other words, they are elements in ecclesiology. See John G. Stackhouse, Jr., "The Renaissance of Religion in Canada," *Books & Culture* 8, no. 6 (November–December 2002): 20.

As moderate religious bodies continue to reduce their tension [with the surrounding social context], they move away from the larger niches and cease to grow.

At any given moment, religious growth will therefore be limited primarily to somewhat higher tension bodies.[28]

Do these sociological observations have anything to say to ecclesiology? I believe they do and suggest four propositions for exploration:

1. Higher-tension and lower-tension churches define the key marks differently. Higher-tension bodies see the marks more as descriptors of the actual life and behavior of the Christian community and Christian disciples, while lower-tension bodies see them more as abstract ideals or overarching theological affirmations.
2. Lower-tension religious bodies tend to prioritize the four traditional marks over the correlative qualities of diversity, charisma, contextualization, and propheticality (which are downplayed or ignored) and tend to interpret the traditional qualities as marks of the church as institution.
3. Higher-tension religious groups tend, partly as a reaction and partly because of a renewed experiential sense of the work of the Holy Spirit, to prioritize or put equal stress on the second set of marks as compared to the four traditional marks.
4. Largely for theological reasons but also presumably for sociological, psychological, and personal reasons, evangelical churches and movements tend to be higher-tension religious groups. But as religious "firms," evangelical churches are subject to the same dynamics that typically lead groups to move from higher to lower tension with the sociocultural environment.

From these rather theoretical considerations we may now move to a more historical discussion of evangelical ecclesiologies.

Sources of Evangelical Ecclesiologies

Due to the circumstances that gave rise to contemporary evangelicalism, twentieth-century evangelicals understandably tended to define themselves primarily in theological terms. This practice contrasted with that of earlier evangelicals; most evangelicals of the seventeenth and

28. Stark and Finke, *Acts of Faith*, propositions 47, 51, 66, 68, 85, and 86 of a total of 99, listed on 277–86 and discussed throughout the book. For some of these propositions, Stark and Finke acknowledge (and critique) the pioneering work of H. Richard Niebuhr, *The Social Sources of Denominationalism* (Cleveland: World Publishing, 1964).

eighteenth centuries, such as those surveyed in W. R. Ward's *Protestant Evangelical Awakening,* made authentic Christian *experience* and *practice* central, not in opposition to doctrine but rather as the intent, meaning, and authentication of doctrine.[29]

Ecclesiologically, however, contemporary evangelicalism is a hybrid. This is true in large measure because ecclesiology necessarily involves not only doctrine but also social practices, manner of life, ecclesiastical structures—in short, the entire spectrum of the social embodiment of the church. Evangelicalism is among other things a social organism, a network of socioreligious bodies. As such, evangelical ecclesiology has a complex range of sources that affects not only its form but also its theological content. The four patterns sketched at the beginning of this essay hint at this.

There are five primary sources of *actual* (not exclusively theological or theoretical) evangelical ecclesiologies:

1. *The Anglo-Catholic and Reformed/Lutheran-Catholic heritage.* Whenever any church or movement gives birth to a new movement, the new body carries a good deal of genetic material with it from its parent. The Reformation, after all, was a *reformation,* not a re-creation or reconstitution of the church. It seems, as many have argued, that the magisterial Reformation was predominantly a reformation of soteriology; much less was it a reformation of ecclesiology. Much medieval Roman Catholic ecclesiology was carried over into all branches of Protestantism (in varying degrees). The principal ecclesiological reforms concerned the sacraments, the centrality of Scripture and therefore of preaching, and perhaps an increased emphasis on congregational life. The main ecclesiological *continuities* were the acceptance of the clergy/laity division (despite the priesthood of believers accent), the state-established church arrangement, and the centrality (in practice and theology) of church buildings and the marginalization or prohibition of house churches or "conventicles."

2. *The Radical Reformation and free church tradition.* More than evangelicals often realize, evangelical denominations and ecclesiology derive from the Anabaptist, believers' church, and free church tradition.[30] Though different shadings of meaning and accents are present in Anabaptist and free church ecclesiologies, broadly they may be con-

---

29. W. R. Ward, *The Protestant Evangelical Awakening* (Cambridge: Cambridge University Press, 1992); and Howard A. Snyder, *Signs of the Spirit: How God Reshapes the Church* (1989; reprint, Eugene, Ore.: Wipf and Stock, 1997).

30. I show how the believers' church tradition influenced John Wesley (and thus to a degree Methodist ecclesiology) in *Radical Wesley.*

sidered one tradition.[31] This stream also, of course, owes something to Roman Catholicism, but much of its understanding of ecclesiology and discipleship has more in common with pre-Reformation sectarian or "schismatic" groups such as the Waldensians than with Catholicism, which persecuted or excommunicated such groups.[32]

As the terms *free church* and *believers' church* imply, ecclesiology is the key issue. What does it mean to be the people of God in actual fact, in history? What social form is the faithful church called on to assume?[33]

A fundamental Radical Reformation critique has always been that the Reformation was incomplete. It failed to carry through to ecclesiology. Faithfulness to Jesus Christ requires that the church be restored to the pattern and dynamic of the early or "primitive" church.[34] Consciously or unconsciously, most evangelical bodies have accepted the free church critique at least in part—accepting the view that church and state should be separate. Yet most have not fundamentally critiqued the clergy/laity division (in other words, they have not adopted the doctrine of the priesthood of believers as a fundamental ministry and ecclesiological principle, even if they have adopted it soteriologically). And for most evangelical bodies, church life and discipleship are centered primarily in church buildings rather than in homes or in the public square.

Because of the double (and in some ways schizophrenic) heritage gained from the magisterial and Radical Reformation, most evangelical bodies have essentially a Lutheran, Reformed, or Wesleyan theology into which are blended or grafted Anabaptist ecclesiological elements.

3. *The revivalist tradition.* In the American experience especially, the picture is complicated by the added influence of the revivalist tradition in its various forms. Although this stream includes some inheritance from eighteenth- and nineteenth-century evangelical awakenings in Europe and the United States, its most potent form is North American

31. See Donald F. Durnbaugh, "Free Church Tradition in America," in *Dictionary of Christianity in America*, ed. Donald G. Reid (Downers Grove, Ill.: InterVarsity, 1990), 450–52; Franklin Hamlin Littell, *The Free Church* (Boston: Starr King Press, 1957); Donald F. Durnbaugh, *The Believers' Church: The History and Character of Radical Protestantism* (New York: Macmillan, 1968); and Barry L. Callen, *Radical Christianity: The Believers Church Tradition in Christianity's History and Future* (Nappanee, Ind.: Evangel, 1999).

32. Gunnar Westin, *The Free Church through the Ages*, trans. Virgil A. Olson (Nashville: Broadman, 1958), chap. 2, "Free Church Movements as Heresies."

33. This was a major theme in the writings of John Howard Yoder.

34. Here primitivism, restorationism, and restitutionism as key ecclesiological impulses might be explored further. See Richard T. Hughes, ed., *The American Quest for the Primitive Church* (Urbana, Ill.: University of Illinois Press, 1988).

revivalism beginning with Charles Finney and continuing in different ways with D. L. Moody and others.

Revivalism tends to reinforce free church ecclesiology through its emphasis on voluntarism, adult individual decision, and the importance of vital congregational life. Revivalism can, of course, flourish in a variety of ecclesiastical contexts.[35] Revivalist ecclesiology, however (to the degree that there is such a thing), is essentially free church. Yet it adds its own distinctive elements. For example, revivalism often inculcates the "revival model" of church life—periodic or seasonal dramatic renewals with implicitly intervening low points or troughs—and accents the value of the emotional experience or appropriation of the faith. It consequently tends to deemphasize steady, ongoing discipleship in simple obedience to Christ, a key accent of Anabaptism. These tendencies were reinforced by the rise and influence of revivalist gospel-song hymnody.

Nineteenth-century American Methodism provides an instructive case study. One can trace in Methodist patterns of evangelism, nurture, discipleship, and to some degree worship a transition from roughly the 1830s on due (in part) to the influence of revivalism.[36] The class meeting (a key Methodist structure for evangelism, discipleship, and socialization) declined as churches adopted revivalistic prayer meetings. The decline of the weekly class meeting and the rise of the revivalistic camp meeting were interrelated developments. Long-term, lifelong discipleship and sanctification were replaced by the revivalist model. To some degree the Holiness Movement, sparked largely by Phoebe Palmer, followed the psychology of Charles Finney more than that of John Wesley.[37]

4. *American democracy.* The democratization of American Christianity has been widely documented and debated.[38] Though the process can be understood in various ways and affected different church traditions unevenly, virtually all North American church bodies responded in one way or another to the spirit of democracy and the democratic ideal.

35. See, for example, Jay P. Dolan, *Catholic Revivalism: The American Experience, 1830–1900* (Notre Dame, Ind.: University of Notre Dame Press, 1978).

36. Clearly, other dynamics were operating as well, some of which illustrate Stark and Finke's propositions.

37. A significant study is Philip F. Hardt, "'A Prudential Means of Grace': The Class Meeting in Early New York City Methodism" (Ph.D. diss., Fordham University, 1998). Using New York City Methodist class records, Hardt documents several divergences from "the original Wesleyan model" of the class meeting. It is important to note, however, that for a variety of reasons the Methodist Episcopal Church from the 1850s on did not for the most part follow Palmer's lead but in its ecclesiological practice and self-understanding moved more toward the Anglo-Catholic side of the spectrum.

38. Nathan O. Hatch, *The Democratization of American Christianity* (New Haven: Yale University Press, 1989).

American democracy (i.e., democratic republicanism) reinforced key aspects of free church ecclesiology, but at the same time it undermined others. Voluntarism tended to replace authoritarian hierarchical structures, but individualism undercut community and covenant solidarity. The result was the American denominational system; denominationalism became "the shape of Protestantism in America."[39] In short, the American experience added another accent and dynamic to the mix that today manifests itself in evangelical ecclesiologies.

5. *American entrepreneurship.* A related and yet in some ways distinctly different dynamic was introduced into American Christianity (and especially evangelicalism) through American entrepreneurship. This was primarily a mid- to late-nineteenth-century phenomenon. The rise of the railroads as America's first big business, the growth of financial capitalism, and in general the American industrial revolution introduced dynamics into U.S. culture that were only latently present at the time of the Revolution. From the 1860s on, the United States became an entrepreneurial nation.[40]

In North America, denominations tend to arise as entrepreneurial enterprises—as do many independent local churches and many evangelistic, missionary, and service agencies. American society provides both the culture and the models for such entrepreneurial ventures. American entrepreneurship influences ecclesiology by providing the opportunity, the mind-set, the models, and the tools for building a certain type of church organization.

Contemporary evangelical ecclesiologies are a blend in varying measure of these five elements: the Protestant tradition tracing back to Roman Catholicism, the free church tradition, revivalism, American democracy, and American entrepreneurship.

Where is the Bible in all this? Strikingly, Scripture is a distinctly remote source in much evangelical ecclesiology; the above five sources

39. Russell E. Richey, ed., *Denominationalism* (Nashville: Abingdon, 1977). Sidney Mead entitled his contribution to this book "Denominationalism: The Shape of Protestantism in America."

40. See Kevin Phillips, *Wealth and Democracy: A Political History of the American Rich* (New York: Broadway Books, 2002), 35–37. Phillips notes that a "surprising number of the commercial and financial giants of the late nineteenth century" at the time of the Civil War were "young northerners" who "used the war to take major steps up future fortune's ladder." Here one might also ponder the significance of the nineteenth-century "benevolence empire" of mission, social reform, and philanthropic societies funded largely by evangelical businessmen and entrepreneurs. See Garth M. Rosell, "Charles Grandison Finney and the Rise of the Benevolence Empire" (Ph.D. diss., University of Minnesota, 1971). The Canadian experience was somewhat different due to Canada's different history.

are primary. To the degree that Scripture is a factor, it is mediated primarily through the Protestant/Catholic and free church traditions. In neither case, however, is Scripture determinative of ecclesiology, though it may be front and center in regard to other doctrines, especially theology (in the narrow sense), Christology, and soteriology—and thus in regard to evangelism and missions.[41]

These five ecclesiological sources are well illustrated in two evangelical leaders of the past: the American Benjamin Titus Roberts (1823–93), principal founder of the Free Methodist Church, and the Canadian Albert Benjamin Simpson (1843–1919), founder of the Christian and Missionary Alliance.

B. T. Roberts gained his essential understanding of the church primarily from the Methodist Episcopal Church, which he joined as a young adult shortly after his conversion. But his ecclesiological thinking was also shaped by Finneyite revivalism and the democratic and entrepreneurial ideas he imbibed from his earliest days in western New York. Given Methodism's roots in Anglicanism, Roberts's ecclesiology may be seen as a blend of the five sources noted above.

Roberts defined his mission and the mission of church he founded as "twofold—to maintain the Bible standard of Christianity—and to preach the Gospel to the poor."[42] These were always the two central notes in Roberts's own theology and ecclesiology. They can be traced to the New Testament but were mediated primarily through Methodism.

In an 1875 article, Roberts discussed the use of *ekklēsia* in the New Testament and other biblical teachings on the church. He described the church as essentially "those whom Christ has called out of the world and who have obeyed the call." The apostle Paul in 1 Corinthians 1:2 "designates the Church, not by its creed, or officers, or history, but by the character of those of whom it is composed."[43] Noting a number of other passages that speak of the holiness and character of Christians, Roberts concluded:

> These, then, are the persons who, united together for the worship of God and the spread of His kingdom, constitute the Church of Christ. The fun-

---

41. In American evangelicalism, Scripture probably has its major ecclesiological impact in the form of primitivism and restorationism. These constitute a key dynamic within the free church tradition, but at some level they have always been at work in the church and always seem to be present in church renewal movements. See Snyder, *Signs of the Spirit*, esp. 40–42; and Hughes, *American Quest for the Primitive Church*.

42. B. T. Roberts, *Doctrines and Discipline of the Free Methodist Church* (Rochester, N.Y.: General Conference [of the Free Methodist Church], 1866), viii–ix.

43. B. T. Roberts, "Who Compose the Church," *The Earnest Christian* 29, no. 4 (April 1875): 101f.

damental thing is—not the creed, nor government, nor history—these may be important—but they are not essential—but the character of its members. . . . This accords, as we understand it, with the definition of "the Church," given in the nineteenth article of the Church of England: "The visible Church of Christ is a congregation of faithful men in which the pure word of God is preached, and the sacraments duly administered."[44]

Assessing the adequacy of this traditional Anglican definition, Roberts wrote, "A congregation of faithful men" implies "those who have those graces of the Spirit, and a life corresponding, which fit men for heaven." "If the congregation is mixed, a part faithful, and a part unfaithful, then the faithful part, however small, constitutes the Church."[45]

Roberts found the Anglican qualification "in which the pure word of God is preached" to be "too exclusive. . . . I would not deny that 'a congregation of faithful men' is a Church, because they may listen sometimes to preaching which is not in every particular 'the pure word of God.'" Similarly, with regard to the sacraments being "duly administered," Roberts said, "I could not insist upon this in its full force and meaning. It is important that the sacraments be duly administered, but where is the passage of Scripture that makes this essential . . . ? I would not deny that a congregation of faithful Quakers belong to the Church of Christ, if they love God with all their hearts, and are led by the Spirit, and have come out from the world and are separate." Roberts argued that the "essential thing to the existence of the Church of Christ is the spiritual state of its members" and quoted John Wesley to this effect.[46]

In a subsequent article, Roberts argued that though the New Testament "does not prescribe any method of church government" as essential, it gives "general principles" that assist the church's effectiveness and efficiency. The Bible in Ephesians 4 and 1 Corinthians 12 "plainly teaches" that "there should be a variety of officers in the church." The New Testament gives no "intimation . . . that any of these gifts has been recalled." Roberts argued that the "whole scope" of 1 Corinthians 12 "is to teach the diversity of gifts, among Christians. Man's work is uniform. In God's work there is unity in variety." Thus, "in the Christian Church—whatever form of government be adopted—there should be a recognition of all the different kinds of orders or ministers which God has appointed." Roberts argued for a pragmatic, functional view of church structure and implied that traditional Protestantism was too restrictive in dividing "the church mainly into two classes—preachers

44. Ibid., 102f.
45. Ibid., 103.
46. Ibid.

and members." The church would be closer to the New Testament pattern, Roberts implied, if it affirmed a wider variety of ministers and "officers," though he did not spell out the implications of this view.[47]

These statements show what Roberts meant by "maintaining the Bible standard of Christianity and preaching the Gospel to the poor." The two accents seem to function as essential ecclesiological marks. The church is an organized, diverse congregation of people who reflect the character of Jesus Christ (love and holiness) and the example of Jesus Christ (ministry to and with the poor). Though he did not explicitly discuss the four classical marks, Roberts implied that the meaning of the marks would be fulfilled in a congregation of faithful disciples who manifest Christ's character and effectively preach the gospel to the poor. Thus, Roberts's ecclesiology is fundamentally evangelical and christological, but traces of the five sources discussed above are clearly discernible.

The same is true with A. B. Simpson. When Simpson resigned his pastorate and his five-thousand-dollar salary at New York City's Thirteenth Street Presbyterian Church in 1881, his central concern was "the neglected classes both at home and abroad." Though Simpson was on good terms with his people, he felt that God was calling him to "radical and aggressive measures," which the church would not accept. "What they wanted was a conventional parish for respectable Christians. What their young pastor wanted was a multitude of publicans and sinners." In announcing his decision, he quoted Jesus' words, "The Spirit of the Lord is upon me because he hath anointed me to preach the gospel to the poor."[48]

Simpson is well known for founding an effective missionary society, the Christian and Missionary Alliance. His intent was not to found a church but to aggressively engage in world evangelization. Because of this, it is easy to miss the important ecclesiological conviction behind his new venture. This ecclesiological thrust was well expressed in a key statement Simpson made in a 1901 article in the *Christian and Missionary Alliance Weekly:*

> We believe the ideal mission is the ideal Church, not a down town chapel where the masses are to be worked upon but a loving brotherhood of Christian equality and fellowship where the rich and poor sit at the same

47. B. T. Roberts, "Officers of the Church," *The Earnest Christian* 29, no. 6 (June 1875): 166–67. Roberts here uses "gifts" and "orders of ministers" interchangeably, based on Ephesians 4:11 and 1 Corinthians 12:28.

48. A. E. Thompson, *A. B. Simpson: His Life and Work,* rev. ed. (Harrisburg, Pa.: Christian Publications, 1960), 85–87; Daryl Westwood Cartmel, "Mission Policy and Program of A. B. Simpson" (M.A. thesis, Hartford Seminary Foundation, 1962), 40; and Donald W. Dayton, *Discovering an Evangelical Heritage* (New York: Harper & Row, 1976), 113.

communion table and the lives rescued from the lowest ranks are put to work in equal fellowship with their more cultured brethren. The educating value of such a Church to the poor is very great, and for the rich no less valuable.[49]

Several themes in Simpson's ecclesiology are captured here. The church is an egalitarian community of believers that gives visible, social witness to the reconciling power of the gospel. But its primary purpose is missions. Simpson believed the church is essentially missional and that the church's mission is essentially ecclesiological. The church is God's missionary movement and as such is broader than any one denomination.[50]

In Simpson's view, however, the church is much more than simply a missionary task force. It is to be a visible demonstration of the power of the gospel. "It is only when we enter into the perfect fellowship of the body of Christ that we can know the fullness of our great salvation," he wrote.[51] As prefigured by the tabernacle and temple in the Old Testament, "God intended His Church to be an exhibition of His glorious Gospel, His heavenly character and the riches of His grace. Its business here is to display Christ, to manifest God and to afford a channel for His revelation and indwelling among men." Jesus Christ is the church's cornerstone, "and only in so far as we are revealing and reflecting Him who is our Head are we accomplishing the object for which the Church was founded."[52]

As the church was in the New Testament, so it is to be today. "There are not two ages of the Church, the apostolic and the modern, but we are the same Church which Christ founded. . . . We have the same promises, the same enduement of power, and should have the same manifestations of the presence and power of God."[53] As the body of Christ, the church is fundamentally "organic," not "mechanical," living and growing by "a force within itself." This means it has a living relationship with its Head: "No one really belongs to the Church of Christ who is not personally united to Christ in regeneration and communion."[54]

49. A. B. Simpson, *Christian and Missionary Alliance Weekly* 26, no. 12 (23 March 1901), 162, quoted in Cartmel, "Mission Policy," 43.

50. Cartmel, "Mission Policy," 36.

51. Albert B. Simpson, *The Highest Christian Life* (Harrisburg, Pa.: Christian Publications, 1966), 70.

52. Ibid., 71f. Based on Ephesians 2–5, Simpson discusses the church as the building, body, and bride of Christ. The "moving tabernacle represented the earthly church, with no continuing city and no inheritance below the skies," while the temple represented the church in eschatological fulfillment (73).

53. Ibid., 73.

54. Ibid., 74.

The unity of the church, Simpson said, means that the church's calling and mission are one throughout history and that the church is "one
in diversity"; its unity is "more perfect because of its diversity."[55] Simpson had seen Charles Spurgeon's tabernacle in London and said that his
own "plan and idea of a church" were like Spurgeon's. A church com-
prises "thousands of members of no particular class, but of the rich and
poor side by side." Simpson did not want a rescue mission but a church
that was a mission and a mission that was a fully functioning, self-sup-
porting church.[56]

Simpson had an essentially functional and democratic view of church
order. He wrote:

> There appears to have been no extremely rigid rule in the New Testament
> about church government further than that a certain body of spiritual
> overseers were appointed out of every church, and they were called elders
> or bishops. . . . Out of these general conditions gradually arose Presbyte-
> rianism on the one hand, and Episcopacy on the other, but neither had
> exclusive warrant of sufficient strength to justify bigotry or controversy.
> It is a safe rule to recognize all these various forms of church government
> as sufficiently scriptural to furnish a frame for the Gospel and the Church
> of God, which is the really essential thing.[57]

Simpson concluded that "the form of government in the Early
Church gradually developed and adjusted itself to conditions, and there
would seem to be, as far as church government is concerned, no great
principle at stake which need hinder the organic union of almost all
evangelical denominations of Christians on some simple basis of compromise and concession with each other."[58]

For Simpson, the key marks of the church are its evangelistic, missionary character (which can be understood as the church's apostolicity) and its calling to be a visible community of worship and nurture,
manifesting the character of Jesus Christ. Given Simpson's conscious
reflection on the nature of the church, it is somewhat misleading to say
(as is sometimes claimed) that the Christian and Missionary Alliance
was from the beginning *simply* a missionary society or parachurch organization. While the Christian and Missionary Alliance did not see itself initially as a denomination, it is clear that Simpson himself was
operating with some key ecclesiological convictions. It is hardly sur-

55. Ibid., 73.
56. Thompson, *A. B. Simpson*, 94.
57. A. B. Simpson, *The Epistles of Thessalonians, Timothy, and Titus* (Harrisburg, Pa.:
Christian Publications, n.d.), 68f.
58. Ibid., 69f.

prising, therefore, that this missionary society eventually became a church (denomination). There were theological/ecclesiological, not just sociological, dynamics at work.

Simpson's own words show how he drew from or was influenced by the five sources traced above. In both Simpson and Roberts, in fact, these five sources are discernible: the Roman Catholic tradition as modified by the Reformation, free church ecclesiology, revivalism, American democracy, and American entrepreneurship.

Importantly—and rather typically for evangelical movements in their early stages—both Simpson and Roberts saw the church movementally, not mainly in institutional or hierarchical categories. In terms of the marks of the church, it is interesting that Simpson is explicit in pairing unity with diversity, and it seems in general that the ecclesiology of both men tends to combine the diverse, charismatic, contextual, and prophetic accents with the traditional emphasis on the church as one, holy, catholic, and apostolic.

Evangelical ecclesiology generally exhibits the blending of, or at least draws from, these five sources. These sources, together with the earlier discussion of marks, could profitably be used as a sort of model in the study of particular evangelical churches and denominations.

Conclusion

This essay has attempted to trace the rather complex trajectories of evangelical ecclesiology. By way of summary, I highlight the following conclusions:

1. The classical marks of the church are only minimally helpful in understanding the theology and sociology of evangelical ecclesiology. The experience and history of evangelicalism point to the limitations of the traditional marks, limitations that are partly overcome by seeing the traditional marks as, in effect, only half the story.

2. Inquiring into the actual sociology of the church can help clarify evangelical ecclesiology. Sociological models (the "religious economy" model, as well as others) add a useful dimension to the theological discussion. They help ground ecclesiology more fully in the actual experience of the church in time, space, and culture.

3. Evangelical ecclesiologies in North America can be understood as so many hybrid manifestations of Roman Catholic ecclesiological elements filtered through the Reformation, the free church tradition, revivalism, and American democracy and entrepreneurship. In this sense, there is what can properly be called *evangelical ec-*

clesiology: a distinctive evangelical ecclesial tradition. Clearly, there is also necessarily an ongoing evangelical ecclesiological agenda: to flesh out—incarnate—an understanding of the church that more fully embodies what the New Testament means by the body of Christ, what it means to form churches that are authentic, visible signs of God's reign.

In closing, I return to the four worship patterns sketched in the introduction. Clearly, all these patterns exist today within (and beyond) evangelicalism. Perhaps the foregoing discussion helps us better understand both the sources and the inherent dynamics of these patterns. The twentieth century added new elements to the ecclesiological mix, especially through the rise of Pentecostal and charismatic Christianity and the emergence of a youth culture (increasingly global) in which rock music plays a central role.

Today, evangelical ecclesiology is (as usual!) in major transition. Precisely for that reason, it faces a large opportunity. What better time to elaborate an ecclesiology that is soundly biblical and evangelical, prophetic and movemental, theologically coherent and sociologically aware, and functional for effective witness to the kingdom of God in an age of rapid globalization?

4

Evangelical Conversion toward a Missional Ecclesiology

GEORGE R. HUNSBERGER

The intentional ambiguity in the title of this essay may be too subtle. Does the title, on the one hand, suggest that evangelical perspective and piety somehow provide resources for the conversion of North American churches toward a missional ecclesiology—an ecclesiology that sees the fundamental missionary character of the church as critical for its self-understanding in a post-Christendom, postmodern setting? Or does it, on the other hand, suggest that evangelicalism *itself* is in need of conversion if it is not to hinder but to participate in such a renewal of ecclesiology? Or does it suggest both?

A number of central accents in the ethos of evangelicalism *may* be useful for an ecclesiology of the sort we need to recover in North America today, *if* they are reformed and transformed by the Word and the Spirit—converted, in other words! Otherwise, those may be the very accents that continue to inhibit transformation in the church's self-understanding in and for the era in which we now stand. Ironically, but perhaps also providentially, key notes of evangelical conviction are at the same time *problematic* as expressions of the church's domestication in and by the culture and *hopeful* as sources for renewal, both for itself (if

105

being a distinct "self" is even appropriate to a thoroughly evangelical identity!) and for companion streams of the church in North America. This essay explores these potential "seeds of renewal" and the path of "falling into the ground and dying" necessary for them to bear fruit.

Before approaching that thesis directly, it is important to indicate what I will *not* be doing in this essay. First, I will not be attempting to trace or analyze the historical roots or tributaries that produced the movement (or "momentum") called evangelicalism. Neither will I be attempting to dissect the movement to offer a comprehensive depiction of its anatomy. Both these tasks are important, but they require historical and sociological competencies other than my own and types of inquiry beyond the scope of this essay.

Of course, we are discussing evangelicalism and ecclesiology, and that means there will be something called "evangelicalism" in my mind as I engage it. Therefore, it will be necessary to show along the way what I take that to be and the basis for it in my own experience. At the outset I should say that I come to this task both as evangelicalism's progeny and as its would-be reformer. Calling for its conversion is to call for my own to continue. In other words, I do not come to the topic of this volume with complete objectivity. The church in whose womb the Spirit birthed my Christian faith was evangelicalism at its best. And the evangelical cast of my formation as a Christian set me on a lifelong quest to see the church renewed according to the gospel, according to Scripture, according to the missionary call of the Spirit. But there is the rub. There are things about evangelicalism that would appear to be inhibitors to the kind of renewal needed. In particular, the quest for communal and missional patterns in the church's life finds itself, at fundamental points, at odds with the strains of individualism that are so strong in evangelicalism. For me, the struggle with individualism is as internal as it is external. The threads of evangelical faith are too pervasive, its birthing force too maternally deep, its convictions too solidly lodged to be dismissed or disregarded. The fact that it set me on such a quest is what leads to my thesis, with hope for new contributions evangelicalism may yet have to make.

Second, I will not be attempting to answer in any definitive way the question, Is there an evangelical ecclesiology? If one takes a look at the many ecclesial bodies that in some way are arguably "evangelical," one finds that they nonetheless come in a variety of forms, each with a heritage of ecclesiology distinct to its tradition. There are Wesleyan and Reformed, Anabaptist and Episcopal, Baptist and Lutheran, charismatic and dispensational bodies that as denominations or otherwise defined communities of congregations bear the marks of evangelicalism and its core ethos. Likewise, there are evangelical congregations scattered among denominations that otherwise do not bear a distinctly evangelical stamp. There are even Roman Catholic and Orthodox parishes in which an evangelical would feel a companion spirit.

Outside either sort of denomination is a host of individual, independent congregations scattered across the North American landscape. Some are urban storefront; some are countryside; some are suburban. Some are small; some are large. Some are multicultural; some are ethnically rooted. Some are "third wave charismatic"; some are dubbed "megachurch" or "seeker church." Some are touted as the "next" form of the church for all of us; some are coming in under the radar as self-consciously "emergent church." A lion's share of these independent churches bears an evangelical ethos. (Perhaps that itself is a clue to something!)

If it is in this array of forms and understandings of "church" that we see the tributaries and deltas of a movement, a momentum, called evangelicalism, then any quest for a distinctive ecclesiology characteristic of its ethos will be daunting. It is likely to be at least as hard as it is to define evangelicalism in the first place.

Third, I will not be attempting to engage ecclesiology from the angles frequently assumed to be its territory. That is, I will not be looking at ecclesiology from the perspective of sacraments, ministry, office, membership, polity, and order, as though that is sufficient for understanding what is believed to constitute the church. I take these issues as important but having more to do with how the church orients and organizes itself—related to ecclesiology yet not ecclesiology per se. Ecclesiology, at the heart of it, is the self-understanding of the Christian community, which then orders its life in a particular way because of that self-understanding. It is what such a company of people thinks it simply *is* and *why* it is.

Nor will I be looking at ecclesiology from the angle of the Reformational discussions regarding the marks of the true church. In those discussions, after all, the Reformers were trying to distinguish the true from the false. They were not trying to define what the church is or construct an entire ecclesiology from their two, sometimes three (and sometimes many more) marks of the true church. But subsequently, in many of our ecclesial communities, we have so emphasized the marks that we have allowed them to *be* our ecclesiology. So we have a heritage—Protestant and evangelical—that defines the church "in terms of what happens inside its four walls, not in terms of its calling in the world," as David Bosch has noted. "The verbs used in the Augustana [confession] are all in the passive voice: the church is a place where the gospel *is taught* purely and the sacraments *are administered* rightly. It is a place where something is done, not a living organism doing something."[1]

The Reformers lived in what was still a Christendom world, and they continued to think and respond to issues of the nature and form of the church with assumptions inherent in that world. It should be no surprise that they did so. But it should surprise us that Christendom ways of thinking of the church still persist in our own time. Evangelicalism, no less than any other of the streams flowing from the Reformation, bears the stamp of the reduction of the church to a *place* where certain things happen.

What was most lost to the church in the period of Christendom was its sense of missional identity. This pervasive eclipse of mission continued to be evident in the Reformational confessions. Wilbert Shenk summarizes:

> Ecclesiologically the church is turned inward. The thrust of these statements, which were the very basis for catechizing and guiding the faithful, rather than equipping and mobilizing the church to engage the world, was to guard and preserve. This is altogether logical, of course, if the whole of society is by definition already under the lordship of Christ.[2]

The gradual emergence of Protestant missionary ventures to newly discovered parts of the world (after a couple of centuries!) does not really contradict this assessment. What is new is that missions are organized apart from the magistrate's initiative and sponsorship. From the time of the Reformation until the eighteenth century, this official directon and support were understood to be chiefly responsible for the evangelization of new regions. But while the emergence of missionary societies and denominational missionary sending agencies added foreign missions to the tasks of the church, recovery in the church's image of itself as essentially missionary was not immediately forthcoming. Missions were sent out by and from the church to newly contacted areas of the world, but in a Christendom-shaped West it was not generally a part of the church's thinking to see itself as a distinct community that itself was sent by God into its own social arena. Too fused were the sinews of church and society for such a thing to be seen. To be sure, there were precedents and anticipations in a number of movements that formed in the eighteenth and nineteenth centuries that lent tangible form to the awakening of a new consciousness. But it was well into the twenti-

---

1. David J. Bosch, *Transforming Mission: Paradigm Shifts in Theology of Mission* (Maryknoll, N.Y.: Orbis, 1991), 249.

2. Wilbert R. Shenk, *Write the Vision: The Church Renewed* (Valley Forge, Pa.: Trinity Press International, 1995), 38.

eth century before the need for a recovery of missional identity came more generally to be grasped. A rapidly decolonizing world helped to spur on a shift from an ecclesiocentric mission outlook, under which the church advanced itself toward other parts of the world, to a theocentric vision of the *missio Dei*, within which the church is understood to be the called and sent people of God, whether in the West or elsewhere. The missional identity this implicates has the following results: The church knows that its reason for being is that it has been sent; the church makes it a missional priority to be a distinctly Christian community in contrast to the perceptions and practices of its surrounding society; the church is continuously shaped by the gospel to be a demonstration of its claims, promises, and invitations; and the church relates itself to its surrounding world, near and far, as a community of the coming reign of God.

The full impact of this shift is still waiting to settle into the consciousness and self-understanding of churches in North America. We have instead continued to follow the script bequeathed us by our Christendom heritage, with an overlay of the Enlightenment's way of viewing persons and societies in terms of autonomous reason, social contract, and linear progress. Increasingly, formal organizational structures are what we use the term *church* to designate. The structures have thus become a functional substitute for the social organism the New Testament calls "church." In the end, in America the church has come to be understood as a "vendor of religious services and goods" in what Roger Finke and Rodney Stark have dubbed our "religious economy."[3] We live then in a world of religious consumers and religious firms in the business of serving them.[4]

What I *will* be attempting to do in this essay is this: I take as my point of departure the ecclesiology side of the evangelicalism and ecclesiology equation. I do that from the specific point of view of a missional understanding of the church, that it is not a "place where certain things happen" but a "body of people sent on a mission"—the mission to represent the reign of God. That vision, as expressed in the book *Missional Church*,[5] grows out of a discernment that the social context of the church in North America has ceased to be even functionally a Christen-

3. Roger Finke and Rodney Stark, *The Churching of America, 1776–1990: Winners and Losers in Our Religious Economy* (New Brunswick, N.J.: Rutgers University Press, 1992).

4. For a more thorough discussion of this contrast between the consumerist and missional models of the church, see chapter 4 in Darrell L. Guder, ed., Lois Y. Barrett, Inagrace Dietterich, George R. Hunsberger, Alan J. Roxburgh, and Craig Van Gelder, *Missional Church: A Vision for the Sending of the Church in North America* (Grand Rapids: Eerdmans, 1998), 77–109.

5. Ibid.

dom one, and therefore, prior assumptions about what the church is for no longer hold. No more is the church the chaplain to an assumed Christian society, nor the moral glue that holds things together, nor the guardian of civility and duty. Bereft of its roles of former times, the church finds itself in the default position of being simply one organization amid a marketplace full of self-interested organizations vying for the time and commitments of members sufficient to sustain its organizational goals, some of them benevolent but many self-serving. We are time after time faced with the evidence that we have come to a cul-de-sac, defining "church" as an entity that provides something for us, its members, rather than as our very selves! We have become immune to how odd it ought to seem when someone says, "Churches today have to decide how best to serve their congregations." Instead, it seems odd to us when someone answers the question "Where is your church?" by assuming that the questioner wants to know where the *people* are right now and not where the *building* happens to be where the church gathers a few times each week!

It is a time for rediscovery when old understandings do not hold and when default understandings do not cohere with the givens of the faith. New understandings must be found. A deep level of self-awareness and self-examination is required for churches seeking their re-formation by the Spirit to be the intended church. Whatever else the new formation will be, it will correspond to the action of the Spirit at the first to call and send, equip and empower the church. The quest is no less than to rediscover our raison d'etre in the intention of God.

If the pressing need of the day is an ecclesiology that is biblically originated, practically evident, and contextually potent, it can only be one that is missional. That does not mean that the being of the church is dissolved into activisms of one sort or another. Nor does it mean that the church is defined purely in functional terms. On the contrary, a missional ecclesiology stresses that the church's *very existence* has been sent into the world. It fulfills its sent-ness as much by its presence and the quality of its life in the gospel as it does by its actions and communications. But the fundamental point is that missions is not peripheral or additional for the church. The fact that it has been sent is of its essential nature, so much so that the sending is implicitly and explicitly formative in all the aspects of its life—its worship, its *koinōnia*, its learning, its witness, its birthing of new communities, its sociopolitical engagements, its compassion and mercy. Holistically understood, Emil Brunner's oft-quoted dictum remains the compass: "The church exists by mission, just as fire exists by burning."[6]

6. Emil Brunner, *The Word and the World* (London: SCM, 1931), 108.

It is against the backdrop of the requirements for recovering a missional ecclesiology that I come then to inquire whether in the core ethos of evangelicalism there are resources for that recovery or whether there are rather hindrances to it. I will do that by looking at the side of evangelicalism that shows up in the "missions" movement. From one angle, this might seem to be the wrong place to begin. It would seem to be more appropriate to explore how evangelical ecclesiologists think about missions and the missionary character of the church. But it may in fact be more telling to see how evangelical missiologists think about the church. Is there a missional perspective that supplies the necessary frame for a renewed ecclesiology? Or is that missional perspective itself lacking precisely at this point? And if so, might that betray what in evangelicalism itself needs to be converted in order to bear fruit?

The question here, in other words, is reversed from the normal way we might put it. It is not the question of whether the evangelical church can recover missions as part of its identity. Clearly, evangelicalism has been marked by its commitment to missions, especially to the evangelization of the world. Engaging in personal evangelism is central to the lifestyle expectations of evangelicals. Given that accent on missions, the question goes the other way around. Is it in evangelicalism's emphasis on missions that it has missed a grasp of what the church is and why it exists? Precisely there the question looms largest: Can evangelicalism recover a sense of the church as a missional community and not merely a sending agency in the missionary enterprise? To put it another way, I will not look at an expression of evangelical ecclesiology to ask how it may be seen missionally. Rather, I will look at an expression of evangelical missiology to see how it imagines the church.

Iguassu Affirmation

The evangelical stream of missions thought is as varied and diffuse as any other, but in recent decades its greatest attempts to forge consensus are probably those found in two movements. One is the Lausanne Committee for World Evangelization (LCWE), begun following the International Congress on World Evangelization at Lausanne in 1974. The other is the former World Evangelical Fellowship (WEF), now World Evangelical Alliance (WEA), particularly its Missions Commission. Both have held numerous conferences and consultations, and from them has come a substantial body of literature documenting the ways missions is viewed.

One of the more recent of those consultations was the Global Consultation on Evangelical Missiology, held October 10–16, 1999, in Iguassu,

Paraña, Brazil. The consultation was convened by the WEF Missions Commission, bringing together 160 "mission practitioners, missiologists, and church leaders" from 53 countries. They came for three purposes. To:

1. reflect together on the challenges and opportunities facing world missions at the dawn of the new millennium
2. review the different streams of twentieth-century evangelical missiology and practice, especially since the 1974 Lausanne Congress
3. continue developing and applying a relevant biblical missiology that reflects the cultural diversity of God's people[7]

The consultation report titled *Iguassu Affirmation (IA)* provides a window into the way ecclesiology figures in the vision of evangelical missiology. While many of the same dynamics can be noted elsewhere, this report is especially important as a case study because of its recent date and the scope of its participation.

The report contains in successive sections a preamble, declarations (nine of them), commitments (fourteen of them), and a concluding pledge. What is most striking on a first read is how rarely the document refers to the church at all. In most cases, the references that are made are more incidental than they are direct attempts to depict the church or construe a particular understanding of it. For the most part, "church" is an object to which the participants relate themselves, not the identity they wear.

To get a sense of the meaning and function of the term *church* in the report, it helps at the outset to catalog the various ways the term is used and the various contexts in which the term is employed. Not all of the occurrences of the word have direct bearing on an ecclesiology of one sort or another. Yet the range of uses and the tendencies that can be observed are ultimately significant with respect to unspoken, unarticulated assumptions about the church or the lack of assumptions.

Two times the word *church* is used simply to designate roles held by some of the 160 participants. The group includes "mission practition-

---

7. World Evangelical Alliance, *Iguassu Affirmation*, Preamble. The *Iguassu Affirmation* will be referenced by section titles and/or numbered paragraphs rather than by page numbers to facilitate searching in either its print-published or web-published versions: William D. Taylor, ed., *Global Missiology for the Twenty-First Century:* The Iguassu Dialogue (Grand Rapids: Baker, 2000), 16–19; and www.worldevangelical.org/textonly/3ig ua-affirm.html.

ers, missiologists and *church* leaders" (*IA:* Preamble, Pledge; emphasis mine, here and in what follows).

In three of the uses, the word occurs to identify churches as part of the sociological reality, with no special comment or meaning attached. It is acknowledged that churches are present and are part of what we have to deal with. In other words, the word is used in a fairly incidental way, and its use gives little clue to an understanding of the church.

". . . agencies, *churches*, and fellow Christians . . ." (*IA:* Commitments, 14)

"Believers, led by the Holy Spirit, are encouraged to create culturally appropriate forms of worship and uncover biblical insights that glorify God for the benefit of the whole *church*" (*IA:* Declarations, 3)

". . . divided over issues of *church* organization, order, and doctrine . . ." (*IA:* Declarations, 8).

In three uses, the point in view is the global spread of the church and the diversity that brings to the picture:

". . . participation by and awareness of the global *church*, as well as mission from people of all nations to people of all nations, are needed for a valid missiology for our time" (*IA:* Preamble).

"The insights of every part of the *church* are needed and challenges in every land must be addressed. . . . We commit ourselves to give voice to all segments of the global *church* in developing and implementing our missiology" (*IA:* Commitments, 8).

Two uses are in the context of recognizing the suffering experienced in various places by the church.

"We acknowledge that our obedience in mission involves suffering and recognize that the *church* is experiencing this" (*IA:* Declarations, 6).

". . . we commit to equip ourselves and others to suffer in missionary service and to serve the suffering *church*" (*IA:* Commitments, 10).

In five cases, the word *church* occurs as the object of the group's collective exhortation or urging. One feels a certain unease about the way the participants, the ever present "we," "us," "our" of the document, see themselves in one way—as other than *being* the church, and viewing the "church" or the "churches" over against themselves—as objects in the direction of which their mission and service are rendered. Here clues begin to develop regarding the kind of ecclesiology functioning in the document.

". . . we *remind* the *church* . . ." (*IA:* Commitments, 10).

"We . . . *call* the *church* to a renewed commitment to holy living" (*IA:* Declarations, 9).

"We commit ourselves . . . to *encourage* the global *church* to become a truly missionary community in which all Christians are involved in mission" (*IA:* Commitments, 3).

"We commit ourselves to *encourage and challenge* the *churches* to respond with a deeper level of unity and participation in mission" (*IA:* Commitments, 3).

"*It is the responsibility* of the *church* in each place to affirm the meaning and value of a people, especially where indigenous cultures face extinction. We *call* all Christians to commit themselves . . ." (*IA:* Commitments, 11).

The closest the participants come in the document to speaking in a voice that presumes they *are* the church is in Commitment 13, but even there they are reluctant. They speak of themselves as "citizens of the Kingdom of God and members of Christ's body," which is their rationale for making a commitment to "renewed efforts at cooperation." The avoidance of the word *church* here makes the reader wonder whether *church* would be too tangible, too practical an accountable community, or whether *cooperation* would be an adequate level of commitment if it were the unity of the churches that was at stake (see *IA:* Commitments, 13).

Among the uses, there are three (the last using the word also in the section's title) that are directly theological affirmations, but once affirmed in a brief assertion, these affirmations are not elaborated.

"The Spirit leads the *Church* into all truth" (*IA:* Declarations).

"Jesus Christ is Lord of the *Church* and Lord of the Universe" (*IA:* Declarations, 1 [title]).

"*Church* and Mission. The *Church* in mission is central to God's plan for the world" (*IA:* Commitments, 3).

A bit more should be said about these references. These alone are the occasions when the word *church* is capitalized. It is uncertain what that means, but it would appear that in these cases something is being said about the church universal, while in the others mention is being made of particular entities, particular sociological phenomena called "churches." Whether this implies some sort of divided mind about the invisible church ("all true Christians") and visible churches needs to be discerned. From a surface reading, it would seem so. The words *visible* and *invisible* are never used, but an evangelical tendency to construe the church in that dichotomous way may be in the background.

Second, the lack of further elaboration on any of the three affirmations is curious, if not telling. In the first instance, the assertion is made on the ninth line of an eleven-line paragraph (in the web-published form). The paragraph focuses on depicting how "all three Persons of the Godhead are active in God's redeeming mission." Five statements are made regarding the Holy Spirit, of which this is the third. It does not appear that the affirmation is really about the church at all. In the paragraph as a whole, and the Holy Spirit section in particular, the dominant language is "we," "us," "our." It seems most likely that the appearance of the word *church* once in the paragraph is more for stylistic reasons, to vary the language with a synonym for "we," "us," "our," though it is largely unspecified here as throughout the document whether the "we" refers to the participants making the declaration or to all Christians.

The notion of the church is not essential to the argument of the paragraph. For all its effort to ground missions in the "three Persons of the Godhead," the paragraph does that solely in terms of the particular activities of each of the persons. No mention is made of the intercommunion of the persons, which many today are finding to provide theological foundations for the communal existence of the people of God. The document later indicates a commitment to "a renewed emphasis on God-centered missiology" in the interests of a "Trinitarian foundation of mission," but its focus even there remains "the operation of the Trinity in the redemption of the human race and the whole of creation" and an understanding of "the particular roles of Father, Son, and Spirit in mission" (*IA:* Commitments, 1).

The notion of the church does not even play a significant role in the vision of the Spirit's intent or activity identified in the declarations paragraph. The Spirit is said to "lead the church into all truth," but apart from its being the object or recipient of that activity, the church does not figure as important to the work of the Spirit. There is not a word about the Spirit forming or inhabiting the Christian community, only forming Christians and their faithful service to Christ in missions. Nothing is said about how the Spirit makes known the mystery and wisdom of God to "the rulers and authorities in the heavenly places" *through* the church (Eph. 3:5, 10). In the end, nothing is really affirmed here about what the church is or how it is implicated in the mission of the Triune God.

The second theological affirmation mentioned above ("Jesus Christ is Lord of the Church and Lord of the Universe") occurs in the title of a section. The paragraph it introduces does not mention the church but speaks only about Christ's lordship extending to and proclaimed throughout the world. What it might mean for Christ to be Lord of the church, or why the phrase is listed alongside (or over against?) the phrase "Lord of the Universe," is never mentioned.

The third affirmation ("Church and Mission. The Church in mission is central to God's plan for the world") occurs in the third commitment. It will be necessary to return to that section again because it is the only place in the document where an ecclesiological affirmation is made and where it is done in missional terms. But at this point it should be noted that no further elaboration is given to explain in what way "the Church in mission" is "central to God's plan for the world." Is it central as the agent God sends, as the fruit missions produces, as a holding place for believers to keep their faith secure until the end, or what? And what exactly is meant by the phrase "the Church in mission"? Is that different from saying simply "the church"? Is mission, in God's plan, an extra feature of the church or inherent in the identity and existence of the church? None of these questions are answered.

A final use of the word *church* makes explicit reference to the doctrine of the church.

"Inadequate theology, especially in respect to the doctrine of the *church*, and the imbalance of resources has [*sic*] made working together difficult" (*IA:* Commitments, 13).

It is interesting that here, where the document considers ecclesiology in a direct way, it is in the form of a confession that what has worked against a balance of resources and genuine mutuality and cooperation in missions is "inadequate theology," especially in regard to a doctrine of the church. An adequate doctrine of the church is not here attempted except in regard to the formation of better attitudes of cooperation.

The confession made here matches one to the same effect in Commitment 3, church and mission, which is the fullest—albeit brief—discussion about the church in the document. Following the affirmation already noted above ("The Church in mission is central to God's plan for the world"), the paragraph proceeds immediately to say, "We commit ourselves to strengthen our ecclesiology in mission, and to encourage the global church to become a truly missionary community in which all Christians are involved in mission." This is an important admission and commitment. Commitment 3 and the document as a whole illustrate the weaknesses in evangelical missiological ecclesiology that need to be strengthened and point to the stronger kind of ecclesiology that is needed.

Three points can be made in that regard. First, the church as community must be recovered. The most hopeful phrase in the document passes by quickly without measuring its importance or seeing how everything else would shift if it were believed. The participants encourage the global church to become a "truly missionary community." It is noteworthy, however, that the word *community* occurs in the document only here and in one other place where "religious *communities*" (of other faiths) are mentioned (*IA:* Commitments, 5). The idea of Christian community might conceivably be in view in the call at another point for "personal and *corporate* holiness, love and righteousness" (*IA:* Declarations, 9), although that reads more into the statement than appears to be there. Community as a concern of missions, or of God, does not arise. The only hint is the broad slogan that God is concerned with "the whole person in the whole of society" (*IA:* Declarations, 4). In that same declaration, the gospel is said to address "all human needs," but one looks in vain for a recognition that the need for community is among them. The document notes neither the shattered relationships, alienations, and fragmentations within or between nations and peoples that mark our world today nor the deep quest for human community among the world's people. Concern is expressed for the "meaning and value of a people" and "the welfare of all peoples" (*IA:* Commitments, 11), and in that regard something of the solidarity and identity of human communities is affirmed. But in no sense, beyond the one phrase in Commitment 3, does it emerge that it is God's intention to establish community, the Christian community, a renewed human community!

Where this absence is most surprising is in the first of the fourteen commitments regarding the "Trinitarian Foundation of Mission." As noted above, commitment is made to "a new study of the operation of the Trinity in the redemption of the human race and the whole of creation," but neither there nor in the trinitarian vision of the preamble is there a hint of the recovery in recent decades of the sense of community within the Godhead and its implications for an ecclesiology wrapped around a fundamental sense of community, of communion with the Triune God (*IA:* Commitment, 1; cf. Preamble). Because the document lacks a theological or even pragmatic vision for the church as community, it is no surprise that in the end, when the document speaks of "proclaiming the Gospel of reconciliation and hope" (Pledge), the language seems to fall flat on its face because no ground has been laid for a notion of reconciliation—unless it is one devoid of human reconciliation—at the heart of Christian missions or of a community called church that bears that mission as its own.

Second, the corporate nature of Christian existence and missions must be recovered. This rides close on the heels of the prior observation but needs mention in its own right. Immediately following the phrase "truly missionary community" in Commitment 3, the meaning it might possibly have had is jarred off the mark by an interpretive clause: ". . . in which all Christians are involved in mission" (*IA:* Commitment, 3).

The same paragraph later says that encouragement and challenge are given to the churches "to respond with a deeper level of unity and participation in mission." This, along with other tendencies of language throughout, begins to bring into sharp relief a portrait of the document's implicit ecclesiology, which is its functional, effective, and operative one. Perhaps it is also the one that too much characterizes evangelicalism in general.

Individualism may be evangelicalism's Achilles' heel. The hallmark of evangelicalism has been its emphasis on personal experience, conversion, and faith. It has characterized conversion to be "accepting Jesus as your personal Lord and Savior." Important as these themes have been historically for renewing the faith of many for whom that faith had lost meaning in sterile forms of ritualism, and for providing an entryway into a life of faith, hope, and love in Christ, the concern of evangelicalism to stress *personal* faith and piety easily becomes the purveyor of the strong strains of Enlightenment-spawned individualism in American culture. In modernity, an epistemology rooted in "I think, therefore I am" has produced the modern self, "the self-contained individual capable of discerning truth and constructing knowledge," providing the basis for achieving personal freedom.[8] Further:

> Freely choosing, autonomous individuals, deciding out of rational self-interest to enter into a social contract in order to construct a progressive society, became the central ideology of modernity. . . . Modernity is the story of this struggle to create society on the bases of objective scientific truth and the construct of the autonomous self.[9]

The convergence of evangelicalism with modernity leaves it vulnerable to a radically individuated form of relationship with God. Resistance to religious intermediaries of any sort and belief in direct approach to God through Scripture, under the personal guidance of the Holy Spirit, contribute to an evangelical bias that sees Christian identity fundamentally as individual. That has the tendency to obliterate the communal, or at least to overwhelm it so that it is not fundamental to the notion of church that shapes Christian practice. Church then tends to take on the modern social form of a *voluntary organization* grounded in the collective exercise of *rationale choice* by its members rather than the form of a communion of saints that is made such by the will of the Spirit of God. There need be no dichotomy between the choices of God and the responses of those whom God calls, of course.

8. Guder, *Missional Church*, 23.
9. Ibid., 25.

But that dichotomy is precisely what emerges from a sense of Christian identity that is first and foremost individual rather than one that knows that human identity is both personal and relational, both individual and communal.

When Christian identity is essentially individual, gathering in fellowship may of course be useful for sustaining and maturing one's faith, as embers gathered together keep the heat from dissipating. But any sense of corporate Christian identity comes hard for evangelicals: "*I* am reconciled to God, and as a consequence of that, you and I are brought together, but corporate identity is not fundamental to my salvation or relationship with God." This is a very different story line from the one apparent in the vision of the apostle Paul, whose reverse logic counters the individualist framework so strongly that it can seem to evangelical sensibilities to be strange or even heretical to the normal way of construing things:

> For he is our peace; in his flesh he has made both groups into one and has broken down the dividing wall, that is, the hostility between us. He has abolished the law with its commandments and ordinances, that he might create in himself one new humanity in place of the two, thus making peace, and might reconcile both groups to God in one body through the cross, thus putting to death that hostility through it. So he came and proclaimed peace to you who were far off and peace to those who were near; for through him both of us have access in one Spirit to the Father.
>
> Ephesians 2:14–18 NRSV

"He has made both groups into one. . . . one new humanity in place of the two. . . . Reconcile both groups to God in one body. . . . Both of us have access in one Spirit to the Father." Not without *you* will *I* be saved, in other words! God saves corporately, joining us together into "a holy temple . . . built together spiritually into a dwelling place for God" (Eph. 2:21–22). An individualist Christian identity is foreign to the Scriptures.

If, for evangelicalism, Christian faith and identity are first personal and individual, its sense of missions tends to be the same. The responsibility to give witness to Christ is one each person bears. The accent rests on personal evangelism, therefore. Any sense of a church's mission grows from this ground. It is the aggregate of the individual callings to be witnesses. Identity and missions are first and foremost individual matters. Missions is not conceived to be first of all the "mission of the church," to which every member is joined. First it is the mission of the Christian, which in the church becomes a collective responsibility.

The *Iguassu Affirmation* has an implicit ecclesiology based on this more individuated notion of Christian identity and missions. To turn immediately from mention of "a truly missionary community" to talk about "all Christians" being "involved in mission" betrays a reluctance to think of the "mission of the church," preferring to think of the "mission of Christians." This distributive sense of missional identity is evident throughout. Elsewhere, when anything like a missional responsibility is indicated, it is taken to be something "we" (either the ones speaking or they together with all other Christians) are to do. It is "our" calling, it is something God wants of "us." Or more directly, it becomes the language of "believers," of "Christians." "*Believers*, led by the Spirit, are encouraged to create culturally appropriate forms of worship and uncover biblical insights that glorify God . . ." (*IA:* Declarations, 3). "The Scriptures command that *Christians* pray for those in authority and work for truth and justice" (*IA:* Declarations, 7). "We call all *Christians* to commit themselves to reflect God's concern for justice and the welfare of all peoples" (*IA:* Commitments, 11). "We encourage *Christians* in environmental care and protection initiatives" (*IA:* Commitments, 12). Churches as churches are not called on in the same way in the document, except when called on to make sure that "all Christians" are doing what they are supposed to do, in other words, that they are "involved in mission."

This is the functional ecclesiology that shows up when the word *church* is used. "Church" tends simply to be a collective term for Christians, either a particular collection of them in one place and group or the larger collection of all Christians, all believers. The word *church,* when it *is* used, functions as a placeholder for the distributive plural language of "Christians" and "believers" and thus signifies a cumulative reality, not a corporal one. It is simply code for Christians considered all together, en masse, as an aggregate. It functions in a way that keeps identity and responsibility individuated and leaves the motivation and action of missions individual matters at root. The document renders implicitly an ecclesiology that is neither corporate nor communal, while it construes a missiology that is (therefore) not ecclesial.

Third, the missional vocation of the church must be recovered. A certain divide between churches and missions has come to characterize evangelical missiology, which is due, I suggest, to the implicit ecclesiology we are noting in the *Iguassu Affirmation.* We have seen that in the end it all adds up to something like this: We have a mission as Christians, not as church or as churches. A "missionary community" is such not because it bears the form of missions but because all the Christians in it are involved in the activity of missions. Missions belongs individually to each and all, and it is defined by what individual Christians are supposed to do. The church as a community is mildly irrelevant to all of that, perhaps tolerated in the picture and at best useful for it. It is certainly guilty if its members are not engaged. But missions in the end does not belong to the church.

For the missions establishment gathered at Iguassu, missions agencies (societies, boards, etc.), unlike churches, are the organizations best designed to gather individual missions responsibility into a joint effort. Missions agencies can do this more effectively and efficiently than churches, which are geared more toward care for their members' needs for nourishment, fellowship, and comfort. A certain dichotomy seems to lurk in the shadows, therefore, between church and missions, churches and missions, settled Christian existence and active missions participation. Noted above were the numerous ways the "we" who authored the document called on churches to encourage all Christians to missions involvement. Such a "we" that is not itself the "us" of the church suggests that they see themselves standing over against, outside of, the church. The church is not expected to have or to know for itself a missional identity or a missional vocation. Here, then, at the very place in evangelicalism where missions is most firmly pursued, at the place where one might expect to find the most fruitful vision for the church's recovery of its missional identity, this identity is not only lacking but appears to be held at a distance. A certain pragmatism of the task, a certain efficiency of achieving it, a certain reaction to the church's ineffective missional past seem to create a divide that keeps an ecclesiology from forming within the missiology the evangelical movement has spawned. More work on the historical roots of the divide will help illumine why this has happened, but for now, it is at least observable in the *Iguassu Affirmation* that what is needed is not forthcoming from this quarter.

It should be added, of course, that in the published collection of papers prepared for the Iguassu Dialogue, there are a variety of voices, some of which reflect the sort of ecclesiology for which I have been arguing.[10] Samuel Escobar's presentations on the "global scenario" and "peering into the future" work from the foundation of a matured missional ecclesiology, although the theme is not so directly mentioned.[11] Valdir Steuernagel, in response to Escobar, underscores the need to "rediscover the role of the community in the life of the church."[12] Ajith

10. Taylor, *Global Missiology.*

11. Samuel Escobar, "The Global Scenario at the Turn of the Century" and "Evangelical Missiology: Peering into the Future at the Turn of the Century," in *Global Missiology*, 25–46 and 101–22.

12. Valdir Steuernagel, "Learning from Escobar . . . and Beyond," in *Global Missiology*, 130.

Fernando, in one of his Bible studies, addresses the importance of the Trinity for thinking about the church, although he signals that importance more than he fulfills it. Nonetheless, he ends by affirming, "Biblical community is an area in which the church will have to present a prophetic alternative in today's society. Yet I fear that this is an area in which we have conformed greatly to the pattern of the world. . . . I fear that many of our structures of community life are derived more from the business world than from the Bible."[13] Stuart McAlister notes concern about the privatization of faith in postmodern societies. "I shudder every time I read another of the popular Evangelical books that serve to reinforce individualism, privatism, and the inward life as if these are the sum and goal of the gospel."[14] He says, "We must reconsider how we do church and then remodel what we are doing."[15]

But these notes are few and far between, illustrating that the lack of a more rigorous ecclesiology in the *Iguassu Affirmation* is not an anomaly. Even in part 6, which offers six case studies on "community, spirituality, and mission," there is surprisingly little reflection on the ecclesiologies of the church traditions in view (Celtic, Nestorian, Moravian, Jesuit, Coptic, and Brazilian Antioch). The study supplied by Clifton D. S. Warren comes the nearest, noting that "Celtic Christians knew of no other way of being Christian but to be a Christian in community. *Peregrini* were sent from a community, with others, to form the nucleus of a new community." He goes on to say, "Community, creation, reflection, asceticism, contemplation, and a robust embrace of life on earth: these are not the typical values of Evangelical mission."[16]

This case study of the *Iguassu Affirmation* shows some of the ways in which a missiology spawned by evangelicalism bears the marks of our contemporary cultural captivity within an individualistic modern culture. Other consultations and documents in the history of the evangelical missions stream could illustrate further the gaps in ecclesiology noted here. But this is sufficient to show some of the tendencies within evangelical missiology that inhibit a meaningful, biblical, gospeled ecclesiology. The question remains, for evangelical missiology and for evangelicalism in general, Might there be ways in which the tendencies that inhibit and hinder also hold some germ of promise, some seed of

13. Ajith Fernando, "The Church: The Mirror of the Trinity," in *Global Missiology*, 254–55.

14. Stuart McAlister, "Younger Generations and the Gospel in Western Culture," in *Global Missiology*, 369.

15. Ibid., 374.

16. Clifton D. S. Warren, "Celtic Community, Spirituality, and Mission," in *Global Missiology*, 493.

renewal for the recovery of a faithful missional ecclesiology? I suggest that there are and offer an indication of the way hindrances may become sources of renewal by reflecting on four themes in evangelicalism's core ethos.

Personal Conversion

It could be said that personal conversion is the essence of the goal of missions in evangelical understandings of it. The importance of a conscious turning to God through faith in Jesus Christ began to be stressed at the time of the Reformation. In the Great Awakenings of the eighteenth and nineteenth centuries, it settled deeply into the psyche of American Christianity. There it flourished in the atmosphere of an expanding sense of individual liberty. The United States was a new kind of nation that from the outset refused to establish a particular religion or religious body, in the interests of personal religious freedom. The confluence led inexorably toward an evangelical conviction that Christian identity is fundamentally a matter of an individual's relationship with God. This, we have already noted, makes it difficult to understand the church in genuinely corporate, communal terms.

A further effect of the founding decision of the United States not to establish a particular church deepens the dilemma. Because of this decision, so say today's rational choice sociologists of religion, the form of religious life in America has come to be that of consumerism and consumption. Rational self-interest governs our religious economy, a religious marketplace of products and services. As Finke and Stark have put it, "Where religious affiliation is a matter of choice, religious organizations must compete for members and . . . the invisible hand of the marketplace is as unforgiving of ineffective religious firms as it is of their commercial counterparts."[17] This, they say, is how religion in America has come to function, and this is the best way to interpret the varying fates of American religious bodies.

There is no escaping the dynamic of this religious consumerism. Churches of every sort are caught in its sway. It constitutes one of the most fundamental elements of the cultural captivity to which we are awakening. Evangelicalism no less than other streams experiences the effects of this deepened form of individualism that militates against the church's rediscovery of its identity and role.

If the individualist tendencies of evangelicalism's accent on personal conversion are more problematic than helpful, then how might it be otherwise? Are there seeds for renewal in these tendencies that can

17. Finke and Stark, *Churching of America*, 17.

help the entire church? A closer look at the way in which evangelicalism has tended to see conversion will yield both a sense of how it inhibits a renewed ecclesiology and how it might, by its own conversion, sow seeds of renewal.

First of all, conversion has tended to be conceived as too momentary an experience. That is, a person's conversion is what takes place at one point in time, when saving faith in Christ commences in a conscious and conscientious way. Conversion becomes, for the converted, something that happened at a past point in time. It is something remembered but not continuing except in its effects. The result is a static quality to conversion, lacking in dynamism and continual renewing power.

Biblically (and for evangelicals that is supposed to make a difference!), it is difficult to find repenting and believing narrowed so much as to be confined to the moment of initial faith. These are qualities presumed to be ongoing, continuous. Faith, hope, and love, the big three in Paul's curriculum, are things he keeps affirming *and* cultivating in every church he writes, expecting these qualities to be always growing and advancing.

Continuing conversion is precisely what is needed in churches that have fallen into a static resignation to things as they have been, stalemated by the memory of a societal role long since vanished and a peripheral place in the current scheme of things. Evangelicalism brings what many other traditions have tended to lack: belief in conversion as a definite change in mind and direction. Cut loose from its static moorings, it has a brisk contribution to make. But it will require a conversion in evangelicalism itself to re-envision conversion in terms of recognizing that the Spirit is always calling out new depths and forms of faith, new degrees of love, and fresh visions of hope. *The Continuing Conversion of the Church* (as Darrell Guder calls it in his recent book by that title) needs evangelical commitment to the constant transforming work of the Spirit.[18]

Second, evangelicalism has tended to see conversion too narrowly as the conversion of an individual person. Those who make the bold claim that God has the power to transform people usually hesitate when asked about God changing society. At that point, people usually resort to the view that when individuals are changed, society is changed. That provides a rationale of sorts for missions to be seen almost exclusively in terms of seeking personal conversions rather than of working for peace or justice. The difficulty is that after all this time, one wonders where the promised payoff is. If it really worked that easily, why haven't

18. Darrell L. Guder, *The Continuing Conversion of the Church* (Grand Rapids: Eerdmans, 2000).

societies in which numerous personal conversions have taken place been transformed?

The problem is not only with mission focus. It also has to do with how communities, including Christian communities, are transformed. They are not automatically changed just because they are made up of converted, transformed people. We find churches in the New Testament, full of converted people, needing to learn some feature or another of life together in communion with God. And that is the need of the moment for church after church in North America. Despite the assumption that churches have it right and know how to be the church, it has become painfully clear that we are in new territory that calls for learning all over again what we are and what we are for. There are no ready-made precedents, no off-the-shelf blueprints, no full-blown models. We are in a time that puts us on a steep learning curve, and it is a communally shared one. Each of us is implicated, but it is not enough to say that when each has been transformed, the community will also be transformed. The community has personhood itself, and that corporate "person" is challenged by conversions that await it in its future! Here again, the commitment to change and conversion in evangelicalism will serve the church well if its own conversion can widen to include the conversion of communities.

Third, conversion in evangelicalism tends to be too oriented to beliefs and morals. Trusting in Christ for forgiveness and salvation and not in works or behaviors is the thrust of evangelical faith and the hallmark of the converted. In addition, a strong evangelical tradition supports the change in moral lifestyle that should accompany faith. The challenge is whether these visions of conversion may be enlarged by biblical visions of the reign of God, which Jesus kept saying was "at hand" by virtue of his presence. Then a moral lifestyle would not be the only thing at stake in the change of life that conversion implicates. Rather, the issue would be a pattern of life that looks for, prays for, and seeks God's reign. This pattern is one of daily response to Jesus' most repeated invitations, to "receive" and "enter" the reign of God. The emerging vision is one of a community more characterized every day by its march to the cadence of a drummer others cannot hear, its loyalty to a Lord others may not recognize, its distinct life as a community oriented to a future others cannot believe will be the future of the world. It means being a distinct community that at many points looks odd to onlookers but in which the "healing of the nations" is already showing up. The challenge for evangelicalism is to embrace a wider range of formative biblical visions and to embody a corporate lifestyle beyond personal morality.

With its own conversions to dynamic, corporate, and lived conversion, evangelicalism has much to contribute to the churches of North America in their struggle to become a "converting community"—in other words, one that is not only converting others but also continuing to undergo its own conversion, deeply and daily. The Reformation dictum may be a helpful reminder at this point: "Reformed, always *being reformed* by the Word of God."

Cross-Cultural Mission

Evangelical faith is characterized by the belief that the message of salvation in Christ is a universal one. In other words, it is true for the whole world and has a bearing on the life of every person. The invitation to put one's faith in Christ is rightly extended to every person, regardless of the person's nationality, culture, or beliefs. Based on this conviction, cross-cultural evangelization has always been defended, at times with more humility and respect for cultural differences than at other times. In recent decades, the accumulated wisdom of many generations of cross-cultural missionaries has coalesced into a substantial body of literature that reflects on the intricacies of cross-cultural Bible translation, the dynamics of living cross-culturally as incarnations of the message, and the riches of the variegated flowerings of insight that have come from each culture in which the gospel has taken root. One of the more important positive contributions of the *Iguassu Affirmation* is its affirmation of those insights and its eagerness to learn from them.

The wealth of anthropological knowledge gained by the evangelical missions movement has a great deal to offer to churches in North America who find themselves in a new cultural context. Churches have begun to discover that they have been domesticated within their culture, overly accommodated to it, and share its most fundamental visions of reality, even when they are at odds with what their own Bible seems to be rendering. They need to learn discernment in order to know their own culture—the one they share with their companions all around them, the one they inhabit by virtue of being reared in it and framed by it. They need to develop the skill of reading the Bible with new eyes for the way it speaks a divergent vision and calls for a frame different from the one they have inherited—not totally other but turned in a new direction toward new assumptions and practices. They need help to decipher what it will mean for them to embody the gospel in a critical contextualization within their own culture without being either so exotic as to be irrelevant or so identifying as to be syncretistic.

For help to be forthcoming from evangelical missiology, however, several conversions will be necessary. Evangelical cross-cultural missions has tended to stress the side of the cross-cultural encounter that has to do with the transmission of the message to someone else, not the examination of one's own culture. It has been concerned with translation of the Bible into each language engaged. It has asked how the message of the gospel can best be said or imagined in that language or culture. It tends, therefore, to be receptor oriented. That is where the important questions are, it is believed—in the translation.

This easily leads to a failure at the very point at which North American churches need help the most. When people focus on the receptor culture and language, they can fail to see that the cultures of both the recipient and the messenger are implicated in the issues of transmission and inculturation. Neither of them is the originator of the message, nor are their cultures and languages those of its original expression. The message bearer is as much in a moment of discovery of the gospel as the one hearing it new. Both cultures, when the message is heard, are called to forms of conversion not anticipated. Neither culture is free of the danger of misconstruing the message, nor is either one incapable of a good and true expression of it.

The danger facing North American churches lies in their tendency to consider their grasp of the gospel so assured that they have ceased imagining that their understanding of it might need to be tested or revised. We in North America need mentors who understand how culture and language function for all human societies, including our own, and who themselves model the willingness to consider that their own culture's grasp of the gospel may have missed the mark and always needs to be revisited. For this, evangelical missiologists will need to check the receptor focus of their work and broaden it to this new territory.

A related problem is the failure to see every church's missionary calling in regard to its own culture, the one it has inside itself. As Lesslie Newbigin has said many times, we in the West are in need of an "inner dialogue" with our own culture.[19] Of course, we have frequently come to that understanding regarding other churches in the world and the inner dialogue they must have with their own, indigenous cultures. But failing to see ourselves as inhabiting a culture, we have not thought the same way about ourselves. Conversion to this agenda is crucial for evangelicalism if it is to serve present needs well.

Overcoming or avoiding these failures is part of this conversion, but another matter has to do with epistemology. Relativism, or even a hint of relativism, tends to draw out a strong reaction from evangelicals, usually in

19. See Lesslie Newbigin, *Foolishness to the Greeks: The Gospel and Western Society* (Grand Rapids: Eerdmans, 1986); and idem, *The Gospel in a Pluralist Society* (Grand Rapids: Eerdmans, 1989), esp. 56ff.

defense of "objective truth" or the like. Evangelicalism's own missionary experience should have prepared it by this time to be ahead of the curve of postmodern critiques of the ways of knowing fostered under the influence of the Enlightenment. If postmoderns claim that all knowing is perspectival, we should have known it already. Missionary experience in every place confirms that all peoples, people of the West included, have socially constructed and historically transmitted ways of knowing and believing and behaving that are the unique perspective through which they experience and interpret the world and everything in it. Each cultural group catches from the gospel, when it is heard, something of its glimmers that no one else has ever seen and misses what it will have to depend on others to help it see. So to qualify all knowing, even of the gospel, as culturally particular and historically conditioned is what we expect when we know God as a missionary God and have had the experience of going with the Spirit to people of other cultures. We learn, as Newbigin has put it, that

> neither at the beginning, nor at any subsequent time, is there or can there be a gospel that is not embodied in a culturally conditioned form of words. The idea that one can or could at any time separate out by some process of distillation a pure gospel unadulterated by any cultural accretions is an illusion.[20]

Utilizing the gifts of evangelicalism's missionary wisdom for the current recovery of the church's missional identity will depend on the ability to welcome the humility and trust in the Spirit that a declaration such as that entails. Without this ability, there will be little to gain for the cultivation of a discerning community whose goal is to know God and to know itself in communion with God.

Biblical Authority

Evangelicalism has always fostered the conviction that Scripture is the "only infallible rule of faith and practice," as was repeatedly said in the congregation of my rearing. Biblical authority is essential to being evangelical, even if there is no clear consensus about how to define the nature of that authority.

Authority may have more to do with the way the Bible is used, the way it functions, than it does with what view of inspiration or inerrancy is espoused. There are those who tend toward a strict, if not wooden, literalism. The text is taken to be a straightforward, direct communication from God to the reader. Wary of the dangers of literalism, others within evangelicalism seek discernible, deducible principles from the text.

20. Newbigin, *Foolishness to the Greeks*, 4.

The instincts these two tendencies represent come into sharp relief in an exchange between Bruce Nichols and Charles Kraft at a Lausanne-sponsored consultation on gospel and culture issues.[21] A full treatment of their views is not possible here, but in essence, Nichols treats the Bible as something of a *textbook* that reveals the shape of a Christian culture as God intends it. Kraft treats it more as a *casebook* that shows in a diversity of settings the contextualization of eternal principles that can be distilled and applied elsewhere. In contrast, Newbigin sees the Bible as a *storybook*, a narrative that "renders accessible to us the actions, character, and purposes of God."[22] For him, the biblical narrative is neither a portrait of an ideal culture nor a source for disembodied principles but a revelation of the meaning and destiny of the world.[23]

The approach Newbigin represents over against those of Nichols and Kraft is worth noticing. It cannot be denied that the Bible comes to us mainly in the form of narrative. If that is so, the critical questions are shifted. How does a narrative have authority? How does it exercise that authority? How do we place ourselves in the way of that authority? How do we imbibe it? For those caught, as many in evangelicalism have been, in a modern complex of rational proofs of God, how does a narrative function apologetically in an alternative way?

Evangelicalism's convictions about biblical authority will be important for the church's recovery of its missional identity, but evangelicalism will be able to contribute in this way only if it takes seriously the actual character of the biblical materials and responds with a hermeneutical approach and apologetic method conducive to narrative. It will also need to show how the Bible as narrative is community-formative.

There are several implications from all of this.

First, evangelicals will have to understand that the biblical narrative renders meaning. Particularly, it renders the actions, character, and purposes of God. The biblical narrative casts a fundamentally reorienting sense of the meaning of the world's life and by doing so draws the community attached to the story into its meaning so that the community imbibes and finally embodies that meaning.

Second, a renewed way of engaging the Bible when it is read, or rather of being engaged by it, is required. The normative way we have dealt with the biblical text is to determine its meaning in the original set-

21. See their essays in John R. W. Stott and Robert Coote, eds., *Down to Earth: Studies in Christianity and Culture* (Grand Rapids: Eerdmans, 1980).

22. Newbigin, *Foolishness to the Greeks*, 55.

23. For a full comparison of these three views, see George R. Hunsberger, *Bearing the Witness of the Spirit: Lesslie Newbigin's Theology of Cultural Plurality* (Grand Rapids: Eerdmans, 1998), 264–70.

ting and then to determine how it is to be understood and applied in the contemporary setting. The problem with the method is that in a subtle way it leaves us largely in charge of the transaction. Our judgments are dominant. Instead, a reading of the text that is missional in character recognizes that the text is in reality reading us! God, through the text, is engaging us, and as readers our responsibility includes welcoming that reading of our world and circumstance. We will recognize that the Spirit asks new questions in the process: How does this text send us? How does it read us? How does it evangelize us with good news? How does it convert us? How does it orient us to the coming reign of God?

Third, the narrative form of the Bible underscores what the Bible itself says, that truth is fundamentally personal. In other words, it is a person, Jesus. Whatever we discern of that truth may and should approximate it and be true to it. But our knowing is not truth in the same way that Jesus is the truth. The modesty of our language needs to correspond with this.

Fourth, narrative stresses how lived the truth is, and it calls from us a commitment to practiced truth. Philip Kenneson has argued, "There's no such thing as objective truth, and it's a good thing too."[24] In his argument, he invites evangelicals to go to their own first principles and to recognize that objective truth assumed to be truth whether or not it is practiced is alien to the evangelical conviction that personal experience and belief translated into transformed life are crucial to Christian life and identity.[25]

An evangelical conversion to patterns such as these, which practice the narrative form of the gospel, holds promise for renewal. Such patterns would cultivate the church to be a storied community, one whose goal is to crawl into the story and take up residence there. This would be a gospeled community, cross-shaped and resurrection-voiced.

"Pure" Gospel

"Where the gospel is rightly preached," the creeds of the Reformation confidently said of the true church. If anything defines evangelicalism it is certainly the evangel, the gospel. What is the gospel in its true, right, and pure sense? While a range of answers is certainly present in

24. Philip D. Kenneson, "There's No Such Thing as Objective Truth, and It's a Good Thing Too!" in *Christian Apologetics in the Postmodern World*, ed. Timothy R. Phillips and Dennis L. Okholm (Downers Grove, Ill.: InterVarsity, 1995).

25. The epistemological shifts sketched in the last few paragraphs are played out in more detail in George R. Hunsberger, "The Church in the Postmodern Transition," in *A Scandalous Prophet: The Way of Mission after Newbigin*, ed. Thomas F. Foust, George R. Hunsberger, J. Andrew Kirk, and Werner Ustorf (Grand Rapids: Eerdmans, 2001), 95–106.

evangelicalism, there are some general tendencies. In the report of the Lausanne-sponsored consultation on "Evangelism and Social Responsibility," the assertion of the primacy of evangelism rested on the ground that it had to do with "people's eternal destiny."[26] The substitutionary atonement and the acceptance of Jesus as one's personal Lord and Savior are undoubtedly parts of it for most evangelicals. While many see the need to stress a much more fulsome sense of the gospel, the tendency is to see the heart of the gospel within a narrow band of ideas such as these.

Gospel people have much to offer the renewal of the church, but it must be asked whether that can happen apart from some serious questions about the scope of the characteristic evangelical understanding of the simple and pure gospel. What exactly is a "personal Lord," for example? And is the eternal destiny of an individual a sufficient description of salvation as Scripture portrays it? How do the narrative Gospels in the New Testament add up to this? How does Jesus speak about the gospel, and how does that impact our own sense of it? At least three lines of conversion for evangelicalism are required.

First, the cross must be central but more fundamentally discerned than in the somewhat mechanistic way that substitutionary atonement notions have tended to portray it. The question to be answered is, What is the connection between the story line Jesus tells (about the reign of God being at hand) and the way the story ends? Without a compelling answer to that question, the atonement is left hanging in midair. This is important because the believing community is invited to take up such a cross and bear it with Jesus. How can a community be cross-shaped apart from understanding the relationship between the cross of Christ and the reign of God Christ announced? And that raises a question about the resurrection as well. Does it overturn the cross? Or confirm it?

Second, a fresh ecclesiology needs to emerge that sees that the gospel of God is intended to be embodied in actual communities. This will give shape to fresh apologetic moves. It is important to this generation to see real people living as though the gospel narrative is true and truly depicts the meaning of the world. The church's missional recovery includes a sense that in the design of God the congregation is the "hermeneutic of the gospel," the interpretive key for understanding it.[27] The missional church is one that knows that its origin is in the gospel and that it is called into being in order to represent the gospel. Evangelicals,

---

26. Lausanne Committee for World Evangelization, *Evangelism and Social Responsibility: An Evangelical Commitment* (Wheaton: Lausanne Committee for World Evangelization and World Evangelical Fellowship, 1982), 25.

27. Cf. Newbigin, *Gospel in a Pluralist Society,* 222–33.

"gospel people," of all people ought to know this and nourish the recovery of the gospel by the churches as their charter story.

Third, there must be a shift in the grammatical structure of the message we hold out as gospel. We have tended to offer as gospel the security of knowing that eternal destiny is secured, the comfort of forgiven sins, the release from guilt, the assurance of the love of God, and the power to live a transformed life. In other words, we try to answer people's "What's in it for me?" question. But by doing so, and thus playing to the consumer instincts of the populace, we have missed what is even more fundamental in the Gospels, namely, that with God's reign at hand, we are commanded/invited to repent and believe this good news, to receive and enter this divine reign as those caught up into the mission of God in the world. Apart from this sense of what is taking place, a deeply missional identity for the church will be difficult or impossible to achieve.

The church, the whole people of God, has the vocation to be a community, to be a certain kind of community, for a divine purpose. Evangelicalism has not always or in all its accents supplied a rich-textured missional ecclesiology. Living its own conversion, mission, Bible, and gospel more completely and being more converted to its own convictions give promise for the renewal of an evangelical ecclesiology and the church's recovery of its missional character.

Part 3
The Best
Ecclesiology?

5

One, Holy, Catholic, and Apostolic

Awaiting the Redemption of Our Body

EDITH M. HUMPHREY

In Search of the Church

"We believe one, holy, catholic, and apostolic church" is a key phrase of self-definition in our ecumenical creed. But how do the multiple "we" called Christians mean this phrase as they describe their church? Do some cross their fingers at this point in the creed's third article? Once said, *what* is the church? And *where* is it? And what should creedal Christians make of their siblings in the faith who do not consider the Nicaeo-Constantinopolitan Creed (along with this phrase) authoritative but important mainly for the historical study of Christianity? How should Christians understand the one, holy, catholic, and apostolic church in an age of pluralism, after centuries of fragmentation and in this time of waiting prior to our final redemption in Christ Jesus? It is clear that if Christians are to continue to speak with any integrity about "the church" and not simply comment in a sociological manner about "churches," these questions require serious attention.

Whenever I begin to think about the nature and condition of the church, I inevitably flash back to my second year in "full-time ministry." Two very young, married Salvation Army lieutenants with an uncharacteristic academic formation, my husband and I were concerned to underscore the continuity of our ecclesial movement (which some even today would not call "a church") with the church historic. In a well-meaning but *not* so well-conceived move, and without enough preparation of our people, we added the recital of the Apostles' Creed to the liturgy of the morning holiness meeting. We argued with ourselves (methinks we were protesting too much!) that this should be no problem in a Salvation Army context because, after all, that very creed, along with the Nicene Creed, was included in the Salvation Army's *Handbook of Doctrine*, which we had studied *in minutiae* at training college for two years. Inevitably, the explosion occurred after service. What we had overlooked was that we were ministering in a beleaguered Quebec English "corps" (i.e., congregation) compiled of a conglomerate of soldiers, not a few of whom had in another life belonged to the Roman Catholic Church and many of whom felt threatened by the ubiquitous presence of that institution, even after the Quiet Revolution of the 1960s and 1970s. At the hand-shaking exit line, my husband was accosted by a livid member with a red face and an unsettled heart who objected vehemently to being asked to say, "I believe one, holy, *catholic,* and apostolic church." "Catholic," in his mind, had a clear meaning, and it did not describe him!

It is highly unlikely that this episode is unique to us, for I find, as I look at the hymnals and songbooks of many Protestant churches, that editors, in reproducing the Apostles' and Nicene Creeds, frequently changed the offending word *catholic* to *universal*—presumably as a preemptive strike to disarm those for whom the connotations of the word have destroyed the denotation. On the other hand, it is true that times have changed. Fewer Protestants, and indeed fewer evangelicals, are ignorant of the importance of catholicity, and indeed some are trying to reclaim this word to describe their own ecclesiologies. Where ecclesiology used to be the proper interest of the Roman, Orthodox, high Anglican, and Lutheran theologian, it is now an increasing preoccupation in other circles—for example, among those attending the Regent ecclesiology conference for which this study was prepared!

In addition to having a newfound comfort with the word *catholic,* many Protestant groups are also turning to their older siblings in the faith—to tradition—for nurture and even for worship patterns. (Witness the success of Robert E. Webber in commending classical worship forms to evangelical communities. See his *Renew Your Worship, Wor-*

ship Old and New, Learning to Worship with All Your Heart, and *Evangelicals on the Canterbury Trail.*) As prophets conscious of our generation's rootlessness, many in the Christian community are deliberately thinking about the church in new ways, not only as a local or present phenomenon but as something integrally connected to the larger body of Christ, including saints of bygone days. Concurrent with this move is the change in perspective among some contemporary theologians and biblical scholars who refuse to continue the pole vault from the fifth century to the Reformation (yes, Virginia, there was a church in the Middle Ages!) and who are listening to that mysterious expression of Christendom, Eastern Orthodoxy, that has been alternately intriguing and foreboding to many Western Christians up until this day.

In this changing landscape, we look around and make our judgments. None of us is as we would like to be. We consider the four "marks" or characteristics of the church (one, holy, catholic, apostolic) and compare these to what we see. On the surface, we might judge that Protestant communities have majored in the holy to the detriment of the one. Catholic has been largely devalued or misunderstood, and apostolic has been explained in two decidedly Protestant dimensions—the sending of missionaries and the keeping of the deposit of faith of the Twelve plus one (St. Paul). As for the Roman Church, it has stressed the oneness, aided by its shape around the papal see, and the apostolic in many dimensions, notably the tangible succession of the episcopate. However, folk wisdom reveals that its ordinary members have not been expected to pursue the holy with much alacrity (that being the purview of a few blessed), and, paradoxically, Rome has not always done so well with catholic, since parts of the communion have not always acted "with reference to the *whole*"—in either a geographical or a temporal sense. As for Orthodoxy, it seems cheeky to comment, since we have not known them for long. The casual observer, however, may sense that the Orthodox have been successful in the catholic and the apostolic (so many nationalities, so much emphasis on continuity of liturgy and creed), but we may have difficulty grasping their notion of the holy. Further, we are given to wonder about the one as we gape at the variety of jurisdictions among the Orthodox—splinter groups labeled "non-canonical" and nationally divided synods in North America.

So where is the one, holy, catholic, and apostolic church? Can we be content that together we cover the gamut, however lopsided one particular expression of the *ekklēsia* might be? Answering the first question (Where is the church?) is a challenge, since Christians are not united in their presuppositions regarding the essence or character of the church. The answer to the second is more obvious, of course—it does not seem good to the Holy Spirit or to us to be content with the status quo, for, of course, the four marks of the church are intertwined and must by their very nature go together, much like the fruits of the Spirit. "One" is indeed defined or explained by the adjectives holy, catholic, and apostolic, just as love is defined by patience, kindness, longsuffering, and so on.

This essay is, more than any other I have written, a meditation and a work in progress. I began my Christian walk looking for Jesus and have continued this journey in my search for the church, the body of Christ. To begin my Christian life, as I did, in a self-described "movement" rather than in a group that delineated itself as a church perhaps meant that I came to feel "semi-deprived." And yet in my community of origin, I learned much about the nature of the church, for where Christ is, there are his people. My search has taken me from a formally non-sacramental body to a eucharistically centered communion, from a group that simply commissions its officers to a body that honors priesthood as a special charism within the priesthood of believers; it has also taken me from a disciplined, evangelistic, and biblically literate (though sometimes rigid) environment to a confusing group that is now threatening to divide along fault lines. These fault lines are not superficial but separate those who have different understandings of holiness, authority, community, evangelization, and the interpretation of Scripture. Both in the more "sectarian" Army and in the so-called inclusivist milieu of the Anglican Church, there have been challenges. The first had no eucharist at all (despite its doctrine that "the Old and New Testaments . . . alone constitute the divine rule of Christian faith and *practice*");[1] the second (despite its emphasis on confession/absolution and its focus on *Holy* Communion) is now overrun by those who want indiscriminately to open the altar. Such challenges have directed me to ask, Where is the church? What is the church? I am sure my story is not the only one like this. Let us approach an answer to such questions by means of investigating the four marks (one, holy, catholic, and apostolic), through considering the present and sacramental nature of the church and through considering its eschatological character and our hope for its *apokalypsis*.

The Four Marks: One, Holy, Catholic, and Apostolic

Despite the Scylla and Charybdis of ecclesial triumphalism and total cynicism, members of all communions today yearn for the visible body of Christ in the world to be whole and healthy. Even those who have no

---

1. Doctrine 1 of 11, produced in *The Song Book of the Salvation Army* (London: Salvationist Publishing and Press, 1955), 474.

use for the methods of contemporary ecumenical "dialogue" pray for the peace of New Zion. There may be those who are uncertain as to the meaning of catholic or apostolic, and others who have no desire to be one with denominations they deem heretical (read catholic?) or hidebound (read apostolic?), but the diagnosis is the same: We yearn to show forth Christ as we are called to do. There is a profound sense of what the church should be, even as many Christian groups are starting to recover what it has been in the past. The extension of our view beyond the local and the present time to past and future is crucial in our coming to see the church as one. It is imperative that we get beyond that new "weasel" expression "Let us *be church*" and start to talk about "the church" without embarrassment and (one hopes) with less confusion. So I will do it.

The Church Is One

This is primary, like the unity of God. We, as well as the ancient Hebrews, take our cue from the character of God himself: "Hear, O Israel, the LORD our God is one." Our oneness springs from the One Who Is, *ho Ōn*. It is as we gaze on him, call on his name, and worship that we are made into his likeness. Envision Moses and the elders in Exodus 24, called up the mountain into the presence of that ineffable One, who beheld God and ate and drank to seal a covenant of love and obedience. Recollect the three—Peter, James, and John—who were called up the mountain (Matt. 17:1–8; Mark 9:2–8; Luke 9:28–36), who beheld their humble Lord Jesus in the presence of Moses and Elijah, transformed before them, with the divine voice left ringing in their ears, "This is my beloved Son, hear him!" The oneness of Israel was typified by this scene in which their representatives worshiped, enjoyed, and covenanted to obey the one God. The oneness of the new Israel is pictured by the three key apostles, overshadowed by the glory of their praying Messiah, who see vividly the continuity between Jesus and the law and the prophets and who are directed to hear *him*—the source, focus, and location of their unity. As the *shekinah* glory lit up the faces of Moses and the three disciples who entered Jesus' glory cloud, so the unity of God tinges our community—and we must not shy away from it.

Notice that this unity from the one God is not some nebulous thing but an actual quality that is describable and measurable. In both Old and New Testaments, the unity is characterized in terms of (dare we say it?) hierarchy alongside mutuality. A mountain! The Holy One, who does not "lay his hand" on his creation but speaks in clear words! The leader (Moses) and King of Kings (Jesus)! The representative leaders—elders and beloved apostles! In the one case, the hierarchy is accentuated and direct—"Now the appearance of the glory of the LORD was like a devouring fire. . . . He called to Moses out of the cloud" (Exod. 24:16–17 NRSV). Despite the awe, the leaders commune with God—they eat the festal meal. In the New Testament, Jesus' excellence and preeminence are undeniable, yet a change in the directness of hierarchy, an exchange, takes place. The humble Messiah *prays* (Luke 9:28), the highest King in solidarity with humanity; his disciples (wonder of wonders!) are allowed to enter the glory of God, fearful though they are. God includes them in his glory and his counsels, for they are about to become his sons by adoption, little dwelling places for his glory. Both stories—exodus and transfiguration—show a marked hierarchy alongside pictures of mutuality and sharing. The scene in the transfiguration is more intimate and more dynamic, for God is there incarnate, within and with them as well as above. Yet the hierarchy is not destroyed in the new covenant scene.

Hierarchy, it would seem, is a bush that is never consumed, however egalitarian we would like to be, however much God calls us "his friends," for oneness requires order if there is to be more than a simple unit. Moreover, this order must be constituted by hierarchy (i.e., with a *hieros*, "sacred"; *archē*, "head" or "source"), if we are speaking about unity among persons with wills and affections. One can imagine order without hierarchy among inanimate objects, as in a crystal or (perhaps, though this is a moot point) an ecosystem. But where persons live together in intimacy, that unity involves (willing or unwilling) acts of direction and response—however mutual and interactive the relationship might be. Practically speaking, any human institution, even those that work by consensus, may be disclosed as hierarchical, with the stronger (however this is determined in any one given situation) leading and others responding. Could it be that such asymmetry is not simply a matter of our fallen condition, not simply a matter of default, but the very means by which any unity is achieved?

Why should we expect otherwise, given the revealed reality of the Trinity, that Three-in-One together adored, with the begotten Son and proceeding Holy Spirit having their source eternally in the Father? How could we think that the church should follow a different pattern? Mutual deference and a hierarchical order are, it seems, the essence of God's own oneness. So are they built into the cosmos he has made. Some moderns have, of course, stressed the mutual perichoretic communion between the persons of the Trinity so as to obscure or mitigate the headship (i.e., *archē*, "source") of the Father and in service of a contemporary egalitarian ecclesiology. They assume wrongly that any talk of paternal monarchy is vicious and fail to notice that a *subtle* hierarchy, articulated *alongside* an expression of the mutuality of the persons,

is the very essence of the creed. Jesus is "God from God"; the Spirit proceeds "from the Father";[2] yet together, Father, Son, and Spirit are worshiped and glorified. This is a puzzling but rich revelation. As Vladimir
Lossky puts it, "The dogma of the Trinity marks the summit of theology,
where our thought stands still before the primordial mystery of the existence of the personal God."[3]

The fathers who defined our ecumenical creeds articulated this mystery with as much precision as possible, following the cues of the fourth
Gospel and St. Paul. We hear in the fourth Gospel of the Son, who dem-
onstrates his love through obedience (14:31) and who goes to the Father—that Father who is, in one sense, "greater" than he (14:28). The
hierarchical language here cannot be softened simply by reference to
Jesus' human nature. Similarly, Paul, in the same letter in which he in-
sists on the oneness of God the Father and Jesus the Lord in a Christianized *Shema* (1 Cor. 8:6; cf. Deut. 6:4), goes on to speak about the
time when the Son "himself will also be in subjection under him [God
the Father], so that God may be all in all" (1 Cor. 15:28, author's translation). Similarly, the Spirit, worshiped rightly as Lord (2 Cor. 3:17),
does not speak of his own but glorifies the Son (John 16:13–14). Our
Triune God is one but not a monad.

Such unity celebrates a nuanced hierarchy-with-mutuality. So it is
with his people, if they are to be one. On a micro-level, the Christian
family is called *both* to mutual deference and to asymmetrical roles expressed in terms of obedience and nurture (Eph. 5:21–22, 25; 6:1, 4). In
the congregation, the larger Christian family, mutual respect is invoked
alongside injunctions to leaders that they "care for the flock" and exhortation to others that they respect, indeed *obey*, their pastors (Phil.
2:4, 12).

Sometimes, *mirabile dictu*, the expected lines of patron and client, or
parent and children, are turned on their heads so that Paul, normatively "father" of his church but also brother to his siblings in the faith,

2. Some might argue that this tension between monarchy and mutuality is apparent
only in the Eastern triadic understanding of the Trinity. Certainly, the mystery is accentuated in this view, which locates the unity of the Trinity in the *person* of the Father
rather than in the abstraction of relationships (Western *ab utroque* theology). However,
appeal to the *filioque* does not, in fact, remove the problem of an eternal source, since
the third article of the creed comes after the second, in which the Father and Son relationship has been outlined. As Augustine (frequently appealed to on behalf of the *filioque*) states, even if the Son is involved, the Spirit proceeds principally from the Father.
This is inherent in the logic and rhythm of the creed. See Augustine, *On the Holy Trinity*
15.26.47 and 17.27.29.

3. Vladimir Lossky, "The Procession of the Holy Spirit in Orthodox Trinitarian Doctrine, in *In the Image and Likeness of God*, ed. John H. Erickson and Thomas E. Bird
(Crestwood, N.Y.: St. Vladimir's Seminary Press, 1974), 90.

receives the patronage of a woman, Phoebe (Rom. 16:2). The lines of hierarchy are not destroyed but radicalized, enriched, and complicated by the absolute parentage of the Almighty and the revolutionizing pattern of Jesus, who was rich and became poor *for us*. The surprising marriage of mutual respect to hierarchy may seem an oxymoron or an intolerable tension to those outside Christ. But for those who know Jesus' pattern of living and who are filled by the Spirit, whose delight it is to glorify others, it becomes the creative dance by which they show forth their nature as God's very children.

The Church Is Holy

The church is called to be one after the pattern of the one God. Thus, the church is *holy*. (That is a declaration, not an expression of wishful thinking!) It is holy because it has been called out *(ekklēsia)* by Christ himself and continues to be called out: "Come out of her, my people," cries the risen and ascended Christ of the Apocalypse (18:4 NRSV). For a very long time, I resisted this kind of talk, because I encountered (or perhaps I only *heard*) a domesticated version of holiness in my Wesleyan-rooted community. Holiness is frequently confused with subjectivist pietism and sometimes offered by means of shortcut methods that deal with only the surface of things or that lead to chronic feelings of inadequacy. But Friedrich Nietzsche is surprisingly right—it is our "long obedience in the same direction" that is desired.[4] And Richard Foster is right—we have lacked discipline, those of us who are in the Protestant West, for a long time.[5] Part of the genius of Methodism was its desire to re-inculcate the ascetic life by means of a methodic and orderly approach to accountability.

What can be done to rid our lives, our communities, of the demons that would take up residence once the room is swept? Our Lord made it clear that "this kind comes out only by prayer and fasting." Fear of legalism and empty form has caused many of us to throw out the baby, or, to change the metaphor, to put aside the very medicine that our older siblings in the church recommend to us as healthful. It is not simply a matter of fasting and praying individualistically or haphazardly when we "feel" that we ought. We are called to fast and pray together: "When *you* [plural!] pray, say . . ."; "When the bridegroom is taken from them, then *they* will fast"; "Confess your sins *to one another* and you will

---

4. Friedrich Neitzsche, *Beyond Good and Evil*, trans. Helen Zimmern (New York: Macmillan, 1907). His phrase has been popularized by Eugene H. Peterson in *A Long Obedience in the Same Direction: Discipleship in an Instant Society* (Downers Grove, Ill.: InterVarsity, 1980).

5. Richard J. Foster, *Celebration of Discipline: The Path to Spiritual Growth* (San Francisco: Harper & Row, 1988).

be healed"; "The sick one should *call upon the elders* and have them pray and anoint them"; "Whoever *brings back* a sinner . . . will save the sinner's life from death." Our prayer together, our confession before one another, our being anointed by those over us in the Lord, our discipline and exhortation of one another—all this makes for the personal purity and the corporate unity the Spirit is forging in us.

Why should we think our being made into his image is an individual affair or an instant accomplishment? Where is that written? Instead, we hear Paul saying, "All of us, with unveiled faces [i.e., transparent to the Lord and one another], seeing the glory of the Lord as though reflected in a mirror, are being transformed into the same image from one degree of glory to another; for this comes from the Lord, the Spirit" (2 Cor. 3:18 NRSV). Confession is *not* a private matter between me and God—we are one. Prayer is *never* private, if by private we mean that it is business only between God and me, though it can be very personal. That is, even when I emulate Jesus' praying in wild places or heed the call to the closet, my prayer is not merely a conversation that involves God and me—I pray, we pray, in the Spirit (Rom. 8:23–27), in the hearing of those who now behold his face, and for the benefit of the whole body of Christ, past, present, and future. Our prayers are presented before God in the heavenlies (Rev. 5:8), handled by others who know him, and mingled together as a savory offering of corporate worship. Even my personal prayer of confession is an occasion for festive celebration among those who are now fully in the light ("There is joy in heaven . . .").

Similarly, healing involves the laying on of hands on another. Even our salvation (in the fullest sense of wholeness) is mediated (1 Cor. 7:16; James 5:19–20), though Jesus alone is the redeemer. From the beginning, then, the historic church has given directions for living, patterns for prayer, creeds for believing, disciplines such as confession and abstinence. It has assumed that we will be involved in one another's lives in an ordered and respectful way. All this works toward our freedom and not for our constraint. Mysteriously, we find that the common pursuit of the holy, and the ineffable work of the Holy One, goes beyond joining us together in unity. We join one another in a characteristic that we share with our Lord, the new human being: At last, we are coming to have faces, to show our charisms and so glorify God, to be real persons! A being who has no face might be worried that in having a face she will be like all the others who possess this quality. But, of course, the very opposite is the case: Faces are diverse, and thus diversity is a correlate of being made holy.

Again, we might assume, given the philosophical discussions of the past few centuries, that our personhood is bound up in the distinction of the I and the not-I. But the Son, who is *toward the Father*, and the Spirit, *who glorifies the Son*, teach us a different way to be. Our identity, corporate and personal, emerges as we live more and more in communion. We have our shared time and key signatures, our common meters and stanza divisions by which to compose spiritual music and write unimaginable sonnets. It is the liturgy, the prayers and structures of two millennia (or more), that gives us the foundations for a lively and fresh word in our own situation. The prayers of our older siblings free us from seeking novelty for its own sake or wondering what on earth the worship leader is up to *now*. In a shared liturgy, past brothers and sisters in the faith gather with us; we take our eyes off the contingent and the individual. We can settle down deep into these prayers, hear the Spirit speak to us directly, and respond confidently with one voice, rather than being distracted by the innovations or eccentricities of a random voice. We realize that to be holy means to be God-centered as we worship, as we come forward to "kiss" our Lord. It does not mean to be seeker-friendly, though our worship will in itself embrace the willing.

Our holiness, our distinctness, is also expressed in what we say together *about* God. It is in reciting together the ecumenical creeds that we become truly called out, truly countercultural in a flabby, accommodating church and a pluralistic, confused world. Again, we speak together *about* our situation and hear God respond: In the humility of confession, we find the freeing power of forgiveness. (And if we find it difficult to confess to our frail brother or sister, make no mistake, we have not really confessed to the holy God, however we mouth the words.) This holiness touches our daily routines as well. It is in the difficult discipline of fasting that we learn gratitude and gain control over other wilder areas of our lives—the sexual appetites, the rush of uninvoked anger, the tendency to self-pity in a world in which many need so much more. Disciplines such as these are transferable, and Paul as well as the ongoing church tradition knew well the importance of mastering the unruly appetites, not because the flesh is bad but because it is not yet in glory. The early church, and many traditions, designated certain seasons and ongoing days as a time when they would exercise together—Advent and Lent, Holy Week, Wednesdays and Fridays. Such common actions are helpful too in forging an actual community in our splintered and scattered cities. Community does not come by chance in a world whose pace, consumerism, and individualism conspire to keep us atomized. Common prayer patterns and patterns of life are tangible ways we are brought together with one another and closer to our Lord. Our holiness, though not complete, is a characteristic we share with one another as the church and within which we are called together to cooperate. The whole church, past and present, has a hand in this wonderful work, because that is how God works.

The Church Is Catholic

What exactly does it mean to be catholic, to be concerned with the whole *(kath' holon)*? Ignatius of Antioch wrote, "Where Jesus Christ is, there is the catholic Church." John Meyendorff, a profound Eastern Orthodox theologian, explains that catholic has two dimensions. It is the opposite of being heretical ("a splitter of truth") and the opposite of schismatic ("a splitter of the community").[6] Frequently, we have made the mistake of thinking that holiness *inevitably requires* splitting. We have played holiness against catholicity, as many outside (and, truth be told, in) the church have played love against truth. We miss the concreteness of the term when we translate it as "universal" and then envisage some nebulous universal church that is, quite literally, only God knows where. To be catholic is to orient ourselves so that we consider and participate in the entire church—past, present, and future; east, west, north, and south—and to recognize our place there. Meyendorff issues this challenge: "There is no way in which one can claim to be a Christian except through concrete membership in the Catholic Church and through a continuous effort at manifesting the catholicity of the Church."[7]

Those are hard words, especially as he goes on to explain that "no human group, however worthy, holy and active, is able to 'create' catholicity: it can only cooperate . . . with divine grace and manifest the divine concern for the life and salvation of the world."[8] In other words, our catholicity comes from the Holy Spirit, who binds us together in one body, and from the finished work of Christ, who has broken down the dividing wall between groups. It is not something we can put into a vision statement and then pursue by sheer force of will and method. The church is an organism, not an institution, or, as Paul puts it, "God's *poiēma*"—his work of art.

So, what then do we make of the turn of evangelistic communities to the ancient liturgical patterns, aided by the likes of Robert Webber? All well and good, wonderful, and a hopeful sign of unity with the church through the ages! Only, let us do this because we are rediscovering what we are meant to be, because we are being grafted into a part of the tradition that we had forgotten, not because it is "esoteric" or "cultured" or even "meeting the needs of this particular congregation"—though I

6. John Meyendorff, *Catholicity and the Church* (Crestwood, N.Y.: St. Vladimir's Seminary Press, 1983), 7–8.
7. Ibid., 9.
8. Ibid., 10.

have no doubt that it will meet needs. And what should we make of the trend toward multiple worship services, each taking a regular place on Sunday or during the week and each aimed at a different peer group? Surely we should think carefully about dividing the worshiping community by age and musical tastes on an institutional and ongoing basis! Such actions impoverish those who are stuck in the contemporary culture and harden the predispositional "traditionalist" in whichever decade or century makes him comfortable—whether using the medieval chant, the Reformation Psalter, or the early twentieth-century gospel song. No, if the church is like a tree, the branches cannot be cut off from one another, and we should delight to sing together, even when we find the harmony difficult to learn. That means treasuring the best of past music and thinking about our common praise rather than privileging the virtuoso performance of a complex traditional anthem or reveling in new worship song after new worship song after new worship song simply because they are new.

Let us therefore "try" the spirits of the new songs to see if they be of God. Let those who use them do so judiciously, well aware of the ubiquitous first-person singular and striving for a full expression of worship toward God, not a simple celebration of "my feelings." And let us not forget the older songs of Zion, for these are the voices of our brothers and sisters, and they have been tested. It is a matter of both truth and love. C. S. Lewis, though he was hardly ever comfortable in corporate worship, considered it essential for the life of the church. He remarked in his essay "On Church Music"[9] that God was pleased whenever the highbrow organist adapted to the abilities of the ordinary communicant who delighted in bawling a gospel hymn and whenever the ordinary communicant was attentive to a musical piece beyond her tastes because she loved the musicians and knew that this was their offering to the Lord. The focus on the "other" and on the Lord is a strong remedy for the culture wars we are experiencing in the church today. It is catholic.

The Church Is Apostolic

Let us begin with a quotation that will make us sit up and listen, even if we disagree with it. It comes from a commentary on the Nicene Creed found on the web that defines the term *apostolic* in such a way that a vague definition is ruled out.

The Church is Apostolic. That is to say, it is the community that Christ founded with the Apostles as nucleus. We read of the first Christian con-

9. C. S. Lewis, "On Church Music," in *Christian Reflections*, ed. Walter Hooper (Glasgow: Collins, 1981), 124–30.

verts added to the Church at Jerusalem that "they continued steadfast in the apostles' teaching and fellowship, and in the breaking of bread, and the prayers" (Acts 2:42). In order to be a Christian, it is not enough to be in the Apostles' teaching. You must also be in the Apostles' fellowship. The Church is a group, just as the Scouts are a group. Suppose that someone found a Boy Scout Manual, and read it, and said, "I like this!" Suppose that he then sat down and memorized the Scout Oath and the Scout Law, and learned to tie 21 different kinds of knots blindfolded, and how to pitch a tent, and how to swim 25 yards underwater, and how to read a compass, and all the other things that a Scout is required to know and to do. Suppose that he further made a point of being trustworthy, loyal, helpful, friendly, courteous, kind, obedient, cheerful, thrifty, brave, clean, and reverent. Would it be accurate to say that he was a Scout? I think the answer is clearly negative. He might be called Scout-like. He would be someone whom the Scouts would gladly welcome aboard. But until he gets in contact with the Scout organization and joins up, he is not a Scout. . . . In like fashion, to be a Christian does not mean simply holding a certain set of beliefs, even if accompanied by appropriate behavior. It means belonging to the Christian community, to the Church. When God sent an angel to the centurion Cornelius (Acts 10), the angel did not instruct him in Christian doctrine and tell him, "Now, if you believe what I have just said, that makes you a Christian." Rather, he told him how to get in touch with the Christian community by sending a messenger to Peter in Joppa. When Saul was on the road to Damascus, Christ spoke to him. But He did not instruct Saul in Christian doctrine. Rather, He told him to go into Damascus and wait for instructions, and then He sent Ananias, a Christian, to receive Saul into the Christian community. And one of the marks of that community is its continuity with the community that Christ founded and upon whom the Holy Spirit descended at Pentecost.[10]

"And one of the marks of that community is its continuity with the community that Christ founded and upon whom the Holy Spirit descended at Pentecost." This is the challenge: to see that because of the incarnation it does not make sense to speak about the "invisible church" or to see the church in a vague way. There is to be a tangible connection of every believing community with those who have gone before, both in word and in truth. The author's point would have been even stronger had he commented on Paul's own words in Galatians that, though he received his revelation directly from Christ, he went to the apostles in Jerusalem to verify his mission (Gal. 2:2). Were correct doctrine and a personal experience of Christ enough to live the full Christian life, such a mission would have been superfluous—especially for the likes of Paul. But that early church leader, so intent on catholic-

10. www.iclnet.org/pub/resources/text/history/creed.church.txt.

ity in his collection for Jerusalem and in his message of reconciling Jew and Gentile believer, also respected the enfleshed character of the church, and so going to the apostles was no mere formality. This did not render any of those apostles (including Peter) infallible, of course, for we hear about the misunderstanding of Peter and James in this same letter. But it does show us that Paul was no mere soloist and that he had a concrete understanding of the body of Christ, for whom his Lord had died, risen, and ascended.

The term *apostolic* can be distorted, it would seem, in three directions. First, it can be restricted in its meaning so that it is used in terms of its etymology only, thus referring simply to missionaries and missions. Certainly, an apostolic church is aware of Christ's *sending* of it into the world, but this does not exhaust the meaning. Second, the term can be confined so as to speak only about the character of the church's beliefs, taking as normative only the idea of the "apostles' teaching" in Acts 2:42. But Luke's wordplay in Acts 2:42 says *tē didachē tōn apostolōn kai tē koinōnia*. The teaching *(didachē)* and the fellowship *(koinōnia)*[11] are *both* gathered around the apostles. It is not that early Christians paid attention to the teaching of the apostles and to fellowship in the abstract. Rather, the apostles, as those who had seen Jesus, formed the center of the believers' belief and life together. As F. F. Bruce puts it (though he does not draw the ecclesial conclusions that I am drawing here!), there is an "apostolic fellowship" connected with the "apostolic teaching."[12] In fact, it could well be said that all of the community's life, including its teaching, fellowship, breaking of bread, and prayers, took place around the apostles, around those who had been with Jesus in a tangible, embodied manner.

Christ is incarnate and did not de-incarnate when he ascended. He identified fully with Israel and brought into the light of day the new Israel, those who are in Christ. Apostles were a prominent part of that new creation, not to be sniffed at as mere institutionalization, and the apostles laid hands on those who were to continue the teaching, the prayers, the breaking of bread, the way of life. To be apostolic, then, means to acknowledge not simply an ideological but an actual historical connection with the first community. We are one household together, and we honor those who have been granted particular author-

11. This reading is possible grammatically, even considering the repetition of the article before *koinōnia*. Given the description of the early church that follows, it is clear that this is the intent if not the grammatical requirement of the phrase, for in everything that follows, not simply in the apostolic decree of Acts 15 but in the life of the body together, the apostolic group is the gravitational center.

12. F. F. Bruce, *The New International Commentary on the New Testament: The Book of Acts* (Grand Rapids: Eerdmans, 1980), 79.

ity (elders/overseers) because they are connected to those who were in time with Jesus. Paul's own claim to be an apostle rested on an unusual "seeing" of Jesus our Lord—not a vision but a resurrection encounter with the risen Jesus himself. How this incarnate and tangible church is to become a complete reality in our divided ecclesial settings is not an easy thing to understand. The first step is to acknowledge its truth in principle and stop bringing closure to the discussion by talk of the "invisible church." The second is for communions to examine the claim of the episcopacy and to reclaim this wonderful structure, which has come to us from the earliest times, even from the first century.

After all, by the time of the writing of 1 Timothy, there is talk of the *episkopos,* though at that time it was not clearly distinguishable from the presbyterate; not many years later, in the late first century, Clement insisted that the apostles foresaw the needs of the church and the possibility of strife over leadership and therefore set up the offices of elder and bishop, not as a novelty but after the pattern given to them in the Scriptures.[13] Again, in the early second century, Ignatius pictured the elders (presbyters) as gathered around the bishop, together representing the council of the apostles, when the earliest apostles gathered around Peter and James.[14] Several decades later, Hippolytus made clear a pattern for ministry and ordination that had obviously been accepted for some time and that he articulated in a time when schism was threatening.[15] By the mid third century, bishops in the church had obviously heard some of the reasoning regarding the making of a congregation that we hear all too often today, and so we hear the warning of Cyprian (Bishop of Carthage, 249–258):

13. *1 Clement* 42:1–44:6. My argument here does not depend on finding the threefold ministry of bishop, presbyter, and deacon clearly delineated in the New Testament per se, although some have thought that they can find this pattern there, at least *in nuce.* Rather, I am asking us not to dismiss the very early traditional development of church along this threefold pattern and questioning the common Protestant prejudice that this structure amounts to the hardening and "early catholicism" (read "institutionalization") of an originally free society. There is, of course, ample evidence of authoritative leadership in the New Testament documents (e.g., Paul's deference to Peter and James), just as there is ample evidence there of the coequal worship of Father, Son, and Spirit (e.g., 1 Cor. 8:6; 2 Cor. 3:18). It is curious that many evangelicals who celebrate the formalization of the latter (trinitarianism) in the Apostles' Creed and Nicene Creed should be so squeamish about embracing the full flower of the former (apostolic church order)! What if this means to reject an essential imprint of the life of Father, Son, and Spirit on the life of the church—heading bishop, ministering presbyter, and nurturing deacon?

14. *Magnesians* 6; *Smyrneans* 8.

15. *The Apostolic Tradition* sec. 2, 8, 9.

You cannot have God for your Father if you have not the Church for your mother. . . . Nor let certain people deceive themselves by a foolish interpretation of Our Lord's words: *"Wherever two or three are gathered in my name, I am with them."* Corruptors and false interpreters of the Gospel, they quote the end and ignore what has gone before, repeating part of it and dishonestly suppressing the rest; just as they have cut themselves off from the Church, so they cut up the sense of a single passage. For Our Lord was urging His disciples to unanimity and peace when He said, *"I say to you that if two of you agree on earth concerning anything whatsoever you shall ask, it shall be done for you by my Father who is in heaven. For wherever two or three are gathered together in my name, I am with them."*— showing that it was not the number but the unanimity of those praying that counted most. . . . He put unanimity first, He gave the precedence to peace and concord. . . . But what sort of agreement will a man make with another if he is out of agreement with the body of the Church itself and with the brethren as a whole.[16]

This brings us to the third way in which the term *apostolic* can be confined. Some may assume that following the apostolic pattern of governance is enough. But not all churches with an episcopal structure are ipso facto fully apostolic. John Meyendorff, who as an Eastern Orthodox theologian is fully committed to the episcopacy as a pattern given by God, explains how there can also be a betrayal of the nature of the church through "passive neglect, weakness, surrender before 'powers and principalities.'"[17] Therefore, a church can be apostolic outwardly but missing the life that should be found therein. One might compare this situation to a hospital that has all the latest equipment and the best-trained doctors but whose residents have no will to heal others. However, the fact that a communion that embraces episcopacy can err in the outworking of its life says nothing about the value or necessity of the structure itself. Moreover, it is simplistic to assume that an apostolic/episcopal structure will quench the Spirit or propel the church toward an uncontrolled hierarchalism. Bishop and people are joined together *in* the same body, not simply one over the other. As Timothy Kallistos Ware puts it, "The Church is not only hierarchical, it is charismatic and Pentecostal. . . . Without bishops there can be no Orthodox people, but without Orthodox people there can be no bishop."[18] Is it possible that the structure is integrally related to that which it contains or embodies? Are we involved in a false dichotomy of spirit and matter,

16. Caecilius Cyprianus, *The Unity of the Catholic Church*, in *Ancient Christian Writers*, trans. Maurice Bévenot, ed. Johannes Quasten and Joseph C. Plumpfe (London: Longmans Green, 1957), 48, 54.

17. Meyendorff, *Catholicity*, 11.

18. Timothy Kallistos Ware, *The Orthodox Church* (London: Penguin, 1964), 249–50.

of abstract faith and works, much as James outlined in his epistle? If Bible-believing Christians were to ask this question again, there would, of course, be much to discuss concerning the relationship between the priesthood of believers and the presbyterate and the episcopate, and even more to consider regarding the episcopate itself in its various assessments of Peter's see.

So the question is, Is it a kind of docetism to ignore the tangibility of the apostolic line when speaking about what is characteristically apostolic and to speak simply about apostolic teaching and action? Have we been so seduced by abstractions that we have forgotten the personal nature of Christ and that the church is made up of persons? In piety, we readily admit the importance of the ancient grandmas or elder teachers of a congregation who showed forth Christ to us when we were children. However, they are often wrongly seen as a mere catalyst that drew us to an abstract body of thinking rather than as an instantiation of the communion of saints that makes up the church. Are we more like a tree or an organism and less like an institution that can be prefabricated? How would we respond to the words of Cyprian, who asked, "The authority of the bishops forms a unity. . . . Can anyone be so . . . mad in his passion for quarrelling, as to believe it possible that the oneness of God, the garment of the Lord, the Church of Christ should be divided?"[19] We must not forestall this discussion because of a contemporary allergy to hierarchy or because of a fear of the imperfect authoritarian communions that we, or our forbears, have experienced.

Here, then, is the template for the church: It is one, holy, catholic, and apostolic. We sense immediately that it is not yet as it should be. For a moment, however, let us consider its present reality and character as we think about the sacramental dimension of the body of Christ.

The Present Sacramental Church

We are not as we should be. Yet we are in Christ, wondrously connected to the one who loves us and thus to one another. Christ's love for the church, far beyond our ken, is a *mysterion*, a *sacramentum*. Yet our present life is in the church sacramental, for it participates in the mystery of Jesus, the God-man who assumed our time and space reality.

From the beginning we see God's people expressing their participation in ways that integrate body, soul, and spirit, taught by their Lord to baptize with water and to celebrate with bread and wine. Though this is not documented in the New Testament, from earliest times oil was also used as a symbol of the sealing of the Holy Spirit—physical oil

19. Cyprianus, *Unity of the Catholic Church*, 47, 50.

was used on the newly baptized as a sign of the tangible descent of the Spirit, as a dove, upon the first anointed One, our Lord Jesus the Messiah. (*Christos* means, of course, anointed.) Everywhere we see physical means and words used to recall, to enact, to bind together our time with the *kairos*, the unique era of Jesus the incarnate One. Jesus' words at the Last Supper can be understood in the indicative as well as the imperative: "Whenever you do this, *you do this* for the remembrance of me." God's word is effective and never returns to him void. When we obey the commands to baptize in the trinitarian name and in water, and to break bread and bless wine for the remembrance of Jesus, something happens. This "something" is not just in our heads—for we are not Gnostics—but concerns the whole community of God and indeed the whole creation as well. We are given to bless, break, and return to God elements he has created that he then uses to effect a change in us and for the sake of the world he has made. We enter into an act that recalls the coming of the Creator into his own world, that witnesses to his continued intimacy with us through the Spirit, and that anticipates the return of the King to this cosmos for the purpose of perfecting it. We are drawn into that point of worship where all roads (past, present, and future) converge. At the font, at the altar and table, we are made one with him and with one another: Eden, Jordan; and Calvary, Vancouver; and Delhi, India; and the New Jerusalem (with its river and banquet) meet. God honors our prayers and our actions, blessing in a way that we can hardly imagine.

The sacraments are the life of the church. This is because they are intimately connected with God's great sacrament, Jesus the Christ, God the Son assuming humanness. In the very words of our master, unless we are washed we are not his; again, we must eat his flesh and drink his blood. The sacraments, then, are utterly significant because they not only express our faith but also enact it, gathering up the past and opening up the future so that the body worships together. The entire liturgy dramatizes the incarnation, life, death, and resurrection of Jesus and does so before the face of the ascended Christ and the indwelling Spirit. A new believer is added to the body in baptism and shares in the same Holy Spirit when sealed. She participates in the mystery of Jesus' life and death, anticipating proleptically the final communion, meeting together with her brothers and sisters across time and space, when she eats and drinks at the Lord's Table. Created in these actions is God's ever present moment, stretching across the *chronos* of human history, intersecting (or perhaps merging) with the *kairos* of the cross and resurrection. In the eucharist, there is a moment of transparence, a mystic joining with those world-transforming events of the first century, whereby we feed on the Lamb slain from the foundation of the earth who is now the standing, slaughtered Lamb in God's presence. It is not that he is sacrificed yet again but that his once-for-all death makes its most profound mark on his own. In this act, which is at once a memorial, a blessing, and an anticipation, past, present, and future find their home in him. So we participate with Christ, our brother and our God, and with one another. As the entire people of God is there, so too is the entire person—physical, psychological, and spiritual. We enter that eternal present, that "time-full" moment, in which everything is fulfilled and has meaning.

What an impoverishment that so many of God's people have relegated this moment to a human expression of doctrine, an intent to follow Jesus (baptism) or a memorial to his death (the Lord's Supper). Paul's strange warnings with regard to an undiscerning participation in the *koinōnia* of the eucharist (1 Cor. 11:30) are a strong intimation of the "much more" that is going on there. It is our communion in the life of Christ, a participation that is real but that can never take away the uniqueness of Jesus or his acts of love for us. Surprisingly, we find that the nurture and life received at this holy place and in this holy moment *fill up* the rest of our "ordinary" moments so that they too take on a sacramental quality. The hymn of the Salvationist Albert Orsborn has it just right:

> My life must be Christ's broken bread,
> My love his outpoured wine,
> A cup o'er-filled, a table spread
> Beneath his name and sign
> That other souls, refreshed and fed
> May share his life through mine.[20]

Such a sacramental life is not a substitute for participation in the ordinances (as Salvationist and Quaker might think) but flows naturally from these. In the holy place of the table or altar, the holy things are for those being made holy—it is unkind, untrue, and indeed dangerous for the unwitting if we baptize indiscriminately and invite to the table those who are unprepared. But the glory we receive in those moments shines on us and in us so that in our daily lives we have a sacramental impact on those who are as yet outside God's family.

Consider, for a moment, Paul's description of God's people in Romans 8, as he is speaking to them about the present life of the Spirit. He describes them as those who, like the earthly Jesus, are "led by the

---

20. *The Song Book of the Salvation Army,* song 462.

Spirit" (8:14)—and Jesus was *led* into the wilderness to be tried and to triumph over temptation. All of us, likewise anointed by the Spirit (Paul says *"sons* of God," pluralizing the term normally reserved for Messiah), are led so that we will "put to death the deeds of the body." "If . . . we suffer with him . . . we may also be glorified with him" (8:13, 17 NRSV). Our sufferings, like those of Jesus himself, are not pointless. The picture that Paul paints in 8:18–25 is that of the church "groaning inwardly" within the pain of the fallen creation, knowing that we and that creation will be set free from mortality, awaiting the final unveiling of all that God plans to do. As the Spirit intercedes for us when we do not have the words, so we in our pleading intercede for the creation of which we are a part and which our human race (through the fall) has consigned, for the present time, to bondage. Our "labor pains" on behalf of the rest of humanity and the creation are not in vain but will issue in God's perfect will: "We know that all things work together for good for those who love God" (Rom. 8:28 NRSV). Thus, the participation in Jesus' death and resurrection, which we experience poignantly in the sacraments, extends into our daily struggle. Those of us who are in Christ are potent signs, God's means of bringing the world to himself. We cannot be separated from God by anything in creation. In fact, the reverse is true: We bring Christ near to that created order into which he was plunged at his incarnation and baptism. In him, we assume a priestly function for the world, starting to learn again the role given to Adam and Eve, the role forfeited or distorted in the fall.

Awaiting the Redemption of Our Body

So the church is given to be one, holy, catholic, and apostolic. And it expresses this sacramentally through baptism and eucharist as well as in its living out the life of Christ, where suffering is transfigured into blessing and life. Part of that reality means acknowledging ourselves to be works in progress, passers-by (or "passovers," as the Eastern Christian tradition would have it), the ongoing *poiēma* (Eph. 2:10) of the Triune God, through the Holy Spirit. What is true of persons, that they are in the process of assuming faces, that they are in the making as individual children of God, seems also to be true of the church as a whole. Established by Jesus, it is also in the process of becoming—it has an eschatological dimension. This is no new discovery, no truth made clear only since the Reformation, with its *semper reformata, semper reformanda.* We hear the poignant plea of the early second-century writer of the *Shepherd of Hermas,* whose love for the church led him to inscribe a series of visions, parables, and teachings about its nature. He builds on the metaphor of Paul, that the church is a temple being built up in

Christ, and also on the vision of John the seer, who saw God's people as a noble lady undergoing trial (Revelation 12). In his visions, Hermas is well aware of the practical problems of a fatigued church and emphasizes the theme of repentance. He also suggests the development of the church through a series of multiple transformations of the lady and through a long sequence in which the tower (also a picture of the church) is built up lovingly and persistently by the workers of God (the angels). The rejuvenation of the lady and the final glory of the tower do not take place in a straight upward curve but through backward and forward movements: Hermas knows well the complexity of the human situation but is assured that God's will is sovereign. What appears at first as a fatigued older woman and a weak tower is seen at the end to be the shining work of God, a mystery of glory and of love.[21]

This realistic yet thoroughly expectant perspective is something that the author of *Hermas* no doubt picked up from Paul. Romans 8, that magnificent chapter that covers virtually every moment of our salvation, again offers us a helpful perspective. Usually the chapter is read in terms of the renewal of creation and the individual resurrection of each member of the body of Christ. Certainly, the chapter speaks to this resurrection hope, as it speaks about life and death, invokes the pattern of the dying and risen Jesus, and looks forward to the eschaton. Yet we are well instructed by N. T. Wright, who reminds us that "what Paul says in chapters 5 to 8 he says to, and of, the church as a whole."[22] Despite this touchstone, and despite the emphasis in Romans 8 on the people of God as a whole and their adoption as part of the glorification of the cosmos, very few[23] have noted a strange detail. In verse 23, Paul says, "We ourselves, who have the first fruits of the Spirit, groan inwardly while we await our 'sonship' [*huiothesia*] the redemption of *our body*" (author's translation). We await the point when we will completely reflect the glory of the anointed One, the Son of God. And that means the redemption, or liberation of "our body." Surprisingly, Wright

21. For further analysis, see chapters 5 and 6 of my *Ladies and the Cities: Transformation and Apocalyptic Identity in Joseph and Aseneth, 4 Ezra, the Apocalypse, and the Shepherd of Hermas,* Journal for the Study of the Pseudepigrapha Supplement 17 (Sheffield, U.K.: Sheffield Academic Press, 1995).

22. N. T. Wright, "The Letter to the Romans," in vol. 12 of *The New Interpreter's Bible: A Commentary in Twelve Volumes,* ed. Leander Keck et al. (Nashville: Abingdon, 2002), 513ff.

23. Of the ancients, Origen is remarkable. In book 7, chapter 5 of his Romans commentary, he opines that "this points to the body of the Church as a whole." See *Commentary on the Epistle to the Romans Books 6–10,* trans. Thomas P. Scheck, vol. 104, in *The Fathers of the Church: A New Translation* (Washington, D.C.: Catholic University of America Press, 2002), 77.

remarks, "Paul uses the singular 'body' rather than the expected plural, as in verse 11, but there seems no particular significance to this change."[24] I wonder. Certainly, Paul has in mind our future personal resurrections, but could it be that he uses the singular to speak about the *corporate* nature of the general resurrection and of our imperfect human life together in the church? Virtually no contemporary commentator takes the phrase this way, as a comment on the longing of the church to be freed, to be made what it is meant to be, but J. A. T. Robinson does comment along similar lines:

> *Soma*, like *sarx*, is essentially a collective term. Hence "our whole body" (verse 23)—the entire mass of human existence in all its relationships redeemed from the death which is its present doom (7:24). The body will then be a body of "glory" . . . as proleptically in the church, the body of Christ, it already is (Ephesians 5:27).[25]

We need not make Robinson's neat division between the church and the unredeemed *sōma* (body) of humanity, for Paul knew the paradox of God's people, who were already redeemed yet waited for what was not yet seen. And he also knew that the present church needs yet to be presented to its Lord as a "chaste virgin" (2 Cor. 11:2). Both he and John the seer issue the Lord's command that the church be separate from the world: "Therefore come out from them, and be separate from them" (2 Cor. 6:17 NRSV); "Come out of her [Babylon], my people" (Rev. 18:4 NRSV). This implies that the church, whose life is hidden in Christ, awaits her full redemption.

In Philippians, as in 1 Corinthians, Paul tackled the major malady that presents itself in our unfulfilled life together: the problem of division of mind and heart. The letter to the Philippians pleads poignantly that the believers be of one mind (3:15), that they put the interests of others first, that they die to self in the pattern of Christ, that they do everything "without murmuring and arguing . . . that [they] may be blameless and innocent, children of God" (2:14–15 NRSV). There, too, Paul envisions the time when this will not be a struggle and when our "body of humiliation" will be conformed to "the body of Christ's glory" (3:21)—all this because our citizenship is in heaven, hidden with Christ.

So infected are we with the disease of individualism that it seems counterintuitive to read Paul's words as referring to anything beyond our individual resurrections and our individual comportment among those who believe as we do. But the early Christians understood their

---

24. Wright, "Letter to the Romans," 598.
25. J. A. T. Robinson, *Wrestling with Romans* (Philadelphia: Westminster, 1979), 102.

personal joys as bound up with the victory of Christ's body. Resurrection was both a personal and a corporate category and not the one without the other. It may be helpful to remember that the earliest teaching (if we believe the New Testament specialists!) on the resurrection was given to people in Thessalonica who were not afraid for their own individual fates. Rather, they feared that the resurrection had passed by those who had "fallen asleep" (1 Thess. 4:13–18). The apostle comforts this community *not* by exhorting them to concentrate on their own individual hope for survival after death. Instead, "they should encourage one another" by means of that grand final vision—a reunion and glorification as "together with them [i.e., all believers]" they "meet the Lord."

Our culture, however, is typified by other concerns—the fear of "losing my identity" and the call to "become myself." Paradoxically, in a time when we are separated by ideology, geography, and fragmented families, our culture urges us to "celebrate diversity." The mantra is found in beer ads and ecclesial wisdom alike. My own teaching institution offers an opening lecture to its new students, warning them to "beware the isms." One of these "isms," friends, is inclusivism. Inclusivism, such as it is preached today, has strangely become the poison of true unity. We will not be one, nor will we have the power to include others in the truth and love of Jesus, until we "think the same," until we become "of one mind" and "one opinion" (1 Cor. 1:10).

The golden-mouthed John Chrysostom commented on what it means to let our manner of life be worthy of the gospel of Christ, to live as though we are citizens of heaven:

> This is what above all things unites believers, and maintains love unbroken, "that they may be one." For a "kingdom divided against itself shall not stand." . . . See how the word "one" is used for concord. See how their souls being many are called one. Thus it was of old. "For they were all," it is written, "of one heart and of one soul, striving together for the faith of the gospel."[26]

The early fathers, when faced with a mystery such as the nature of the Son or the Trinity, wisely worked with negatives, erecting boundaries of thought, as well as making positive statements. Given the complexity of our actual situation in the believing community and given the mysterious nature of the church as it is envisaged, let us try to erect

26. John Chrysostom, *Homilies on Philippians,* in *Nicene and Post-Nicene Fathers; Chrysostom: Homilies on Galatians, Ephesians, Philippians, Colossians, Thessalonians, Timothy, Titus, and Philemon,* ed. Philip Schaff, 1st ser., vol. 13 (Peabody, Mass.: Hendrickson, 1994), 200.

some boundaries, some negative statements, to prevent unfruitful thought. Here are some that emerge from our discussion and that I offer for critical analysis:

> The church is not a human institution, yet the church is not abstract (i.e., it is concrete, visible, made up of real people).
>
> The church is not to be confused with the Son, yet the church cannot be understood except in communion with the Son.
>
> The church is not atemporal (i.e., it cannot be denied in its local appearances and cannot be recognized except by connection with Christ and the apostles), yet the church is not time-bound and embraces the fellowship of the saints.
>
> The church is not yet perfect, yet the church's eschatological dimension must not be denied.
>
> The church comes fully into being where Word and sacrament are present, yet it must not be denied where two or three gather together.

Let us conclude on a more positive note. What would it mean to live as citizens of heaven, within the polity of the kingdom? It would mean recognizing our marks as one, holy, catholic, and apostolic and listening to one another about what these characteristics mean in a practical and observable sense. It would mean following Chrysostom's cue and looking to the times "of old" as well as to today for an understanding of the nature of the church. It would mean delighting in the family ways of the church, the prayers and patterns of our older siblings, while also allowing new shoots to spring from that ancient tree. It would mean consciously placing ourselves before the face of God and in the context of his entire church, to be catholic rather than blinkered and parochial. It would mean remembering that, despite the battles of old and of today and the divisions in the church that seem entrenched and irreversible, our God is the one who specializes in resurrection. (To the scattered dry bones God spoke by the prophet Elijah, and they arose, a great army.) It would also mean avoiding premature institutional unity with one another (and for some, this would also mean avoiding premature communion),[27] while we continue to pray and work together as with one mind and one heart. It would mean not being scandalized by the differences we perceive nor glibly downplaying them for the sake of

27. The ecumenical breezes of the second half of the twentieth century have blown so strongly that it is now considered uncharitable when Christians decline to share the table with those from other communions. It should be remembered that the open table is a novelty and that for Christians through the ages, as well as for many today, communion has been understood as an expression of mutual and profound theological and ecclesial

a false unity. It would mean trying to sort out what is healthful diversity and what is compromise with the world or departure from the apostolic family. And above all this, it would mean recognizing that the church belongs to the Lord and that he will complete the work he has begun in us.

"We ourselves, who have the firstfruits of the Spirit, do indeed groan inwardly while we keenly anticipate our adoption, the redemption of our body" (Rom. 8:23, author's translation).

"Now to him who by the power at work within us is able to accomplish abundantly far more than all we can ask or imagine, to him be glory in the church and in Christ Jesus to all generations, forever and ever. Amen" (Eph. 3:20–21 NRSV).

---

agreement. That is, for many, the eucharist enacts not only vertical intimacy with God but also horizontal intimacy around the bishop—and this beyond a minimalist "Jesus is Lord!" confession. The radical way in which this idea has been changed is now seen in those congregations that are opening the table not only to other Christians but to anyone present, in a mistaken gesture of hospitality. It is hoped that those who practice a table open to all those professing Christ will be charitable to their brothers and sisters for whom the Lord's Supper has a distinct ecclesial meaning. When these latter decline to partake with their fellow believers across communal lines, it should in no way be read as an insult or a declaration that they consider themselves better than other Christians. Rather, it is an honest and time-honored response to the divisions we now experience and is often coupled with an expression of hope in the God who will make all things known to us, as we pray and live together. Instead of offering indiscriminate communion that renders inconsequential deep theological differences, those who do not practice an open table may well foster the hospitality of offering a "blessing" to their friends. Indeed, it would be helpful if this ecumenical gesture were offered by the "freer" denominations as well so that those with particular scruples regarding the table might be included when worshiping with friends outside their own ecclesial community. I offer my creedal Roman brothers and sisters the greatest respect when I respect the wishes of their bishop and do not seek the host in their assembly—but I will gladly be blessed by them!

6

Free Church Ecclesiology and Evangelical Spirituality

A Unique Compatibility

ROGER E. OLSON

For several decades now, many evangelical Christians raised in the free church tradition have been following high-church pied pipers along the Canterbury Trail toward magisterial Reformation churches with their historic episcopates, ancient liturgies, and creedal commitments. Some have even gone beyond Canterbury to Rome or Constantinople—a natural progression in the eyes of their free church friends and families. My own pilgrimage has been somewhat similar, though far less extensive. I was raised in the thick of the classical Pentecostal movement, which eschewed not only formal liturgy but even printed orders of worship in church bulletins! My journey has led me not to bells, smells, and bishops but to baptistries, printed orders of worship, and battles over conventions and confessions. I became Baptist at a time when some evangelical Baptists were becoming Episcopalian. But I have remained free church, and therefore, there is more continuity than discontinuity in my pilgrimage.

That claim surprises some of my friends and acquaintances from other traditions. I suspect that is because they, like many outside the free church tradition, do not perceive it as a coherent tradition that holds together diverse manifestations such as Pentecostals, Baptists, Mennonites, Churches of Christ, Brethren, Evangelical Free, Evangelical Covenant, and Christian and Missionary Alliance (not to mention many more denominations). On several occasions well-meaning persons have casually commented to me that the free churches lack an ecclesiology. They regard my tradition as a bunch of churches that reject or neglect ecclesiology. That's like someone who values baroque architecture saying to a person who lives in a Frank Lloyd Wright house, "But your house doesn't have architecture!" I have come to believe that the free church tradition and its ecclesiology are not only widely misunderstood but also often maligned by many Christians, including many evangelicals who should know better. Some of them were born into and spiritually nurtured within free churches and have rebelled against their heritage. Others simply have not taken the time or the trouble to investigate the free church tradition, with its often more implicit than explicit ecclesiology.

I would like to provide some information about and insight into the free church tradition and recommend it to suspicious magisterial Protestants (and especially evangelicals in the so-called mainline churches). I would like to go even farther and propose an unprovable thesis for consideration—that free church ecclesiology, properly understood, is more compatible with the evangelical Protestant ethos and spirituality, properly understood, than its alternatives. I will not argue that free church ecclesiology is *normative* for evangelicalism; that would be presumptuous and insulting to my valued evangelical friends of other traditions. I have no interest in boundary setting and patrolling. When it comes to evangelical identity, I believe that ecclesiology and especially polity are secondary to the gospel itself. However, I do suspect that free church ecclesiology is more conducive to life centered around the gospel—that is, evangelical spirituality—than alternative visions of the church and churchly practices. That is my modest claim, and I hope it will not offend anyone.

Before setting forth that claim and the argument in its favor, however, it will be necessary and helpful to discuss the problem of defining the key categories of this paper: *free church* and *evangelical*. Eventually, I will provide my own definitions or descriptions of those categories, and only then will others know whether they can agree with my thesis.

That is because there are such widely varying understandings of both categories. Both are notoriously slippery; I would go so far as to suggest that they are essentially contested concepts. There is no universally agreed on, standard definition of free church or evangelical. Both concepts have been and remain the subjects of great controversy.

Before delving into those matters, however, I would like to engage in a little meta-discussion of religious and spiritual categories in general. There are two general approaches to such category identification and description: bounded set and centered set.[1] A bounded set is a category with clear and precise boundaries; an entity (person or organization) is in one of three possible relations to the category: within it, outside it, or on its boundary. Usually, being on the boundary of a bounded set is a precarious position and often possible only temporarily if at all. An example of a bounded set category is United States citizenship. A person's citizenship may be in question, but that is not the same as being truly ambiguous. A court must decide whether it exists or not. The situation is like being pregnant; one cannot be somewhat a U.S. citizen anymore than one can be somewhat pregnant. Of course, one can hold dual citizenship, but that does nothing to alter the fact that one either is or is not a U.S. citizen. Definite criteria for determination of genuine citizenship exist even if their application to a specific case is a matter of difficult adjudication.

A centered set is a category with a clear and definite center of gravity but no unambiguous boundaries. Persons and organizations (and possibly other entities) are not necessarily either within or outside the category; they are in some relation to its center, which warrants their being identified more or less by the category label. Whereas a person cannot be more or less a U.S. citizen or more or less pregnant, he or she can be more or less politically liberal or conservative or more or less healthy or ill. These categories are defined by centers with no definite circumferences. There are generally agreed on criteria for determining whether a person is politically liberal or in good health, but a person can be ambiguously liberal or only generally healthy and still be labeled "liberal" or "healthy." The determination is made by reference to a core of factors and the person's relationship to them. A person with borderline blood pressure may still be healthy, especially if his or her pressure is improving; a person who believes in capital punishment may still be liberal, especially if his or her attitude toward it is anxiety-ridden and surrounded by doubts and qualifications.

1. For this distinction and description I am indebted to Paul G. Hiebert, "Conversion, Culture, and Cognitive Categories," *Gospel in Context* 1, no. 4 (October 1978): 24–29.

Free church and evangelical are both centered-set categories. They are relatively ambiguous categories defined by sets of core commitments to beliefs, practices, and experiences. They have no definite, unambiguous boundaries; persons and organizations may be more or less free church and more or less evangelical. In my own opinion, much is decided by which way a person or organization is facing and moving—away or toward the center of the category. The only alternative to this perspective on these categories is to recognize a formal magisterium with power to decide who is within and who is outside the categories. Since the best scholars cannot decide on the boundaries and there is no magisterium such as a supreme court with the power to decide and enforce matters of inclusion and exclusion, these categories must remain centered sets rather than bounded sets. This does not mean they are meaningless. It simply means that in some and perhaps many cases we cannot say with absolute certainty who is genuinely free church[2] and who is authentically evangelical.[3] We must often settle for degrees, qualifications, and ambiguity when deciding such matters.

Evangelical Ethos and Spirituality

A great deal of controversy surrounds the task of identifying the category "evangelical." In part, that is because the term has been used in so many ways in the last century. Some use it as a synonym for Protestant, while others use it as a synonym for fundamentalist or even fanatic. For some it is simply a label for any missionary endeavor, while for others it designates a low-church wing of the worldwide Anglican communion. For most of us who are involved in the North American subculture of evangelicalism, the term has come to designate an ethos or flavor of Protestant Christianity rooted in the Reformations of the sixteenth century and renewed and reformed by the Pietist and revivalist movements of the eighteenth century. Some of us involved in this multidenominational evangelical movement emphasize its Puritan roots, while others highlight its continental Pietist and Wesleyan roots. Donald Dayton has helpfully delineated two paradigms of evangelical history and ethos: one that interprets evangelicalism and its theology as normatively reformed, rooted in the magisterial Reformation and its Puritan and Presbyterian manifestations in Great Britain and New England, and another that interprets evangelicalism and its theology as

2. For example, some scholars consider Methodist churches to be within the free church tradition, and some do not.

3. For example, some scholars consider Seventh-Day Adventists to be evangelicals, and some do not.

normatively revivalistic, rooted in radical Protestantism, Pietist spirituality, the Great Awakenings, and the Holiness movements.[4]

My own view is that both paradigms are correct and incorrect. They are correct in pointing to evangelicalism's roots and incorrect in portraying one set of roots as normative for evangelicalism. It seems clear that evangelical Christianity—as a relatively distinct but diverse religious movement—derives from two main sources and that its defining center is bipolar. On the one hand, evangelicalism is profoundly marked by commitment to the Reformation ideals of *sola gratia et fides, sola scriptura,* and the priesthood of believers, especially as these were interpreted and communicated by divines of the Puritan tradition in Great Britain and New England. On the other hand, evangelicalism is profoundly marked by commitment to the experiential ideal of what has been called *conversional piety,* which arose especially among the continental Pietists and revivalists of the Great Awakenings. But, of course, the Puritans also valued conversional piety, and the Pietists and revivalists embraced and promoted Protestant orthodoxy. Their differences were matters of emphasis and ethos. During the First Great Awakening of the 1730s and 1740s, their interests coincided, and evangelicalism as we know it was born as a mass movement within British and American Protestantism. Ever since then, evangelicalism has been a large tent (metaphorically speaking), featuring two main characteristics: commitment to general Protestant orthodoxy (especially the authority of Scripture and the atoning death of Christ) and the experience of conversion to Christ by repentance and faith, resulting in justification, regeneration by the Holy Spirit, and an intimate, personal relationship with Christ marked by prayer, holiness of life, worship of God, and active participation in the church of God's people. The bipolar center of the evangelical category, then, is doctrinal and experiential.

But the movement has always been denominationally diverse—transdenominational and multidenominational—rather than identified with any one particular Reformation ecclesiological tradition. Cooperation between diverse confessional traditions within evangelicalism was enhanced in the twentieth century first by common bonds of opposition to liberal theology and destructive biblical criticism and then, later, by shared opposition to radically sectarian, separatistic fundamentalism. In spite of profound differences of opinion regarding important details of the evangelical character and ethos and in spite of controversy among post–World War 2 evangelicals about the move-

4. Donald W. Dayton, "The Search for the Historical Evangelicalism: George Marsden's History of Fuller Seminary as a Case Study," *Christian Scholar's Review* 23, no. 1 (September 1993): 12–33.

ment's boundaries, most leading evangelical scholars have come to regard it as *both* experientially *and* doctrinally defined. That is, evangelicalism is identified by commitment to *orthodoxy* and *orthopathy*—right belief and right experience. Of course, one could also throw in *orthopraxy*—right living manifested in Christ-honoring works of love and righteousness.

Two evangelical scholars of the last two to three decades have been especially helpful in highlighting evangelicalism's experiential identity. They are Donald Bloesch and Stanley Grenz. In his *Future of Evangelical Christianity: A Call for Unity amid Diversity,* Bloesch emphasized both evangelicalism's firm commitment to generous orthodoxy and its passionate promotion of the experience of salvation. With regard to the latter he wrote, "It is not enough to believe in the cross and resurrection of Christ. We must personally be crucified and buried with Christ and rise with Christ to new life in the Spirit."[5] Without diminishing the importance of generous orthodoxy, including absolute commitment to ancient and Protestant doctrinal essentials such as the deity of Christ, the Trinity, and justification by grace through faith, Grenz describes the evangelical ethos just as much in terms of a shared understanding of spirituality focused on a vibrant, personal relationship with the living Lord Jesus Christ as in terms of a shared understanding of the authority of the Bible and basic Christian orthodoxy. For him, the heart of evangelical faith lies in the shared evangelical story of "testimony to the reality of a personal, life-changing transformation" by grace from sin into relationship with Christ.[6]

In this account of the essence of evangelicalism, then, an irreducibly *individual*—not individualistic or autonomous—element lies at its core; to be evangelical is to have a relationship with God marked by *mediated immediacy.* Conversional piety may begin with a sacramental experience of God's grace (which is something debated among evangelicals), but it requires a personal, I-Thou encounter with God at some time after that. And that encounter cannot be automatic or wholly mediated; it must include a conscious, willing, responsible response to the divine initiative that cannot be accomplished for a person. The person must respond for himself or herself. Evangelical hymnody and devotional writing are filled with references to this mediated immediacy of the evangelical relationship with God: "Blessed assurance, Jesus is mine; . . . I in my Savior am happy and blessed" and "I come to the gar-

5. Donald G. Bloesch, *The Future of Evangelical Christianity: A Call for Unity amid Diversity* (Garden City, N.Y.: Doubleday, 1983), 17.

6. Stanley J. Grenz, *Revisioning Evangelical Theology: A Fresh Agenda for the Twenty-First Century* (Downers Grove, Ill.: InterVarsity, 1993), 33.

den alone; while the dew is still on the roses. . . . And he walks with me and he talks with me and he tells me I am his own." Many scholars— including evangelicals—have scoffed at these lyrics and ones like them as if they reduced Christianity to a lone-ranger relationship or a Gnostic spiritual individualism. Be that as it may, and I have no doubt they have been misinterpreted individualistically at times, such lyrics and similar devotional phrases express something at the heart of evangelical spirituality: the personal relationship of immediacy between the repentant sinner's soul and the merciful God of forgiveness, comfort, and strength.

Of course, this can at times devolve into sentimentalism; all spiritualities are in danger of distortion. At its best, evangelical spirituality has always supplemented the individualism of the personal relationship with God through Jesus Christ with the mediation of Scripture and church. Neither Bloesch nor Grenz could ever be accused of neglecting the importance of Bible and community in evangelical spirituality. Nevertheless, the inner logic of that spirituality—as I have identified it, following them and many other commentators on evangelicalism—inexorably includes a strong emphasis on the priesthood and prophethood of every believer.[7] The truly converted person who has entered into and maintains (by God's grace) a strong relationship with the living God through Jesus Christ in the power of the Holy Spirit cannot help but realize a communication with God that cannot be absolutely confined to the final authorities of creed, clergy, or state. In the words of Jürgen Moltmann, such persons will inevitably become experts and specialists in their own spirituality—not over against the community of God's people but on its behalf, and not over against tradition but in order to keep it alive in continuing reformation.[8] The life of conversional piety—continuous, personal transformation through mediated immediacy with the Spirit of Christ—falls into tension with human spiritual authority that quenches "new light breaking forth from God's Word" into the converted person's mind and heart. Secular and sacral hierarchies tend to quench such reforming light when it is being kindled in and by "ordinary" Christians without rank or office. Evangelicalism is a spiritual and theological renewal movement of individuals bound together by the Spirit of God in community; it has arisen and

7. On the prophethood of all believers, see Roger Stronstad, *The Prophethood of All Believers: A Study in Luke's Charismatic Theology* (Sheffield, U.K.: Sheffield Academic Press, 2001).

8. Jürgen Moltmann, *God for a Secular Society: The Public Relevance of Theology* (Minneapolis: Fortress, 1999), 221–23.

thrived because of ordinary Spirit-filled individuals who have heard a word from God and have called the church to renewal and reform.

Free Church Ethos and Ecclesiology

The free church tradition is as notoriously difficult to pin down as is evangelicalism. To verify this, all one has to do is read a number of encyclopedia articles on the subject or examine the definitions and descriptions of free church provided by scholarly books and articles. If one wishes to be totally confused, he or she can investigate the subject on the world wide web! Some time ago I overheard a Christian university administrator and evangelical scholar refer to the free church tradition. Out of curiosity I asked him for a rough definition. His response indicated that for him the category includes virtually all non-Roman Catholic and non-Anglican denominations. He mentioned Presbyterians as a model of free church. This is, of course, one respectable approach to the subject. The *Encyclopedia of Christianity* defines free church over against state church or church territorial: "As compared with a state church, a national church, or a territorial church, the free church is structurally a type of church that rejects any equation of the civil and Christian community, any marriage of throne and altar . . . any related religious uniformity imposed by ecclesiastical or governmental compulsion."[9] According to the same article, the term *free church* appeared in 1843 with the formation of a Free Presbyterian Church of Scotland in protest against the increasing control of the national Presbyterian Church by the government. Throughout the nineteenth century, however, many church bodies in Europe, Great Britain, and North America began to use "free church" to identify themselves not only over against state and territorial churches but also in contrast to the so-called mainline Protestant bodies, even where they did not enjoy state support.[10] These preferred the label "free church" to Ernst Troeltsch's "sect-type" designation, even though the latter fit them quite well in many cases. In the United States, especially since 1832, when all formal relationships between state governments and particular denominations were abolished, all denominations have been free churches in the strictest and most formal sense. Even the Roman Catholic Church

9. *The Encyclopedia of Christianity*, vol. 2, s. v. "free church" (Grand Rapids: Eerdmans, 2001), 346.

10. Franklin H. Littell, "The Historical Free Church Defined," *Brethren Life and Thought* 9 (autumn 1964): 78–90. Littell defines free church over against any coerced faith, including social patronage of a particular denomination that amounts to "social establishment."

in the United States is formally and legally a free church in that it enjoys no state sponsorship or support.

Especially in the United States, then, a second definition or description of the free church heritage arose—one that went beyond separation of church and state to general opposition to formal ecclesiastical hierarchies, sacerdotalism, creedalism (not confessionalism), and "mixed assemblies." Donald F. Durnbaugh, author of *The Believers' Church: The History and Character of Radical Protestantism*, prefers to call this tradition "the believers' church" and "radical Protestantism." Nevertheless, for all its ambiguity, many of us still prefer "free church" while admitting very little difference between it and "believers' church."

According to Durnbaugh and other scholars of the free church tradition, such as Franklin Littell, the free church tradition's essence—its core or center—is constituted by a pattern of attitudes that gives rise to its ethos. This pattern may be found first (after the primitive church) in embryo form in the medieval Waldensian churches of northern Italy, but its first full flowering was in the Anabaptist communities of the sixteenth century and then in the dissenting and separatist movements among the Puritans in England and North America in the seventeenth century. It may now be found in a variety of Protestant church bodies and movements, including Baptists, Congregationalists, Pentecostals, Mennonites, Brethren, Churches of Christ, Evangelical Free, and Evangelical Covenant churches. According to both Durnbaugh and Littell (as well as a number of other scholars), the chief characteristic mark—the controlling characteristic—of the free church ethos is *voluntarism* (or *voluntaryism*). Durnbaugh expresses this well: For free church Christians "the church consists of the voluntary membership of those confessing Jesus Christ as Lord. To them an uncoerced faith is the mark of true religion."[11] Of course, there is a sense in which all church membership in the United States and many other countries is voluntary. Durnbaugh and others who stress voluntarism as the essence of the free church ethos expand it to include rejection of not only formally and legally coerced faith but also any full church membership that is not strictly voluntary and participatory (including enjoyment of social patronage).

Voluntarism is closely related, on the one hand, to rejection of state sponsorship (which privileges persons who belong to churches recognized and supported by the state) and, on the other hand, to a nonhierarchical church polity. Most free churches believe that where bishops rule, kings cannot be far behind and that the rule of bishops over

11. Donald F. Durnbaugh, *The Believers' Church: The History and Character of Radical Protestantism* (New York: Macmillan, 1968), 32.

churches stands in stark tension with the priesthood of believers. The label "bishop" may be used by some free churches, but it means nothing more than pastor or overseer and never designates a special clerical office of spiritual authority. Free churches believe that hierarchy stifles full participation and soul competency—both of which are necessary to genuine believers' priesthood and prophethood. Most free church bodies extrapolate from the principle of voluntarism (which is itself an extrapolation from priesthood of believers) to autonomy of local congregations, which are free to enter into association with other congregations for purposes of mission.

This account of the free church ethos may sound hopelessly individualistic to some, and that criticism has dogged free churches for centuries. It would be good to remember, of course, that Protestantism itself appears hopelessly individualistic to adherents of the Eastern Orthodox and Roman Catholic traditions. Martin Luther felt free to stand against a thousand years of tradition and against the authority of the hierarchical church and empire of his day. This was for him not an expression of personal autonomy but of priesthood and prophethood. He was compelled by the Word of God and reason. And yet, at least according to the free church perspective, he reneged on that courageous insight and act when he turned to the power of the prince to squelch the *Schwärmer* ("enthusiasts"), many of whom were simply attempting to carry forward the true impulses of the Protestant Reformation. The same happened in Zurich under Zwingli and the city council and in Geneva under Calvin and the magistrates.[12]

Are the free church ethos and ecclesiology individualistic as charged? No doubt they have been corrupted by autonomous individualism at times, just as hierarchical ecclesiologies have been corrupted by dominating power. But their individualism is not the individualism of the Enlightenment, as some critics believe, but the strong belief in the priesthood of believers that energized the Protestant Reformation and especially radical Protestantism of the sixteenth century—a century and more before the Enlightenment began. Littell argues cogently throughout his book *The Free Church* that voluntarism (which he calls voluntaryism) in the free church tradition has nothing to do with any modern principle of individualism. It has to do only with a "readiness to be guided by the Scriptures."[13]

Of course, this particular "readiness" implies a strong distrust of human hierarchical power and an equally strong trust in the ability of

---

12. Leonard Verduin, *The Reformers and Their Stepchildren* (Grand Rapids: Eerdmans, 1964).

13. Franklin H. Littell, *The Free Church* (Boston: Starr King Press, 1957), 42.

the converted believer to interpret Scripture and speak prophetically. The free churches have generally emphasized community as the context for their principle and practice of voluntarism. Christian community, however, is defined not as a mixed assembly of true Christians and nominal Christians led by a clerical hierarchy but as the gathered people of God seeking consensus about the leading of the Holy Spirit. Individuals choose voluntarily (freely and responsibly) whether to participate, but once they choose to participate, the community holds them accountable for full and right participation. At their best, free churches have never exalted the individual above the community; they have simply exalted the community—composed of persons in relationship with God—above the hierarchical powers of state and bishop. As Miroslav Volf has demonstrated in his excellent defense of free church ecclesiology, *After Our Likeness: The Church as an Image of the Trinity,* a community of equal persons bonded together by love can be a better analogy of the Trinity than can a hierarchy of powers.

Free churches have historically also interpreted voluntarism as being in tension with strong creedalism and formalism of worship. This tendency is not as clearly tied to the inner logic of the free church ethos as are separation of church and state, equality of believers, and local congregational autonomy. Nevertheless, many, if not most, of the historical free churches have eschewed requirements that members and clergy formally swear allegiance to or sign creeds. There may be exceptions, and they depend very much on how one defines free church and creed. If one defines free churches as "non-creedal," as some do, then the matter is settled. However, if one identifies voluntarism as the center of the free church ethos, then creedalism or a rejection of creeds is not crucial.

Still, there is some reason why many free churches have opted for confessional statements that express the consensus of the belief of the gathered church over creeds that express what persons must believe in order to be saved or to be Christian. One reason is historical and not strictly logical or theological. Many free churches emerged as renewal movements out of territorial churches or denominations that functioned as national or state churches, and many of the latter used creeds to stifle dissent and reform. Many free churches began with the insights and reforms of a person who discovered a new interpretation of Scripture that flew in the face of an authoritative creed or creed-like statement. They believed that the valued Reformation principle "reformed and always reforming" required taking human statements of belief as fallible authorities at best. Many such churches have written confessional statements that express publicly the consensus of their belief, and they ask potential members and leaders to respond to them, but these statements are usually considered open to revision as the Spirit of God leads the people to discover new insights in Scripture.

The same situation applies with regard to free churches and liturgy. There is no necessary logical or theological link between free church tradition and ecclesiology, on the one hand, and informal worship, on the other hand, but many free churches believe that the gathered church of priests unto God and prophets of God must leave space in worship for the moving of God's Spirit in new and surprising ways. Of course, in most free churches, worship does come over time to be structured in ways that tend to do the opposite. As every free church member knows, "informality" can become its own liturgy. Originally, however, many of the free churches eschewed formal liturgy such as that practiced in the Church of England and among Lutherans in order to emphasize the priesthood and prophethood of all believers. There is no reason *in principle* why any ordinary Christian cannot, within the free church context, lead worship, preach, celebrate the sacraments or ordinances, and speak spontaneously for the benefit of the entire congregation.

What, then, is free church ecclesiology? I have been describing its ethos. What view of the church does it support? Here one finds among free churches more agreement in theory than in practice. Following the principle of voluntarism, most free churches view the church as the local congregation—a voluntary gathering of regenerated believers in Jesus Christ who are equally priests and prophets and who covenant together for worship and mission. They reject the identification of the church with any historic, visible episcopate or with any state or its government. They do not eschew offices of leadership such as deacon, elder, and pastor (and sometimes bishop), but they regard their holders as servants of the people of God without any special spiritual power or authority other than what is given them by God through the congregation. Some free churches opt for a hybrid of congregational and presbyterian church polity in which certain leaders are given authority by several or many congregations, but they are never considered spiritually superior or possessed of supernatural powers or authority apart from or over the people of God, who elect them.

Free churches do affirm that the church is one, holy, catholic, and apostolic. The unity of the church resides in the Holy Spirit, who unites individuals into the temple of the Holy Spirit; hierarchy detracts from unity. Unity also resides in common belief and unified worship as well as in fellowship and service. The church is holy in that it consists of only truly repentant, regenerated believers who share a common faith and commitment to Jesus Christ. Mixed assemblies detract from the church's holiness. The church is catholic in that it stands in spiritual continuity with all true churches of Jesus Christ throughout the centuries and across cultures. Universality is undermined by artificial boundaries of humanly devised creeds and liturgies that exclude believers who do not share the same confessional or liturgical identity. The church is apostolic in that it is rooted in the teaching of the apostles.[14] Free churches all strive to be New Testament churches. A strong restorationist impulse runs through most of the free church tradition. Visible, historical, apostolic succession often conflicts with the spirit of apostolicity, which consists in being sent by Christ and being his true suffering agents in world transformation by means of the gospel. In response to detractors and critics who claim that the free church tradition lacks the marks of the true church because it lacks apostolic authority, free church apologists point to the bishops of some of the churches of historic episcopacy and their manifest apostasy.

Is the true church, then, merely a formality? Free church ecclesiology does not include a necessary polity, but it does tend toward congregationalism because of its perceived consistency with the priesthood of believers and voluntarism and because of the perceived dangers of other polities, especially hierarchical ones, which have historically seemed to quench the spirit of renewal.

Free Church Ecclesiology and the Evangelical Church

If my accounts of the evangelical ethos and the free church ethos have some validity, it seems they are especially compatible with each other. Certainly, many evangelicals have found this to be the case. A case could be made that free church ecclesiology has become the sociological norm for most of the evangelical subculture in North America, and there can be little doubt that most of the younger churches of the two-thirds world, including evangelical churches and movements, have adopted a free church style. My concern here, however, is not to promote the free church ethos or ecclesiology as normative for authentic evangelical faith but only to assert the much more humble claim that the two are peculiarly compatible. That compatibility lies in the individualistic impulses of both. By "individualistic" I do not mean what many take it to mean: autonomous self-assertion. I mean only the emphasis on the integrity of the personal relationship with God as irreduc-

14. For a fascinating defense of the apostolicity of free churches (especially focused on the Pentecostal movement), see Veli-Matti Kärkkäinen, "The Apostolicity of Free Churches," *Pro Ecclesia* 10, no. 4 (fall 2001): 475–86.

ibly immediate, even if mediated by the context of the gathered community and its hearing and heeding of the Word of God.

Unfortunately, our hyper-individualistic American culture (especially in the United States) distorts this immediacy into autonomy, but that is not the fault of the principle of the individual before God. The declaration "Ain't nobody but Jesus going to tell me what to believe"[15] does not reflect the true ethos of either evangelical or free church individualism. The individual's identity is achieved only in community, but it is the individual's identity that is being achieved. A maxim of evangelical folk religion is "God has no grandchildren," and there is some truth in that maxim. Ultimately, evangelicals believe, the person—not isolated or alone but unique, free, and responsible—stands before God in an I-Thou encounter and makes a decision. Ultimately, no one can make that decision for a person once he or she reaches a level of moral maturity in the awakening of conscience. That is not to deny the evangelical identity of paedo-Baptists but only that baptismal regeneration apart from the necessity of a later repentance and confession of faith is fully evangelical. The two grandfathers of modern evangelicalism, Jonathan Edwards and John Wesley, agreed on this even though they practiced and defended infant baptism.

As much as we today like to emphasize community, we should not deny that evangelicalism contains a crucially important emphasis on the individual. The call of the gospel is to individuals; ultimately, only individuals can accept the transforming power of the Holy Spirit and embark on lives of discipleship to Jesus Christ. Nations and families may be discipled but not collectively without personal response by their citizens and members. In the matter of salvation, individuals are saved first, and through their salvation, collectives may be saved and discipled. Walter Rauschenbusch taught us much about the collective natures of sin and salvation, and yet he was well aware of the primacy of the individual's response to the gospel.[16] Even evangelicals who embrace the social gospel and the Christian nurture model of spiritual development recognize that a personal relationship with God is a matter of mediated immediacy and that each believer is both a priest and a prophet within the community of God's people—a subject of spirituality and not merely an object of collective bargaining.

What ecclesiology fits the evangelical spiritual ethos better than that of the free church tradition? How can a person who stands before God

15. Attributed to a leading free church spokesman for separation of church and state in "Sex, Sin, and Salvation," *Newsweek*, 3 November 1998, 37.

16. Walter Rauschenbusch, *A Theology for the Social Gospel* (New York: Macmillan, 1917), 95.

in an I-Thou relationship of mediated immediacy be imprisoned in a hierarchical framework that quenches the Spirit of renewal and prophecy by denying that he or she can be an expert in his or her own spirituality under God? How can a congregation of gathered believers passionately committed to receiving and following new light breaking forth from God's Word and to being enlivened by fresh winds of the Holy Spirit be controlled by a formal, human hierarchy that so often defends the status quo and resists reform? Free church ecclesiology is renewal ecclesiology; it is structured to enhance and promote personal experiences of the Holy Spirit and personal interpretations of God's Word for the benefit of the whole people of God. It is servant ecclesiology that eschews dominating power over in order to enhance mutuality and community among all God's people. It is responsible ecclesiology that demands participation and accountability from all God's people. It is conversional ecclesiology that recognizes the transformation of individuals into priests unto God and prophets of God as the most important facet of the church's mission. Only the principle and practice of voluntarism promote this evangelical vision of the church and its mission consistently.

But what about the other pole of the bipolar core of evangelical faith—the pole of generous orthodoxy? Do not the free church ethos and ecclesiology undermine the unity of the faith within the church and give rise to doctrinal anarchy and chaos? How can voluntarism protect the doctrinal deposit of the faith and guard it against fanaticism and liberalism? After all, have not some of the worst manifestations of both arisen within the free church tradition? Are not Unitarianism and Mormonism offshoots of the free church movement? Without a hierarchical magisterium and authoritative creeds, what is to prevent the rise of new heresies within the church? Such questions made some sense in times when the hierarchy of the churches of the historic episcopate was generally doctrinally sound. The question now sounds quaint. It reminds one of the attempts by Ronald Knox to link free churches with "enthusiasm" as two manifestations of the same religious pathology. In an age in which bishops in apostolic succession and the priests they ordain and supervise proclaim the necessity of "taking leave of God"[17] and call for radical revision of basic Christian belief under the guns of modernity,[18] fear of heresy among free churches appears odd to say the least. It is becoming all too apparent that neither clerical hierarchy nor formal creedalism prevents heresy and even apostasy within the churches.

17. Don Cupitt, *Taking Leave of God* (New York: Crossroad Publishing, 1981). Cupitt is an ordained priest of the Church of England.
18. For example, retired American Episcopal bishop John Shelby Spong.

What, then, is the free church's protection against heresy? How does the free church maintain orthodoxy? It does so within the local congregation and between congregations by means of accountability networks. Free church conferences, conventions, and associations adopt confessions of faith that reflect the beliefs of congregations and ask their affiliating churches to join in affirming them. It is always possible, of course, for individual members and congregations and even entire networks to stray from historic Christian orthodoxy. This happened, for example, with the Unitarian movement among Congregationalists in the late eighteenth and early nineteenth centuries. What is instructive is that the majority of Congregational churches and associations isolated those that repudiated the trinitarian faith and confession of Jesus Christ as God and Savior and rejected their claims to be true Christian bodies while defending their right to believe and confess whatever they wanted to.

What is the alternative? The only workable alternative, so it seems, is state support of orthodoxy. A hierarchical denomination seems unable to enforce orthodoxy within its own ranks any better than a free church association. It can push out heretics, but it cannot stop them from claiming to be Christian or Episcopal or evangelical without government help. Free churches recognize this situation and embrace the right of every person to believe, worship, and confess without government restriction. Furthermore, free churches are highly suspicious of calls for stronger sanctions against heretics and "false brethren." Who would exercise and enforce those sanctions? Free churches prefer the risk of doctrinal chaos and anarchy over the risk of government or even quasi-government interference in religious liberty. That does not mean free churches are unconcerned about orthodoxy; some are more concerned to maintain theological correctness than others. The same is true in the magisterial Protestant denominations and within the Roman Catholic Church. Some bishops and synods enforce doctrine and some do not; ultimately, there is little or no protection against a bishop who falls into heresy or immorality. Anyone who thinks that a hierarchical system guarantees maintenance of orthodoxy simply is not familiar with developments in the Episcopal churches in the United States. Free churches prefer to put their trust in the Spirit of God and the power of the Word of God for maintenance of orthodoxy and to leave the door open for possible reconsideration of traditional doctrinal formulations as God breaks forth new light from his Word through the priests and prophets who constitute the body of Christ.

Some evangelical scholars have decried the free church tendency to ignore ancient and Reformation creeds and confessions of faith. D. H.

Williams's *Retrieving the Tradition and Renewing Evangelicalism: A Primer for Suspicious Protestants* is a sustained polemic against free churches' lack of adherence to ancient Christian creeds and the rule of faith of the church fathers. The ironic situation is that in spite of their non-creedalism, the vast majority of free churches in North America has managed to maintain basic Christian orthodoxy better than most of the magisterial, mainline Protestant denominations that are formally creedal and have hierarchies that are supposed to preserve and protect the traditional faith. Apparently, requiring clergy to swear allegiance to creeds is no guarantee that their preaching and teaching will remain orthodox. Without requiring adherence to creeds, most free churches in North America have managed to be more functionally Nicene than their formally Nicene counterparts in the world of mainline, magisterial Protestantism. I am not arguing that free churches are automatically more orthodox than others; I am simply arguing that they are not automatically less so.

Conclusion

The case I have made for a special consistency between evangelical spirituality and free church ecclesiology is indirect and informal. I do not expect that everyone will see it as I and many evangelicals in the free church tradition do. My case depends heavily on particular angles of vision with regard to evangelicalism and free church ecclesiology, but I believe they are shared by reputable scholars of both. To sum it up briefly: Evangelicalism is a spiritual as well as a theological renewal movement; it is identified as much by a specific orthopathy as by Protestant orthodoxy. That orthopathy includes an irreducibly individualistic dimension that is often informally described as a personal relationship with God through Jesus Christ and that I have here labeled conversional piety. Within the context of the community of God's people, an individual responds freely (whether freedom is interpreted as compatible or incompatible with divine determinism) to the initiative of God and enters into a transforming relationship that is marked by a mediated immediacy of God's presence to the individual soul. Evangelical spirituality includes a high estimation of a believer's priesthood and prophethood; it underlines a believer's responsibility to relate directly with God in a mutual I-Thou encounter that is new every day. While none of this excludes the importance of tradition or community, the evangelical ethos highlights the individual's relationship with God.

The free church ethos and ecclesiology fit well with this evangelical spirituality because they also prize the priesthood of believers and leave room for them to become experts in their own spirituality so that they can speak a needed word of guidance, correction, exhortation, and reform to the community without hindrance from bishop or king. Free church ecclesiology, like evangelical spirituality, binds the conscience of the church to the Word of God alone and permits—even requires—members of churches to participate in the processes of renewal and reform. For evangelical free church adherents, the free church tradition (ethos and ecclesiology) and the evangelical faith are twin extensions of the Protestant impulses of the sixteenth century. We look back at magisterial Reformers such as Luther and Zwingli and notice how they drew back at crucial moments and declined to move consistently along the trajectories on which they had begun their reforming works. At first Luther wanted the evangelical church to be separate from the state; later he considered that unrealistic and harshly criticized the radical Protestants who moved farther in that direction. The same is true of Zwingli, who, even more than Luther, began his reforming work in Zurich on a trajectory that would have led him to become Anabaptist. Later he drew back out of fear of the city council.

The free church tradition regards itself as *consistent Protestantism.* Many free church apologists go farther and claim for their tradition the restoration of the true New Testament church. But caution is in order because it is notoriously difficult and perhaps even impossible to draw from the New Testament a particular structural ecclesiology; only the vaguest outlines of ecclesiology may be discerned from the New Testament, and they do not include clear guidance for decisions about authority and power in churches after the apostolic age. (The questions left unanswered are who appoints or elects officers after the apostles and who oversees groups of churches after the apostles.) Strong cases can be made on the basis of the New Testament for several political structures of the church. Free churches claim that their polity is overall and in general supported by the New Testament and by the evangelical Protestant ethos.

7

The "Gift" of the Church

Ecclesia Crucis, Peccatrix Maxima, *and the* Missio Dei

MICHAEL JINKINS

"The Church has always existed, and it will always exist," wrote Heinrich Bullinger in 1561, at that time leader of the branch of the Protestant Reformation founded by Ulrich Zwingli and successor to Zwingli as pastor of the Great Minster in Zürich, Switzerland. "Because God from the beginning would have humankind saved, and to come to the knowledge of the truth (1 Tim. 2:4), it is altogether necessary that there always should have been, and should be now, and to the end of the world, a Church."[1]

1. Bullinger's words may be found in the Second Helvetic Confession. Lesser known than its cousin, the Heidelberg Catechism, the Second Helvetic Confession proved to be an influential statement of faith in the history of the Reformed tradition and continues to exert some influence today, not least as it stands in the *Book of Confessions* of the Presbyterian Church (U.S.A.). See *The Constitution of the Presbyterian Church (U.S.A.), Part 1: The Book of Confessions* (Louisville: Office of the General Assembly), 52–116; and Jack

179

The church, according to Bullinger, exists in history for the sake of *missio Dei*, "God's mission." As such, it lives, suffers, and lays down its life to serve God's creative and redemptive mission to the world. However one may construe ecclesiology, and in the essays in this volume we have been offered a considerable variety of ecclesiological perspectives, a doctrine of the church that hopes to be true to the gospel of Jesus Christ is grounded in the *missio Dei* revealed in his life, death, and resurrection. No such doctrine of the church is complete without recognition of the cross of Christ, in which the church's identity is forged as in a crucible and to which the church is called in discipleship as *ecclesia crucis*, "the community of the cross." No such doctrine of the church is complete without recognition of the sinfulness of the church, indeed, recognizing the church to be *peccatrix maximus*, "the greatest of sinners," in its failure to live up to its calling, while at the same time recognizing the gracious faithfulness of God in Christ, who alone reveals the character of the church's failure—and whose mercy is immeasurably greater than the church's sin.

The ecclesiological concerns and issues arising from the essays in this volume are broad indeed: Roger E. Olson and Bruce Hindmarsh provide theologically and historically informed perspectives on evangelicalism and the church. Olson's argument that there is an essential compatibility or affinity between evangelical Protestantism and free church ecclesiology is particularly interesting and, at many points, very persuasive, though this affinity is also, at times, problematic for both evangelical theology and various free church traditions. George R. Hunsberger's essay, with its subtle but provocative title "Evangelical Conversion toward a Missional Ecclesiology," raises fundamental questions regarding a "conversion for evangelicalism" and draws attention to certain weaknesses in evangelical ecclesiology, particularly with reference to its pervasive individualism. Kerry L. Dearborn and Edith M. Humphrey bring the conversation about evangelical ecclesiology into a larger theological and ecclesiological context. Dearborn's eloquent engagement with the trinitarian faith of Celtic Christianity seems especially promising. Personally, I would like to see the implications of her thought pursued farther, perhaps in conversation with Ian Bradley's *Colonies of Heaven: Celtic Models for Today's Church* and George MacLeod's classic manifesto *Only One Way Left*.[2]

Rogers, *Presbyterian Creeds: A Guide to the Book of Confessions* (Philadelphia: Westminster, 1985), 96–139.

2. Ian Bradley, *Colonies of Heaven: Celtic Models for Today's Church* (London: Darton, Longman & Todd, 2000); and George MacLeod, *Only One Way Left* (Glasgow: Iona Community, 1956).

The present essay argues that voluntaryism is for Protestant ecclesiology a two-edged sword, that while it has contributed much to the vitality of the evangelical movement in history and to the liveliness of many contemporary evangelical churches, its cost, including its tendency toward an alienation of persons in pursuit of individualism, is too high a price to pay (and is an unnecessary and theologically inappropriate price as well). The church is not called to define itself according to the cultural and religious individualism that has resulted in what Stanley Hauerwas describes as the "buyer's market" of church competition, which has more to do with entertainment and marketing than with the gospel. Rather, the church is called to a life of communion in the very likeness of the Triune God, Father, Son, and Holy Spirit, and to the mission of God in the world, a mission inseparable from the way of the cross. The themes around which this essay is constructed, therefore, are: (1) the promise and peril of ecclesial voluntaryism; (2) the character of the Triune God of grace as life and pattern of Christian community in the world; and (3) the significance of the cross for the church's vocation.

The Promise and Peril of Ecclesial Voluntaryism

An Ecclesiological Challenge

Some time ago, I came across a fascinating statement in a sociological journal:

> Christianity is a faith that is *chosen*; one only becomes a Christian by a conscious and individual act. It was, in fact, this quality that made Christianity so threatening to the Roman Empire, as it gave rise to the possibility of a multi-sited organization not subject to central control. For such choice to be possible, however, all Christian religions must share what David Little has called "conscientious individualism," that is the understanding that such choice as to join the Church was made possible by the fact that each individual possessed an authoritative moral conscience that had explicitly to choose to join the Church. . . . No one is *born* a Christian.[3]

This sociological understanding of Christian faith, and its corresponding ecclesiology, not only accords generally to the message of evangelical Protestantism but also reflects something like a "commonsensical view" of the acquisition of faith, values, and allegiances that

---

3. Tracy B. Strong, "Setting One's Heart on Honesty: The Tensions of Liberalism and Religion," *Social Research: An International Quarterly of the Social Sciences* 66, no. 4 (winter 1999): 1144.

has tended to dominate Western thought at least since the mid seventeenth century.[4] The nascent cultural and political individualism implicit to this way of looking at the world is not altogether separable from religious individualism, despite sincere protests to the contrary by many evangelical scholars.[5] John Locke, the child of Puritan Calvinism and the ethos of philosophical, political, and scientific inquiry that characterized what Alfred North Whitehead once called "the century of genius," famously defined the church:

> A Church, then, I take to be a voluntary society of men, joining themselves together of their own accord in order to the public worshiping of God in such manner as they judge acceptable to Him, and effectual to the salvation of their souls. I say it is a free and voluntary society. Nobody is born a member of any church; otherwise the religion of parents would descend unto children by the same right of inheritance as their temporal estates, and everyone would hold his faith by the same tenure he does his lands, than which nothing can be imagined more absurd. Thus, therefore, that matter stands. No man by nature is bound unto any particular church or sect, but everyone joins himself voluntarily to that society in which he believes he has found that profession and worship which is truly acceptable to God. The hope of salvation, as it was the only cause of his entrance into that communion, so it can be the only reason of his stay there. For if afterwards he discover anything either erroneous in the doctrine or incongruous in the worship of that society to which he has joined himself, why should it not be as free for him to go out as it was to enter? No member of a religious society can be tied with any other bonds but what proceed from the certain expectation of eternal life. A church, then, is a society of members voluntarily uniting to that end.[6]

4. For two particularly interesting perspectives on this issue, see Marsha G. Witten, *All Is Forgiven: The Secular Message in American Protestantism* (Princeton, N.J.: Princeton University Press, 1993); and Robert N. Bellah, "The Protestant Structure of American Culture: Multiculture or Monoculture?" *The Hedgehog Review* 4, no. 1 (spring 2002): 7–28. Also note the critical, theological response to these issues in Dale T. Irvin, *Christian Histories, Christian Traditioning* (Maryknoll, N.Y.: Orbis, 1998); and Kathryn Tanner, *Theories of Culture: A New Agenda for Theology* (Minneapolis: Fortress, 1997).

5. See, for example, my papers "Elements of Federal Theology in the Religious Thought of John Locke," *The Evangelical Quarterly: An International Review of Bible and Theology* 66, no. 2 (April 1994): 123–41; and "John Cotton and the Antinomian Controversy, 1636–1638: A Profile of Experiential Individualism in American Puritanism," *Scottish Journal of Theology* 43, no. 3 (1990): 321–49.

6. John Locke, "A Letter Concerning Toleration," in *On Politics and Education* (New York: Walter J. Black, 1947), 27–28. Also see a recent critical edition, John Locke, *Political Essays*, ed. Mark Goldie (Cambridge: Cambridge University Press, 1997), which includes "An Essay on Toleration" (1667), as well as minor essays on toleration, religion, and other social concerns.

Herein we glimpse a seed of the evangelical liveliness, the vitality, the energy, that is typical of the transdenominational evangelical movement in church history and of many contemporary evangelical congregations. This vigor starkly differentiates this movement and these congregations, their worship, Bible study, enthusiasm for distinctively Christian living, and evangelism, for example, from the languishing state and national churches of Western Europe. Herein lies also a hint of the alienation of persons, the dissension and spirit of schism, as well as the impulse to exclusion that has been inseparable from the story of Protestantism in general and of North American evangelicalism in particular. Recent studies, theological, sociological, and historical, have chronicled both aspects of voluntaryism that issue forth from the vision of church that John Locke stated with such clarity and force.[7]

A Personal Reflection

I recall being taught in the Southern Baptist Church of my childhood that a church is a voluntary gathering or association of individual believers. We understood ourselves, as members of the church, to be persons who had responded individually to the preaching of the gospel by trusting Jesus Christ as our Lord and Savior, by giving our lives to Jesus and following him through the waters of baptism to a "risen life" in Christ. Though we did not know it at the time, we were in agreement with the aged Reformed theologian Karl Barth, who in the final fragment of his *Church Dogmatics* wrote, "The first step of this life of faithfulness to God, the Christian life," is a person's "baptism with water, which by his own decision is requested of the community and which is administered by the community, as the binding confession of his obedience, conversion and hope, made in prayer for God's grace, wherein he honours the freedom of this grace."[8]

Later, while in seminary, I came to believe that, as profound and valuable as this understanding of Christian faith and Christian baptism

7. Donald E. Miller, *Reinventing American Protestantism: Christianity in the New Millennium* (Berkeley: University of California Press, 1997); Stanley Hauerwas, *In Good Company: The Church as Polis* (Notre Dame, Ind.: University of Notre Dame Press, 1995); Robert William Fogel, *The Fourth Great Awakening and the Future of Egalitarianism* (Chicago: University of Chicago Press, 2000); Robert D. Putnam, *Bowling Alone: The Collapse and Revival of American Community* (New York: Simon & Schuster, 2000); Robert Bellah et al., *Habits of the Heart: Individualism and Commitment in American Life* (Berkeley: University of California Press, 1985); Robert N. Bellah and Frederick E. Greenspahn, *Uncivil Religion: Interreligious Hostility in America* (New York: Crossroad, 1987); and Barry A. Kosmin and Seymour P. Lachman, *One Nation under God: Religion in Contemporary American Society* (New York: Harmony Books, 1993).

8. Karl Barth, *Church Dogmatics*, vol. 4, *The Doctrine of Reconciliation*, part 4 (fragment), ed. G. W. Bromiley and T. F. Torrance (Edinburgh: T & T Clark, 1969), 2.

is and however much I respect those who hold to this perspective (including my pastors and professors at that time), it tends to shift both one's theological emphasis and ecclesiological attention *from* the faithfulness and freedom of God *to* one's own faith and freedom. Indeed, my change in theological perspective precipitated my own move from the Baptist to the Reformed tradition. I came to the conviction that when we are baptized, our baptism is wrapped by the Holy Spirit in the baptism of Jesus Christ, in whom and by whom, with whom and through whom we are called by God, and that Christ's baptism sweeps over our own baptisms and sweeps us up in the indelible, sacramental sign of God's act of pure, unmerited grace. Thus, I came to believe that infant baptism represents the grace of the Triune God more fully and more appropriately than does believers' baptism, so much so that as a Presbyterian pastor, I preferred that adults take their baptismal vows *after* the act of baptism to symbolize that their act of faith (given to them by God) is a response to the faithfulness of God in Christ on their behalf.

I make these personal and autobiographical statements not so much as an *apologia* for infant baptism as to clarify two very different ways of thinking about what it means to belong to the church and thus two very different understandings of church. The church as voluntary association or religious society represents a vital ecclesiological understanding, and it reflects particularly well the evangelical emphasis on a transforming encounter with God (believers' conversion) as the necessary condition for full participation in the community of believers. This encounter with God, according to evangelical theology, demands a corresponding response in one's life and includes joining together with others who have experienced Christian conversion. While the event of conversion is individual, the converted are compelled not to forsake the fellowship of the faithful.

The church as a gathered body, by contrast, represents a clear alternative of ecclesiological perspective, perhaps complementary, perhaps competing, in which belief in God's faithfulness and freedom is understood to be expressed through *the community's* inclusion of those (often, but not always, children) who have not yet recognized the gospel or made it their own by faith.[9]

The first ecclesiology (the voluntary association) tends to emphasize transformation over formation; the second (the gathered body) tends to understand transformation as a product of formation. The first emphasizes the I-Thou encounter at the heart of personal faith and sees the work of God as that which breaks through into the midst of individuals, some-

9. This issue has often had a kind of "early versus later generations" feel about it, as is evidenced in the conflicts among New England Congregationalists. See, for example, Jonathan Edwards, *The Works of Jonathan Edwards*, vol. 12, *Ecclesiastical Writings*, ed. David D. Hall (New Haven: Yale University Press, 1994).

times in the life of the church and sometimes despite the church; the second understands the divine encounter both as an aspect of the faith preserved and conveyed instrumentally through the community of faith and also as an aspect of the life of God, Father, Son, and Spirit, in relation to members of the community. As such, it is sometimes in tension with or even contradicts the traditions of the community.[10] These two ecclesial perspectives inevitably compete, given the nature and limitations of our humanity, and there is an undeniable and irresolvable conflict between them; yet they are also ultimately complementary. The church catholic, in other words, would be poorer were we to lose either perspective.[11]

There are obviously dangers to any ecclesiology that assumes that because all members are baptized, then all members have heard and responded obediently to the call of Jesus Christ to discipleship. There is, in my view, even more danger to the perspective in certain state and national churches that virtually equates citizenship with church membership. It is possible, as Søren Kierkegaard reminds us, for people to receive just enough Christianity to be effectively inoculated against the

10. I am particularly indebted to James E. Loder, *The Transforming Moment*, 2d ed. (Colorado Springs: Helmers & Howard, 1989); and C. Ellis Nelson, ed., *Congregations: Their Power to Form and Transform* (Atlanta: John Knox, 1988). Recently, I have returned to two classics to contemplate the relationship between Christian transformation and formation: Rudolf Otto, *The Idea of the Holy* (1923; reprint, New York: Oxford University Press, 1950); and William James, *The Varieties of Religious Experience* (1902; reprint, London: Penguin, 1985).

11. The idea that deep theological/ecclesiological diversity entered the history of the church at the Protestant Reformation (or after) is fundamentally at odds with the realities of the preceding millennium and half of the church's existence. From the pages of the New Testament through the rise of various monastic traditions, the church has been blessed (not plagued) with a variety of ecclesial forms of life. Did they represent sometimes incommensurable values? Yes, of course. Would not the church be poorer, however, if the New Testament omitted the epistle of James (representing a peculiar form of Christian community) in favor of only Pauline or Petrine letters (both of which offer quite different understandings of Christian community)? Would not the church be poorer if there were no Franciscan tradition, if only Benedictines (for example) had flourished? However uncomfortable ecclesial diversity may be at particular moments, judging by the profound diversity of God's creation, I have a hard time imagining that such diversity is a curse. Rather, even the diversity among Christian forms of community seems to me a blessing and evidence once again of the wisdom and wonder of the Triune Creator. The extent of this diversity and the fact of the church's ambivalence toward it have in recent years been the subject of considerable scholarly attention. See, for instance, Everett Ferguson, ed., *Doctrinal Diversity: Varieties of Early Christianity* (New York/London: Garland Publishing, 1999); and idem, *Forms of Devotion: Conversion, Worship, Spirituality, and Asceticism* (New York/London: Garland Publishing, 1999), volumes 4 and 5, respectively, in the series Recent Studies in Early Christianity. In the editorial introduction to volume 4, Ferguson writes, "A principal theme characterizing recent study of early Christianity is the diversity in the Christian movement, present from its

virus of Christian faith.[12] Christian formation is not complete until persons have responded to the faithfulness and freedom of God by entrusting their lives to Christ in personal discipleship. But there are also dangers in an ecclesiology that so places the emphasis on the faith and faithfulness of individuals that the church becomes a kind of holier-than-thou club. These dangers take the shape of endless schisms, the bottomless pit of introspective tests for authentic experiences of faith and faithfulness, and the perpetual and self-righteous exclusion of those who do not conform, all in the name of God.

A Theological Response

C. S. Lewis, in a letter to a friend, offered a critique of ecclesial voluntaryism, arguing for the church as the "body of Christ in which all members however different . . . must share the common life, complementing and helping one another precisely by their differences."[13] Lewis's observation resonates with the biblical accounts of Jesus' calling of his disciples.

---

beginning and continuing even after orthodoxy was firmly institutionalized" (ix). "Diversity was already evident in the early history of the church in the differences between Jewish and Gentile believers" (x). Indeed, as Andrew Louth writes in the first essay in the volume, "I think we need to remind ourselves just how diverse and disparate the communities of the fourth century—and not just the Christian communities—were. The basic unit was the city—πόλις, civitas—with its surrounding countryside. Except in the case of a few great cities, especially Rome and Constantinople, the city and its surroundings were a self-contained economic unity. . . . Their loyalties were primarily local, which found expression in the local religious cults that Christians were to call 'pagan'" ("Unity and Diversity in the Church in the Fourth Century," 3–4). Further, he notes, "The local church, with its growing number of local saints, came to do at least as good a job of defining and expressing local loyalties and local identity as the local pagan cults had done, while at the same time expressing a sense of belonging that transcended the merely local" (7). Louth explores the texture of diversity in the first centuries of the church's history, with special reference to the fourth century and the struggle the church experienced in some cases affirming, in others denying, and in still others condemning its diversity. He explores the rhetorical devices, the ecclesiastical-political instruments, and the liturgical acts that attempted in various ways, with varying degrees of success, either to reinterpret the church's diversity in terms of unity (if not uniformity) or to enforce unity of some sort (variously defined). While considerable attention has been given in recent years to the subject of diversity in the early church, Louth also reminds us that especially since the Protestant Reformation, scholars have repeatedly explored patristic history, specifically exploring its doctrinal and liturgical diversity. This essay was previously published in *Studies in Church History* 32 (1996): 1–17. Other essays in the same volume explore diversity in the early Christian communities with reference to particular doctrines. See also Roger E. Olson, *The Mosaic of Christian Belief: Twenty Centuries of Unity and Diversity* (Downers Grove, Ill.: InterVarsity, 2002), 287–305.

12. Kierkegaard's comment, "We can be baptized *en masse* but can never be reborn *en masse*," of course speaks to the larger point. See Søren Kierkegaard, *Philosophical Fragments/Johannes Climacus*, ed. and trans. Howard V. Hong and Edna H. Hong (Princeton, N.J.: Princeton University Press, 1985), 18–20.

13. C. S. Lewis, *Letters of C. S. Lewis*, ed. W. H. Lewis (New York: Harcourt Brace Jovanovich, 1966), 224.

What a strange assembly that group of first disciples must have been: at least one political zealot and at least one collaborator with the Roman occupation (I wonder how they got along), some hotheads (the sons of thunder), a chronic but well-intentioned vacillator (the promise of Peter, the Rock, was long deferred in Simon), and a self-righteous prig or two (Judas included). These people did not choose to join this band. They were called and chosen by Jesus. And to this day, only God knows what was in their hearts. Their unity resided not in themselves, their behavior, their beliefs, or their affections but in the Christ who called and chose them to follow him.

An ecclesiology that begins from the assumption that the church consists of individuals who have chosen to follow God, individuals who join together because they share the same faith, are similarly faithful in their behavior, or share similar faith experiences (the tests of orthodoxy, orthopraxy, orthopathy), is built on the shifting sand of human frailty and variability. It is so easy to equate difference with ungodliness, so tempting to confuse diversity with perversity, and so utterly impossible for persons (even for sincere Christians) to know the heart of another that we must count on something other than shared affinities, beliefs, aspirations, morals, values, religious experiences, and commitments to unite us in fellowship and community. We must count on God in Christ for this. Whatever unity means, and whatever it means to belong to the community of Christ, it cannot depend on us. The church is one because the church is, as Paul tells us, the one body of our Lord Jesus Christ (Romans 12; 1 Corinthians 12). Dietrich Bonhoeffer's reflections on the body of Christ are particularly profound and pertinent:

> For those who belong to him, Jesus' departure does not mean a loss but rather a new gift. For the first disciples the bodily community with Jesus did not mean anything different or anything more than what we have today. Indeed, for us this community is even more definite, more complete, and more certain than it was for them, since we live in full community with the bodily presence of the glorified Lord. Our faith must become fully aware of the magnitude of this gift. The body of Jesus Christ is the ground of our faith and the source of its certainty; the body of Jesus Christ is the one and perfect gift through which we receive our salvation; the body of Jesus Christ is our new life. It is in the body of Jesus Christ that we are accepted by God from eternity.[14]

14. Dietrich Bonhoeffer, *Discipleship*, trans. Barbara Green and Reinhard Krauss (Minneapolis: Fortress, 2001), 213. This is the new critical edition of Bonhoeffer's *Nachfolge* previously translated into English as *The Cost of Discipleship*.

Listen again to Bonhoeffer's claim. "Our faith must become fully aware of the magnitude of this gift. The body of Jesus Christ is the ground of our faith and the source of its certainty." We belong to the body of Christ. By the grace of God in Christ, we are members of the body of which Christ himself is head. The sinews of God's Word and Spirit hold us together. Our unity is not sure because of our hold on one another. God's hold alone is sure. And God alone holds the church. Thus, the Heidelberg Catechism asks the question, "What is your only comfort in life and in death?" and answers, "That I belong—body and soul, in life and in death—not to myself but to my faithful Savior, Jesus Christ, who at the cost of his own blood has fully paid for all my sins and has completely freed me from the dominion of the devil: that he protects me so well that without the will of my Father in heaven not a hair can fall from my head; indeed, that everything must fit his purpose for my salvation. Therefore, by his Holy Spirit, he also assures me of eternal life, and makes me wholeheartedly willing and ready from now on to live for him."[15]

In my mind's eye, I imagine this question asked of the whole church. The Heidelberg Catechism is an ecclesiological confession. This the church confesses. The church belongs body and soul, in life and in death not to itself but to our faithful Savior, Jesus Christ. The church, its salvation won, its debts paid, freed from the dominion of Satan, belongs to God in Christ. And we belong to God in Christ here and now as members of Christ's body, the church. "*We* belong!" As Karl Barth once observed, we "exist eccentrically"; we "belong to this Lord completely." "Do you not know that . . . you are not your own?" (1 Cor. 6:19 NRSV).[16] Our "belonging" is never our "possession."

The Character of the Triune God of Grace as Life and Pattern of Christian Community in the World

An Ecclesiological Challenge

James Torrance has often reflected on the distinctive problem certain Protestant churches have with sectarianism, the belief that the true, pure, and faithful church (as some have called it, the "invisible church") is both separate and separable from the church at large (the "visible church"). He relates the story of how as he emerged from an ec-

15. Allen O. Miller, M. Eugene Osterhaven, Aladar Komjathy, and James I. McCord, eds., *The Heidelberg Catechism with Commentary* (New York: United Church Press, 1962), 17. This edition is especially helpful because of the wealth of scriptural cross-references provided in the footnotes and the excellent theological commentary.

16. Karl Barth, *Learning Jesus Christ through the Heidelberg Catechism*, trans. Shirley C. Guthrie, Jr. (Grand Rapids: Eerdmans, 1964), 30.

umenical worship service in Belfast, Northern Ireland, he was confronted by a Protestant churchman who asked bluntly, "How can you, a Scottish Presbyterian minister and Reformed theologian, worship with Roman Catholics?" "My answer," said James, "was that God does not accept us because we offer Protestant worship, or Roman Catholic worship, or some beautiful Anglican liturgy, or 'free prayers'! God accepts us by grace alone, not because of any offering we sinners can make, but only for what we are in Christ and on the ground of that one offering which he has made once and for all."[17] He continues:

> For four hundred years, from the time of the Reformation, the Reformed churches have stressed *sola gratis* on the vertical plane, that God accepts us freely and unconditionally for what we are in Christ by faith alone, be we Jews or Gentiles, male or female, black or white. But so often we betray this gospel by not working it out on the horizontal plane, by failing to accept one another as freely and unconditionally as God in Christ has accepted us. The New Testament knows no divorce between the vertical and the horizontal.[18]

"But what has this to do with ecclesiology?" one might well ask. James, himself, answers the question by contrasting sectarianism and an ecclesiology grounded in the grace of Christ alone.

> As I see it, sectarianism arises when two things happen: first, when any group or church makes an absolute identification between their formulations of the truth and the Truth, and then, second, says, "We shall only accept you IF you accept our formulation of the Truth!"—and the gospel of grace is betrayed by what is sometimes an arrogant self-righteousness, which can even lead to the active persecution (by violence or "godly discipline"!) of those who do not agree with the group. God does not accept us on the ground of our *formulations* of the doctrines of grace (or our assent to the truth of the doctrine of "justification by faith alone"). He accepts us by *grace* for what we are by faith in Christ. When then should we impose a condition of acceptance on others, which God does not?[19]

None of the authors writing in this volume has claimed the kind of exclusive or self-righteous proprietorship of "Truth" against which Tor-

---

17. James B. Torrance, "The Ministry of Reconciliation Today: The Realism of Grace," in *Incarnational Ministry: The Presence of Christ in Church, Society, and Family*, ed. Christian D. Kettler and Todd H. Speidell (Colorado Springs: Helmers & Howard, 1990), 131.

18. Ibid., 132.

19. Ibid., 133. See also James B. Torrance, *Worship, Community, and the Triune God of Grace: The Didsbury Lectures* (Carlisle: Paternoster, 1996).

rance warns. They all represent in their essays the grace, modesty, humility, respect, and hospitality that could serve the church well as a model for theological dialogue. There is, however, in the voluntaryism and individualism, in the quest for a pure and holy fellowship that lies close to the heart of evangelical faith and ecclesiology, an element of exclusion and a tendency to self-righteousness that are sometimes manifested in terms of church discipline.

David Wiley, in an essay on John Calvin's ecclesiology, writes, for Calvin, "however much one might identify the visible church with its marks—the Word preached and heard and the sacraments rightly administered," the faithful and true church "is ultimately invisible, eternal, and invincible because of the sure foundation of divine election." The pure and faithful church "is distinct but not separate from the visible church"; according to Calvin, "the church is always mixed."[20] Calvin's thought brings to mind an ecclesiological application of Jesus' parable of the sower (Mark 4:1–20) and the promise of the Lord of the harvest, who alone can winnow this crop.[21] Ecclesiology, for Calvin, cannot be divorced and abstracted from Christology. To do so lands us in the realm of insecurity with reference to God's eternal election. And assurance, for Calvin at least, is of the very essence of faith. Better to understand the election of the elect as subsumed in the person of Jesus Christ. Christ, in other words, is elect for us, and the church is elect in Christ. This we apprehend by faith alone.[22]

A Personal Reflection

A few years ago, an evangelical colleague at a sister seminary raised a question related to my interest in ecclesiology. He was particularly in-

20. David N. Wiley, "The Church as the Elect in the Theology of Calvin," in *John Calvin and the Church: A Prism of Reform*, ed. Timothy George (Louisville: Westminster John Knox, 1990), 96–97.

21. Heinrich Bullinger's sermon "Of the Holy Catholic Church" makes much the same point: "But let us hear what the evangelical and apostolic testimony says. The Lord says plainly in the Gospel that cockle grow up in the Lord's field, being sown by a wicked man, and he forbids it to be plucked up, lest the corn should be plucked up also. Behold, cockle sown by an evil man (I say) by the devil himself, which is not corn, and yet it increases and it is in the Lord's field. Again, the Lord says in the Gospel: 'The kingdom of heaven is like unto a net, which, being cast into the sea, draweth all manner of things up with it; and when it is filled, it is brought to the shore; and there men sitting reserve that which is good in a vessel, and that which is evil they cast away.' Behold again, how you may see both good and bad drawn in one and the same net, and therefore both good and evil are to be reckoned in one and the same kingdom" (G. W. Bromiley, ed. and trans., *Zwingli and Bullinger*, Library of Christian Classics [Philadephia: Westminster, 1953], 296–97).

22. See, for example, Karl Barth's discussion of "The Covenant as the Presupposition of Reconciliation," *Church Dogmatics* IV.1.22–66.

trigued by a remark I had made paraphrasing G. K. Chesterton: The difference between a schismatic and a saint is that the schismatic loves his criticisms of the church more than he loves the church, while the saint loves the church more than his criticisms of it. My colleague said that it struck him as strange that I should focus so much on the church and on our relationship to the church, whereas he tended to focus more on one's relationship to Christ than to the church.

I have thought often about my friend's words, especially as I read these essays, each of which attempts to make critical and constructive statements more or less toward an evangelical ecclesiology. As I read the essays, I found myself agreeing more and more deeply with my friend's preference to focus more on Christ than on the church. And I was reminded of another passage from Chesterton:

> The saint is a medicine because he is an antidote. Indeed that is why the saint is often a martyr; he is mistaken for a poison because he is an antidote. He will generally be found restoring the world to sanity by exaggerating whatever the world neglects, which is by no means always the same element in every age. Yet each generation seeks its saint by instinct; and he is not what the people want, but rather what the people need. . . . Therefore it is the paradox of history that each generation is converted by the saint who contradicts it most.[23]

My friend played the role of Chesterton's "saint" for me (assuming that a saint can be a cantankerous gadfly, and I think many of the most interesting saints are), and I want to return the favor, though I make a very shabby saint indeed. The more we talk about the church, the more we reflect on the constituency of the church's membership, the godliness and piety and purity of Christians, the marks of the true church, and so forth, the more I want to divert our focus to Jesus Christ and the nature of the church's relationship with Christ.

C. S. Lewis's hesitance to endorse even the most pious self-reflection is partly at work here. Lewis insisted that whenever his attention was fixed on himself, he became overwhelmed by the zoo of lusts and bedlam of selfishness that he observed in his own heart.[24] I am convinced of the truth of a paradoxical axiom related to the church's identity that we neglect at considerable loss: The more we think about our identity and

23. G. K. Chesterton, *Saint Thomas Aquinas: "The Dumb Ox"* (London: Doubleday, 1956), 23–24.

24. This is wonderfully communicated in a letter C. S. Lewis wrote on July 31, 1954, to a Presbyterian pastor, the Reverend Dr. F. Morgan Roberts, in which Lewis cautions against introspection in prayer. Instead, we should "always . . . turn the attention outwards to God" (from the collection of the Louisville Presbyterian Seminary Library). See also C. S. Lewis, *Prayer: Letters to Malcolm* (London: Geoffrey Bles, 1964).

integrity as people of God, the less we have to do with Christ, who alone gives the church its identity and integrity. Only by the route of self-forgetfulness—"lost in wonder, love, and praise" at the grace and mercy of God in Christ—does the church arrive at its intended destination.[25]

I do not mean to belittle or minimize the significance of any attempt to inquire closely into the doctrine of the church, to make critical and constructive contributions to the church's self-understanding. I do, however, want to exaggerate the opposite move, calling on us to inquire even more closely into the character of Christ and of the church's relationship to God in and through Christ.

This is where John Calvin's perspective on sanctification can be of great service to ecclesiology, even for non-Calvinists. Calvin entreats us to look upon Jesus Christ, the mirror of our sanctification, "in which we can contemplate that which the weakness of the cross obscures in us,"[26] because, as Calvin argues elsewhere, "our righteousness is not in us but in Christ. . . . We possess it only because we are partakers in Christ; indeed, with him we possess all its riches."[27] According to Calvin, my friend Trevor Hart explains, "What is his [Christ's], has become ours."[28] Indeed, Calvin, in his introduction to the theme of the epistle to the Colossians, says that "all parts of our salvation are placed in Christ alone, [and] that they [the Colossians] may not seek anything elsewhere." Thus, Paul bids the Colossians to "rest in Christ alone."[29]

Who and what the church is (its identity and mission, its righteousness and integrity, its holiness and purity) is gifted to the church in Jesus Christ. Christ is the mirror of our personal sanctification—meaning that if we wish to see our progress in grace we must look not to ourselves but to Jesus Christ—because Christ is the mirror of the church's sanctification.[30] There is nothing other than Jesus Christ to which we may look for our sanctification. And it is in and

25. The quoted phrase comes from Charles Wesley's soaring hymn of praise, "Love Divine, All Loves Excelling."

26. John Calvin, *Commentary on Galatians, Ephesians, Philippians, and Colossians,* ed. David W. Torrance and Thomas F. Torrance, trans. T. H. L. Parker (Edinburgh: Oliver and Boyd, 1965), Commentary on Ephesians, 136.

27. John Calvin, *Institutes of the Christian Religion,* ed. John T. McNeill, trans. Ford Lewis Battles (Philadelphia: Westminster, 1960), III.xi.23.

28. Trevor Hart, "Humankind in Christ and Christ in Humankind: Salvation as Participation in Our Substitution in the Theology of John Calvin," *Scottish Journal of Theology* 42, no. 1 (1989): 79. This essay is the most wonderful extended reflection on Calvin's understanding of "substitution" I have ever read.

29. Calvin, *Commentary on Galatians, Ephesians, Philippians, and Colossians,* Commentary on Colossians, 298.

30. George Hunsberger's essay, "Evangelical Conversion toward a Missional Ecclesiology," is particularly trenchant at this point.

through the church that we find ourselves sanctified in Christ. Neither is there anything but Christ to which the church may look to find out who the church is and why it exists. The identity and purpose of the church, and the identity and end of every member of the church, lie in its belonging to Jesus Christ. This means, at least in part, that our theology of the church is subject to the character of the God revealed in Christ and that our various concepts of church membership, adherence to particular formulations of faith and church discipline, conformity to particular standards of behavior and practice, and so forth are all always subject and subordinate to the veto of God's grace in Jesus Christ.

The church's focus on Jesus Christ does not divert our attention from the Triune God of grace. Christocentrism is not in conflict with theocentrism or trinitarianism. This must be clearly understood. Jesus Christ is our window on the life and character of the Triune God. Through Christ we know God as Father, Son, and Spirit. As Robert Jenson observes, "Christocentrism and trinitarianism cannot coherently be used to balance each other, since they are the same thing." Commenting on Karl Barth's theology, Jenson writes:

> The fundamental identification of God is, according to Barth, that he is the one "who has revealed himself in Jesus Christ." Thus the doctrine of the Trinity is "analysis of the concept of revelation." Barth does not mean that we come to the doctrine of the Trinity by analysis of a general concept of "revelation"; the doctrine results from analysis of the way in which Scripture describes the particular historical event Jesus Christ, as in fact revelation of God.[31]

31. Robert W. Jenson, "Karl Barth," in *The Modern Theologians: An Introduction to Christian Theology in the Twentieth Century*, vol. 1, ed. David F. Ford (Oxford: Basil Blackwell, 1989), 41–42. Barth himself, in a chapter titled "The Root of the Doctrine of the Trinity," writes, "The miracle that we cannot stress too strongly corresponds simply on the one side to the mystery of God from which revelation comes forth and by which it is always invested and then on the other side to the paradox that in revelation God really does come forth out of His mystery. This is how it is with God's being revealed. Without God's being historically revealed in this way, revelation would not be revelation. God's being revealed makes it a link between God and man, an effective encounter between God and man. But it is God's own being revealed that makes it this. In this respect too, with reference to the goal, our statement that God reveals Himself as Lord is confirmed. The fact that God can do what the biblical witnesses ascribe to him, namely, not just take form and not just remain free in this form, but also in this form and freedom of His become God to specific men, eternity in a moment, this is the third meaning of His lordship in His revelation" (331). A particularly relevant analysis of Barth's understanding of the revelation of the Triune God in Jesus Christ is provided in William Stacy Johnson, *The Mystery of God: Karl Barth and the Postmodern Foundations of Theology* (Louisville: Westminster John Knox, 1997), particularly 43–65.

As the medieval mystic Lady Julian of Norwich says in her *Revelations of Divine Love*, when we look upon Jesus, especially when we see Jesus on the cross, we are beholding in his face the Triune God; indeed, she says that wherever Jesus is spoken of, "the blessed Trinity is always to be understood."[32] This is why, in the final analysis, one must do the fundamental theological work suggested by Kerry Dearborn if an evangelical ecclesiology is to represent anything more than sectarian dogma.

A Theological Response

"The Church," wrote John Zizioulas in the opening passages of surely one of the most influential ecclesiological studies in the twentieth century, "is not simply an institution. She is a 'mode of existence,' *a way of being*."[33] While the church can be approached sociologically and historically, psychologically and politically, and certain aspects of its life can be illuminated using the tools of these disciplines with their specialized theoretical approaches and technical vocabularies, the church must also be understood theologically if it is to be understood properly, because the church, as "a way of being" among humanity, reflects God's own being-in-communion.[34] T. F. Torrance writes:

> The Church may be described as the place in space and time where knowledge of the Father, the Son and the Holy Spirit becomes grounded in humanity, and union and communion with the Holy Trinity becomes embodied within the human race. Expressed the other way round, the Church is constituted by the Holy Spirit as the empirical counterpart of his sanctifying presence and activity in our midst, for in the Spirit we are made members of Christ the incarnate Son and through him have access to the Father. The "one holy Church" is thus, as it were, the complement of the "one Holy Spirit." As Irenaeus in his major work expressed it: "This Gift of God has been entrusted to the Church, as breath was to the first created man, that all members receiving it may be vivified, and the communication of Christ has been distributed within it, that is, the Holy Spirit, the earnest of incorruption and the confirmation of our faith, and the ladder of ascent to God. . . . For where the Church is, there is the Spirit of God; and where the Spirit of God is, there is the Church, and

32. Julian of Norwich, *Revelations of Divine Love,* trans. Clifton Wolters (London: Penguin, 1966), 66.

33. John Zizioulas, *Being as Communion: Studies in Personhood and the Church* (Crestwood, N.Y.: St. Vladimir's Seminary Press, 1985), 15.

34. See also Edward Schillebeeckx, *The Church with a Human Face: A New and Expanded Theology of Ministry,* trans. John Bowden (New York: Crossroad, 1990), 5–6; and Miroslav Volf, *After Our Likeness: The Church as the Image of the Trinity* (Grand Rapids: Eerdmans, 1998).

every kind of grace; but the Spirit is truth." As such the Church is constituted by Christ to be the receptacle of the Gospel proclaimed and handed on by the apostles, which Irenaeus described as a continuously "rejuvenating deposit" *(depositum juvenescens et juvenescere faciens)*. It is significant . . . that while Irenaeus regarded the Church thus entrusted with the Gospel as the empirical *vis-à-vis* of the Holy Spirit, he nevertheless thought of it as oriented so completely beyond itself that he spoke of the Gospel as "the pillar and ground of the Church."[35]

The wholeness and holiness for which the church, as the body of Christ and people of God, yearns already belong to the church by virtue of the God who calls the church into existence and sustains it in being through God's own life-giving Spirit and Word. In a manner that corresponds to God's unique, continuing, and incomprehensibly vulnerable act of creation, bringing into existence, by the power of God's Spirit and Word, all things *ex nihilo* and entrusting to this creation the gifts of life and freedom, God brings into being the church as communion, entrusting God's Spirit and Word to this human community.[36] With the Spirit of God in its lungs, the church breathes forth the Word of God, the gospel of Christ. And the gospel of Christ, though spoken by the church, remains altogether "beyond" the church, having the power to rejuvenate that which itself proclaims the gospel.

The Triune God of grace is, therefore, the very life of the church, even as the character of the Holy Trinity—the Father, whose life is poured out eternally for the divine Other, "a flowing wellspring with no holding-trough beneath it";[37] the Son, whose life is in eternal reciprocity, grateful submission, giving without limit as imageless image of the Father;[38] and the Spirit, who is the eternal love and life and gift of the Father and the Son[39]—is the eternal pattern to which the church is called on behalf of the world God loves. Hans Urs von Balthasar writes in his meditation on the Apostles' Creed:

> [God's] first gift is the Church. That she exists and is known is presupposed; the individual believer, who says "I believe" (not "we believe"), does so within this sacred community. What she is remains, since she is the work

35. Thomas F. Torrance, *The Trinitarian Faith* (Edinburgh: T & T Clark, 1988), 256–57.

36. Although theologians have long tried to communicate a sense of this divine vulnerability with reference to the church, Annie Dillard has trumped them all in her remarkable essay, "An Expedition to the Pole," in *Teaching a Stone to Talk: Expeditions and Encounters* (New York: Harper & Row, 1982), 17–52.

37. Hans Urs von Balthasar, *Credo: Meditations on the Apostles' Creed*, trans. David Kipp (New York: Crossroad, 1990), 30.

38. Ibid., 38–39.

39. Ibid., 39, 45–47.

of the triune God, mysterious in many respects. *Ecclesia* means she who is "called out," and the beginning of this call was the choice of Israel to be a "kingdom of priests and a holy nation." . . . The Church, permanently rooted in Israel, elevated through the Son's Eucharist to being his incarnate Bride, and qualified through the Spirit to give worthy answer, is definitely a structure of the triune God that brings creation to completion.[40]

"The glory of the gospel of Jesus Christ is the revelation of God's Triune nature and the outpouring of God's healing love into our world," writes Kerry Dearborn.[41] God, in Christ, reveals God's purpose for all humanity, the secret locked in the heart of creation: that we might share in God's eternal life and love and gift for the other. Jesus Christ, through the power of the Holy Spirit, constitutes us as a people of God after the likeness and in the character of the Triune God, whom Christ reveals, and calls us beyond everything that might make us smaller of heart and meaner in spirit to live as God lives, to love as God loves, and to give of ourselves to others with God's own extravagant selflessness.

The church of Jesus Christ, stretching through time and into eternity, cannot be encapsulated and contained in a single ecclesial movement or institution. Nor does the church of Jesus Christ depend on our faithfulness for its faithfulness. We rest in the assurance that Jesus Christ is Lord of the church and that the church's past, present, and future are in God's hands. These are not abstract mutterings of piety. These statements represent the essential witness of the church to its constituency in the life of God and its creaturely boundaries. What God hath joined together, let no one put asunder.

The Significance of the Cross for the Church's Vocation

An Ecclesiological Challenge

Alan Lewis once observed, "Ministry is theology's polygraph, its infallible lie-detecting test, revealing the truth of what the church believes and the identity of whom she worships—the God of the cross or the false deities of her cultural ideology."[42]

What did Lewis mean when he wrote these words? In what sense is the church's ministry theology's polygraph? Do our busy programs and our entrepreneurial zeal, our pursuit of pop entertainment in the guise of the worship of God, our user-friendly yet biblically uninformed, spir-

40. Ibid., 83–84.
41. Kerry L. Dearborn, "Recovering a Trinitarian and Sacramental Ecclesiology."
42. Alan E. Lewis, "Unmasking Idolatries: Vocation in the *Ecclesia Crucis*," in *Incarnational Ministry*, 113. I deliberately evoked Lewis's employment of the phrase *ekklēsia crucis* in the title for this essay.

itually vapid sermons and market-driven responses to religious consumerism really have a story to tell to the nations about the vacuity of our theology? Or can we simply disconnect the church's ministry (what we pragmatically do to serve the institutional needs of the church) from our essential beliefs, from our treasured hopes and aspirations, from the fundamental understandings of who God is and who we are called to be in Jesus Christ, from our theology? If strapped to a lie detector of our own theological making, should the church sweat?

Ecclesiology is haunted by the specter of the church's indentured servitude to the world's standards of success, the enduring temptation to craft the church's ministry and mission so as to cause neither scandal to the world's sensibilities nor shock to the world's values.[43] What sublime seduction is this that leads the church to believe it can save its institutional life and secure the souls of the world by offering the world a religious version of the world's own sorry sentiments![44] To win in this endeavor is to lose—and to lose big. Christ's words pursue the church down through history:

> Then he began to teach them that the Son of Man must undergo great suffering, and be rejected by the elders, the chief priests, and the scribes, and be killed, and after three days rise again. He said all this quite openly. And Peter took him aside and began to rebuke him. But turning and looking at his disciples, he rebuked Peter and said, "Get behind me, Satan! For you are setting your mind not on divine things but on human things." He called the crowd with his disciples, and said to them, "If any want to

43. This is nothing new. Reinhold Niebuhr, in 1928, wrote in his journal, "Detroit observed Good Friday today as never before. Sixteen theatres and many churches besides were filled to capacity during the three-hour period. I wonder how one is to understand this tremendous devotion of this pagan city. How little place the real spirit of Christ has in the industrial drive of this city. And yet men and women flock by the thousands to meditate upon the cross. Perhaps we are all like the centurion who helped to crucify Jesus and then was so impressed by the whole drama of the cross that the confession was forced from his lips, 'Surely this was the son of God.'—Before going to the theatre service I passed a Methodist church with a message on its bulletin board that explains many chapters in American church history. It was: 'Good Friday service this afternoon. Snappy song service.' So we combine the somber notes of religion with the jazz of the age. I wonder if anyone who needs a snappy song service can really appreciate the meaning of the cross. But perhaps that is just a Lutheran prejudice of mine" (Reinhold Niebuhr, *Leaves from the Notebook of a Tamed Cynic* [1929; reprint, New York: Harper & Row, 1980], 172).

44. C. Ellis Nelson, in his landmark study *How Faith Matures* (Louisville: Westminster John Knox, 1989), 66–71, critiques the institutionalization of the church and what Max Weber called "the routinization of charisma," drawing on research from Thomas O'Dea. He observes the process by which a religious community adjusts its beliefs to the world to ensure its institutional survival. See also Thomas F. O'Dea, *The Sociology of Religion* (Englewood Cliffs, N.J.: Prentice-Hall, 1966), 90–97; and idem, *Sociology and the Study of Religion: Theory, Research, Interpretation* (New York: Basic Books, 1970), 240–55.

become my followers, let them deny themselves and take up their cross and follow me. For those who want to save their life will lose it, and those who lose their life for my sake, and for the sake of the gospel, will save it. For what will it profit them to gain the whole world and forfeit their life? Indeed, what can they give in return for their life? Those who are ashamed of me and of my words in this adulterous and sinful generation, of them the Son of Man will also be ashamed when he comes in the glory of his Father with the holy angels.

Mark 8:31–38 NRSV

Throughout the Gospels, again and again, one finds Jesus addressing Peter. And whenever one finds Peter locked in Jesus' gaze, one hears a word directed from Christ specifically to his church:

- In this passage from Mark, after Jesus spells out the meaning of his mission, he says to Peter (and, by extension, to the church): "Get behind me, Satan! For you are setting your mind not on divine things but on human things."
- At the Last Supper, when Jesus prophesies his betrayal and Peter protests, "Though all become deserters, I will not," Jesus says, "Truly I tell you, this day, this very night, before the cock crows twice, you will deny me three times" (Mark 14:29–30 NRSV).
- After Jesus is raised from the dead, he speaks to Peter: "Simon son of John, do you love me more than these?" . . . "Tend my sheep." . . . "Feed my sheep" (John 21:15–17).
- Then, in a personal message regarding "the kind of death by which he [Peter] would glorify God," Jesus says to Peter, "Very truly, I tell you, when you were younger, you used to fasten your own belt and to go wherever you wished. But when you grow old, you will stretch out your hands, and someone else will fasten a belt around you and take you where you do not wish to go" (John 21:18–19 NRSV).

Peter's triumphalism, whether in his unwillingness to embrace the cruciform mission of the Messiah or in his desire to remain on the mount of transfiguration (Luke 9:18–36), prefigures the struggle of the church to define and pursue a mission that allows it to bask in the glow of the world's admiration while also clinging to the message of the crucified God.[45] Lewis's critique of an ecclesiology built on lies and idolatry

---

45. In another context, I have critiqued the anxiety and defeatism that stand at the opposite end of this continuum: M. Jinkins, *The Church Faces Death: Ecclesiology in a Postmodern Context* (New York/Oxford: Oxford University Press, 1999), 8–32.

stings like alcohol on a fresh scrape. "Look at our power and wealth!" so many contemporary churches seem to say. "Witness the numbers of people we attract and the cleverness of our marketing plan! See the greatness of our building programs, so impressive, so solid, so permanent."

Certainly, Lewis notes, the church is not called merely to renounce power. There is nothing particularly righteous about powerlessness. But we are called, in the name of Christ, to renovate power, to find in the cross of Jesus a radically new conception of power—divine power, creative power, resurrected power.[46] The church is given this renovated power by the crucified and risen Christ himself, power to forgive and to serve, to liberate and to create, "that repentance and forgiveness of sins . . . [may] be proclaimed in his name to all nations" (Luke 24:47 NRSV). Perhaps Jesus' prophecy regarding Peter's future—that one would bind his hands and lead him where he would not want to go—does not refer, at least in the first instance, to Peter's physical death at the hands of Rome but to the more immediate consequences of Peter's calling: his death to self and self-directedness, his death to old concepts of God and God's expectations, the death of his understanding of who God would accept into the fellowship of the faithful, and his corresponding resurrection in Christ that allowed God to bind his hands and to lead him in a direction he would never have chosen as he bore witness to Jesus across the ancient world (Acts 10). How else can we explain a Palestinian Jewish fisherman on the streets of cosmopolitan Rome?

A Personal Reflection

Recently, I was involved in a research project on the state of ministry in North America.[47] One of the focus groups I moderated was made up of evangelical pastors from a variety of denominations. When the group was asked to comment on the meaning of "good ministry," their responses were as varied as their experiences, but common themes soon emerged. Repeatedly they said that the essence of "good ministry" lies in the ways that members of a congregation express the love of Christ in their lives. Some pastors placed the emphasis on the Spirit's working through the people of God to show God's love. Other pastors placed the emphasis on the ways in which people lived out the Word of God in serving others in the world. But over and over again they saw ministry as the people's embodying of the presence of Christ in the world for the sake of others.

46. Lewis, "Unmasking Idolatries," 119–20.
47. "Pulpit and Pew: Research on Pastoral Leadership," Jackson W. Carroll, project director, Duke University Divinity School.

Students of Avery Dulles, the Jesuit scholar best known for his classic ecclesiological study *Models of the Church,* might be more than a little surprised by the responses from this group. I certainly was. After all, evangelical pastors are supposed to have a fairly narrow understanding of the church and its mission. Being in the tradition of Protestant revivalism, shouldn't evangelical pastors see the church solely as a "preaching point"? And as such, shouldn't they have a one-dimensional notion of the mission of the church as the "herald" who preaches the Word of God? Indeed, Dulles identifies a variety of theologians (mostly Protestants in the Reformed and evangelical traditions) whose understanding of the church is so limited that they say the church is merely an event, a point of encounter with God, with little or no historical continuity.[48] Yet while these pastors saw preaching as central to the life and ministry of the church, they also saw the mission of the church in a far more complex and holistic manner.

The church, according to these pastors, is called together into what Dulles describes as a "mystical communion," a quality of Christian community that is represented in the German contrast of a *Gemeinschaft* (or *Bruderschaft* or *Personengemeinschaft*) over against a *Gesellschaft.*[49] In other words, the church, as mystical communion, is more a fellowship than an institution, more an extended family than a society. As such, as a fellowship drawn together by the tethers of the Holy Spirit and in response to the Word of God, the church is sent forth into God's

48. Avery Dulles, *Models of the Church* (New York: Doubleday, 1987), 77. While Karl Barth is frequently and justifiably placed by Dulles in this category, largely on the strength of Barth's *Letter to the Romans* (2d ed., 1921), one may also find in Barth's thought a sense of the church as servant. Certainly, he understood, with Calvin, *omnis recta cognito Dei ab oboedientia nascitur* ("true knowledge of God is born out of obedience"). See Karl Barth, *Evangelical Theology,* trans. Grover Foley (Garden City, N.Y.: Doubleday, 1964). The category "The Church as Herald" makes strange bedfellows of Rudolf Bultmann and Billy Graham, again, not without some justification.

49. Ibid., 47–48. Dulles's analysis draws on not only the sociological research that describes the characteristics of "primary groups" (in Charles H. Cooley) but also the theological work of Reformed scholar Emil Brunner in his *Misunderstanding of the Church* (Philadelphia: Westminster, 1953). In this monograph, Brunner writes, "The *Ecclesia* of the New Testament, the fellowship of Christian believers, is precisely *not* that which every 'church' is at least in part—an institution, a something. The Body of Christ is nothing other than a fellowship of persons. It is the 'fellowship of Jesus Christ' or 'fellowship of the Holy Ghost,' where fellowship or *koinōnia* signifies a common participation, a togetherness, a community life. The faithful are bound to each other through their common sharing in Christ and in the Holy Ghost, but that which they have in common is precisely no 'thing,' no 'it,' but a 'he,' Christ and His Holy Spirit. It is just in this that resides the miraculous, the unique, the once-for-all nature of the Church: that as the Body of Christ it has nothing to do with an organization and has nothing of the character of the institutional about it. This is precisely what it has in mind when it describes itself as

world to be a sign and symbol of God's grace and mercy (the church as sacrament) and to serve others selflessly in the Spirit of Christ (the church as servant).[50] For these pastors, there was simply no conflict between the kerygmatic and the sacramental (though the evangelical pastors in the group who were from the free church traditions never used the term *sacramental*), between the symbolic and the service-oriented, between the fellowship-enhancing and the public-embracing aspects of the church's mission. They constitute a seamless garment.

the Body of Christ" (10–11). Brunner elaborates on the connection between God and this mystical communion in the third volume of his *Dogmatics:* "The social form of the Ekklesia was a necessary consequence of their [the first Christians'] faith. For since God had communicated Himself to them in Christ, it followed that they must communicate themselves to each other. From the knowledge of reconciliation, the fellowship which we have with Christ, there followed immediately the 'fellowship which we have among ourselves.' The *agape*, the love of God which was communicated to them through Christ, was now living and present in them and united them to one another. This means that the social character of the Ekklesia resulted from its spiritual character as an association of men through the Holy Spirit, through the love of Christ. And that itself was the structural law of this social entity" (Emil Brunner, *The Christian Doctrine of the Church, Faith, and the Consummation*, vol. 3 of *Dogmatics*, trans. David Cairns and T. H. L. Parker [Philadelphia: Westminster, 1960], 29). Here Brunner manages to argue for an ecclesiology that characterizes the church as a believers' fellowship while avoiding both the voluntaryism and individualism that characterize and threaten most conventional evangelical ecclesiologies, especially in North America.

50. Ibid., 63–102. Dietrich Bonhoeffer is virtually unique among theologians for having argued for four distinct ecclesiological models over the course of his short life: mystical communion, herald, servant, and fellowship of disciples. See Dulles, *Models of the Church*, 48, 94–95, 225. In Bonhoeffer's doctoral dissertation, *Sanctorum Communio: A Theological Study of the Sociology of the Church*, he advances the concept of the church as mystical communion, writing, "The [Christian] community is constituted by the complete self-forgetfulness of love. The relationship between I and thou is no longer essentially a demanding but a giving one." This passage is cited in Dulles, *Models of the Church*, 48. The new critical edition of Bonhoeffer's *Sanctorum Communio* is translated by Reinhard Krauss and Nancy Lukens (Minneapolis: Fortress, 1998). Bonhoeffer's *Life Together* also reflects a sense of the church as mystical communion: "Christian community means community through Jesus Christ and in Jesus Christ. There is no Christian community that is more than this, and none that is less than this. . . . We belong to one another only through and in Jesus Christ" (Bonhoeffer, *Life Together/Prayerbook of the Bible*, trans. Daniel W. Bloesch and James H. Burtness [Minneapolis: Fortress, 1996], 31). Dulles notes that Bonhoeffer, in *Ethics*, "moves toward a more kerygmatic position" (undoubtedly, at least in part under the influence of Barth's thought): "The intention of the preacher . . . is not to improve the world, but to summon it to belief in Jesus Christ and to bear witness to the reconciliation which has been accomplished through Him and His dominion" (Dulles, *Models of the Church*, 94). In his remarkable, posthumously published *Letters and Papers from Prison*, however, Bonhoeffer issues an uncompromising call for the church to serve others in the world (and thus to improve the world): "The Church is the Church only when it exists for others. To make a start, it should give away

Were these pastors just being idealistic and unrealistic when they described good ministry? Is the reality of the church even close to the church they envision theologically? In other words, can the ministry of the congregations these pastors serve pass their own theological polygraph test? No. And yes.

What I mean to say is this: I have found comfort as well as confrontation in a biblical text so familiar that it has almost become a cliché in our cynical culture (almost; the Word of God manifests an astonishing ability to resist even our best efforts at reductionism). Jesus offers a man (Mark 10:17 calls him simply "a man," while Luke 18:18 refers to him as "a certain ruler"; we commonly call him "the rich young ruler") the opportunity to follow him as a disciple. The man appears to be well qualified to be an ideal disciple: righteous and zealous. He is even prosperous. He is a person of some power and influence. This is a person who would certainly be at the top of most "prospect lists" in most Protestant congregations. But when Jesus tells him how much discipleship costs, the man goes away empty.[51]

Jesus, watching this sad young man slip through the crowd, says, "How hard it is for those who have wealth to enter the kingdom of God! Indeed, it is easier for a camel to go through the eye of a needle than for someone who is rich to enter the kingdom of God" (Luke 18:24–25 NRSV). We (especially we preachers) have tried so hard to save the church from Jesus, to make it clear that Jesus did not mean to say what he clearly said. As one pundit put it: For two thousand years we have tried to breed smaller camels and forge larger needles. Trying to spin-

---

all its property to those in need. The clergy must live solely on the free-will offerings of their congregations, or possibly engage in some secular calling. The Church must share in the secular problems of ordinary human life, not dominating, but helping and serving. It must tell men of every calling what it means to live in Christ, to exist for others. In particular, our own church will have to take the field against the vices of *hubris*, power-worship, envy, and humbug, as the roots of all evil. It will have to speak of moderation, purity, trust, loyalty, constancy, patience, discipline, humility, contentment, and modesty. It must not under-estimate the importance of human example (which has its origin in the humanity of Jesus and is so important in Paul's teaching); it is not abstract argument, but example, that gives its word emphasis and power" (Bonhoeffer, *Letters and Papers from Prison*, ed. Eberhard Bethge [New York: Macmillan, 1972], 382–83); Dulles, *Models of the Church*, 94–95, quotes from this larger passage. Finally, in Dulles's revised taxonomy of models, he adds the category of "The Church: Community of Disciples." And, of course, Bonhoeffer, perhaps more eloquently than any other theologian, has spoken of the church as a community of disciples in his *Discipleship*, where he writes, "Whenever Christ calls us, his call leads us to death" (87).

51. One can hardly imagine a better instance to conflate two biblical texts: Mary's song of praise to God, who lifts up the lowly and sends the mighty and the rich away empty (Luke 1:46–55), and this paradigmatic text of discipleship that finds the eager supplicant fade into sadness and slink out of the crowd. Jesus was his mother's boy.

doctor the proverb simply undoes Jesus' own commentary. "Those who heard it said, 'Then who can be saved?' He replied, 'What is impossible for mortals is possible for God'" (Luke 18:26 NRSV). The starkness of the passage is not incidental, and it is definitely not accidental. Jesus apparently meant what he said.

Here's where I find comfort: What is impossible for us is possible for God. That's it! Even the impossible is possible with God.

There is a gap between the church's espoused faith and its practice of faith so big that we could drive a whole herd of camels through it. The church is as hypocritical as any Pharisee of old, as timid of the cost of discipleship (the cost to wealth, power, influence, possession, prestige) as the rich young ruler, as squeamish about associating with those whom our society brands "sinners," as tightfisted in giving away the grace we have so marvelously received, as Judas himself. If we are a sacramental presence among the nations, it is because the world can see among us the living parable of the God whose grace is greater than all our sin. If we are a servant people, it is often because the Spirit shames the church into feeble acts of generosity where great acts of gratitude are called for. But the church's message is not "Behold our goodness!" It is "Behold God's grace!"[52]

A Theological Response

George MacLeod, founder of the Iona Community and surely one of the most prophetic voices of the twentieth century, in his restatement of the church's mission, *Only One Way Left*, wrote:

> "God was in Christ, reconciling the world to Himself, not counting against them their trespasses, and having committed to us the word of reconciliation." That is, if the Cross is first a catharsis, and then an inexpressible comfort, it must have a "contemporaneous," ongoing, consequence. We are to be to others what Christ has become for us. The condition of our continuing conciliation with Him, is that we embark on the same unconditional reconciliation to others as He has extended to us.[53]

Jesus Christ is *missio Dei*. Christ's church, Christ's *ecclesia crucis*, this community of the cross and of the crucified, is bound in Christ to God's mission, a mission to a world that God creates and seeks, re-

---

52. Nigel Biggar, in his superb study of Karl Barth's ethics, argues for the church's primacy as hearer of the Word of God. He writes, "The Word of God establishes among its hearers a fellowship of open and critical dialogue. Accordingly, it is as members of that fellowship that it addresses individuals: 'the Word of God is not spoken to individuals, but to the Church of God and to individuals in the Church'" (Biggar, *The Hastening That Waits: Karl Barth's Ethics* [Oxford: Oxford University Press, 1993], 124).

53. MacLeod, *Only One Way Left*, 35.

deems and reconciles in love. It is God's mission that redefines and radicalizes such terms as *secular* and *sacred;* this world—every part of it down to its very toes—was created by God, belongs to God, and is loved by God. And so MacLeod writes:

> I simply argue that the Cross be raised again at the center of the marketplace as well as on the steeple of the church. I am recovering the claim that Jesus was not crucified in a cathedral between two candles, but on a cross between two thieves; on the town garbage-heap; at a crossroad so cosmopolitan that they had to write his title in Hebrew and in Latin and in Greek (or shall we say in English, in Bantu and in Afrikaans?); at the kind of place where cynics talk smut, and thieves curse, and soldiers gamble. Because that is where He died. And that is what He died about. And that is where churchmen should be and what churchmanship should be about.[54]

Ecclesia crucis is not an enclave of distracted Platonists handing down idealistic pronouncements from on high. Neither is *ecclesia crucis* a company of politicians bartering competing self-interests and ideologies at the altars of *Realpolitik*. *Ecclesia crucis* succeeds in existing in the marketplaces and at the garbage dumps, on crossroads as well as in the small churches and great cathedrals of the world, in the compromised, frailty fraught struggle to trust and obey God—recognizing that the church needs to repent even of its repentance—only by virtue of the fact that its faltering obedience and shabby repentance are judged and graced by the obedience and repentance of Jesus Christ. The ecclesiology of *ecclesia crucis* recognizes, as did Martin Luther, that "there is no greater sinner than the Christian church."[55] As Lutheran theologian Eberhard Jüngel observes:

> Luther does not simply take over the early church's language of *casta meretrix* (pure harlot). For although this tradition had stated that "the Church is made up of sinners" whose "great prayers are the prayers of sinners: 'Forgive us our trespasses.' . . . Sin is in the Church, contagious and ineradicable, like the weeds in the field that are forever obstinately encroaching": nevertheless it saw itself as "a continuation of Christ and so as a source of holiness and therefore as faultless."[56]

This paradox, this dialectic, this tension coheres to the church and gives the church the gift of its peculiar message to the world and of its distinctive mission to the world in the name of Jesus. This dialectic is

---

54. Ibid., 38.
55. Quoted in Eberhard Jüngel, *Theological Essays*, trans. J. B. Webster (Edinburgh: T & T Clark, 1989), 211.
56. Eberhard Jüngel, *Theological Essays*, trans. J. B. Webster (Edinburgh: T & T Clark, 1989), "The Church as Sacrament?" 211.

irresolvable. The presence of the Holy Spirit (true God of true God) in the church does not eradicate the dialectic or resolve this tension.[57] The Paraclete, the Comforter, speaks forgiveness, but the breath of God is not identical to the breath of the church, nor the Word of God to the words of the church. Creator remains Creator; creature remains creature. We have this treasure in a clay pot. So Jüngel continues:

> According to the insights of the reformers, on the other hand, the union
> of the church and its Lord, understood by analogy from the soul's mar-

57. I have in mind a concern with the ecclesiology of Reinhold Hütter, *Suffering Divine Things: Theology as Church Practice* (Grand Rapids: Eerdmans, 2000), 107–10, which in his rejection of the role of dialectics in speech about God stands in real danger of lapsing into a kind of absoluteness about the church's theological language that is, at least potentially, idolatrous. Hütter's rejection of the dialectical theology of Karl Barth seems to imply that the church can somehow preempt the freedom of God in its speech about God. He writes, "Because Barth ascribes no unique work of any concretion or duration to the Holy Spirit, eschatology must become the outstanding epiphany of the 'empty' place that through conscious reproduction of absence creates a kind of presence. But precisely this is the fulcral point: The work of the Holy Spirit does not leave this place empty. It is always 'salutarily' occupied in word and sacrament. . . . As Christ's Spirit, it is Christ's consoling presence, one that generates faith even though it is not yet 'seeing,' and one that nonetheless assures the reliability of the *vita passiva* and relieves theology of dialectics, if not *peregrinatio*. Christ's 'place' is thus never really empty. Rather, it is occupied unequivocally by Christ in the Holy Spirit, with an unequivocalness that itself is the ground of faith such that theology, too, can be engaged with the unequivocalness of faith (albeit not with the unequivocalness of eschatological perception, but neither with the equivocalness of a dialectic that must also behave as if God takes with one hand what he gives with the other)" (107–8). He seems to assume that if Christ is present, there is no need for dialectical language about God. If this is accurate, his theology would be consistent with the view that plurality, diversity, and conflict are evidence not of richness but of failure and untruth. Barth's dialectical approach to the knowledge of God reminds us, however, that even God's name consists in God's refusal to be named. To say this is not an admission of failure but a celebration of the freedom of God and the mystery of God. If Barth is correct, it would be perilous indeed to attempt to move from the reality of God as the ground of faith to the unequivocality of human faith and a corresponding unequivocality of human speech about God. Does such a move, if Barth is correct, not risk precisely a transgression of the first commandment, a confusion of that which is human with that which is God? This seems to have been Barth's concern. Again, and perhaps even more fundamentally, is not such a confusion of unequivocality with the reality of God's revelation already a move toward idolatry? Again, this seems to have been Barth's concern, and it is a concern that presses us toward a more complex understanding of God and a more pluralistic conception of the world than that which Hütter understands. See Karl Barth, *Church Dogmatics*, ed. G. W. Bromiley and T. F. Torrance, trans. G. W. Bromiley (Edinburgh: T & T Clark, 1957), II.1.60–61. See also Cynthia Rigby, "On Earth as It Is in Heaven: Toward a Reformed and Feminist Eschatology by Way of the Ascended Christ" (paper presented at *"Eskatologi og den teologiske diskurs,"* sponsored by the theological faculties of the Universities of Copenhagen, Aarhus, and Lundt, Karreb-ksminde, Denmark, 16–19 May 2000).

riage to Christ, and the holiness which flows from that union, must lead the church to understand itself as *peccatrix maxima* (the greatest sinner), and thus—to put the matter with Luther's phrase summing up the intention of the Epistle to the Romans—to "magnify" sin. It is precisely through the church's understanding of itself as *peccatrix maxima* that the intimate relation between church and Jesus Christ is expressed. And thereby Jesus Christ is taken seriously as the Son of God who in his holiness is not simply concerned with "his own person" but with "all sinners" so that in the power of his holiness he became "a sinner of sinners." His holiness, because it is a holiness which takes pity on sinners, makes him into the *peccator peccatorum* (sinner of sinners) *in their place;* the holiness of the church, on the other hand, leads it to recognize itself as *peccatrix maxima*. As the *peccator peccatorum*, Christ is holy because he wipes away our sins, whereas as *peccatrix maxima* the holy church remains ever dependent upon the fact that its sins have been wiped away. He is the sacrament which the church receives, to which the church can only testify and which the church must hand on as a recipient. And so prayer for the forgiveness of its own sins is the criterion by which we decide whether, in representing and presenting the sacramental event, "mother church" understands itself *secundum dicentem deum* or whether it misunderstands itself as self-representation.[58]

The gift of the church, then, is none other than Jesus Christ, in whom the church receives all the riches of God's grace. God's gift of Jesus Christ to the church is identical to God's gift to the world. But the church, in the power of the Spirit, is also God's gift to the world because the church is the body of Christ, of whom Christ himself is head. The church embraces its identity and pursues the *missio Dei* inasmuch as and precisely to the extent that the church bears witness in its life to the grace of God in Christ and lives (as George MacLeod said) to be to others what Christ has been to the world.

The church, *ecclesia crucis*, because it knows itself to be the community of the crucified, knows itself to be *peccatrix maxima*. This community is baptized into the crucified God, and the life to which the church is raised is a crucified life. The church, indeed, understands itself properly and in an appropriately theological sense (as opposed to merely as an expression of its morbidity or neuroses) as *peccatrix maxima* only because it is the community who has found itself, has located itself, in the crucified God, and has found in Christ the humanity for which it was created and the vocation to which it is called.

The church's holiness is real but derived holiness. Its purity is authentic but not its own. The church's righteousness, as much as its unity,

58. Jüngel, *Theological Essays*, 211.

lies not in anything the church believes, hopes, or does but in Jesus Christ alone, who is the righteousness of God for us.[59] All the church possesses, even the faith by which it holds fast to Jesus Christ and through which it "possesses" all the riches of Christ, it holds in and through Christ, who, as the pioneer and finisher of our faith, has the faith we need *on our behalf*. *Missio Dei* is the church's mission, and the church pursues this mission in the world as it takes its rest in and entrusts itself in all it does to the grace of God crucified.[60]

59. Luther's understanding of Christ's possession of all that is required of us is especially powerful when we reflect on this teaching ecclesiologically. See E. P. Rupp and Benjamin Drewery, eds., *Martin Luther* (London: Edward Arnold, 1970), a collection of seminal texts from Luther's writings: "At last," Luther wrote in 1545, remembering his own evangelical breakthrough, "as I meditated day and night, God showed mercy and I turned my attention to the connection of the words, namely—'The righteousness of God is revealed, as it is written: the righteous shall live by faith'—and there I began to understand that the righteousness of God is the righteousness in which a just man lives by the gift of God, in other words by faith, and that what Paul means is this: the righteousness of God, revealed in the Gospel, is *passive*, in other words that by which the merciful God justifies us through faith. . . . There and then the whole face of scripture was changed; I ran through the scriptures as memory served, and collected the same analogy in other words, for example *opus Dei*, that which God works in us; *virtus Dei*, that by which God makes us strong; *sapientia Dei*, that by which He makes us wise; *fortitudo Dei, salus Dei, Gloria Dei*" (6). Luther here parallels Calvin's conviction that all parts of our salvation are complete in Jesus Christ, a theological insight that, when applied ecclesiologically, invites us to reconceptualize membership in the church in terms of membership in Christ, our union with Christ being understood as both the ground of our union with one another and that by which we receive all we need. In a letter to Melanchthon (dated August 1, 1521), Luther writes, "If you are a preacher of grace, then preach grace that is true and not fictitious. . . . God does not save fictitious sinners. . . . We must sin as long as we are here; this life is not the dwelling-place of righteousness, but as Peter says [2 Peter 3:13] we look for new heavens and a new earth, in which righteousness dwells. It suffices that through the riches of God's glory we have come to know the Lamb that takes away the sin of the world; sin will not tear us away from him" (73). These streams of thought converged in an even earlier letter to George Spenlein (dated April 7, 1516), in which Luther writes, "Beware, my brothers, at aiming at a purity which rebels against being classed with sinners. For Christ only dwells among sinners. . . . Therefore thou wilt only find peace in him when thou despairest of self and thine own works. He himself will teach thee how in receiving thee he makes thy sins his, and his righteousness thine" (8).

60. George Hunsberger's reflections are especially instructive when he observes, "An individualist Christian identity is foreign to the Scriptures. If, for evangelicalism, Christian faith and identity are first personal and individual, its sense of missions tends to be the same. The responsibility to give witness to Christ is one each person bears. The accent rests on personal evangelism, therefore. Any sense of a church's mission grows from this ground. It is the aggregate of the individual callings to be witnesses. Identity and missions are first and foremost individual matters. Missions is not conceived to be first of all the 'mission of the church,' to which every member is joined" ("Evangelical Conversion toward a Missional Ecclesiology"). His challenge to evangelicalism is both timely and critical to the future of the evangelical movement if it is to embrace a more thought-

Closing Reflections on the Discipleship of the Church

This essay opened by recalling a confessional statement from the Reformed tradition that Heinrich Bullinger wrote in the sixteenth century. It will close by reflecting again on this confession, not because it is the finest or the fullest ecclesiological statement in existence but simply because it communicates so clearly the church's unique role in God's mission of creative love and redemption on behalf of the world.

"The Church has always existed, and it will always exist," wrote Bullinger. "Because God from the beginning would have humankind saved and to come to the knowledge of the truth (1 Tim. 2:4), it is altogether necessary that there always should have been, and should be now, and to the end of the world, a Church." This statement reflects the source and purpose of the mission for which God sustains the church. This statement also indicates that the church is the object of God's power to create, sustain, and resurrect.

The church exists in the history of the world for the sake of *missio Dei*, and for no other reason. God's eternal love is the source of God's mission. Indeed, God's mission is the incarnation of God's love. The character of this mission is revealed *in our humanity* in the life, death, and resurrection of Jesus of Nazareth. God's mission cannot be undone by the church's failures. Frail creature of dust, and feeble as frail the church may well be, but it is specifically this church, *peccatrix maxima*, "the greatest of sinners," that Christ calls to take up its cross and follow him.[61] The church is called to discipleship by and in and through Jesus Christ. The unconditional ground of the discipleship of every disciple of Christ is this calling of the whole church to live into its identity as *ecclesia crucis*. As Bonhoeffer has taught us, whenever Christ calls someone, Christ bids that one come and die. This is true even if that one whom Christ calls and bids to come and die is the one, holy, catholic, and apostolic church.

The church that follows Jesus Christ always runs the risk of dying. Bullinger indicates that the church will always exist. Yet this does not mean that the church survives from age to age. The church's adaptability, the church's resourcefulness, the church's capacity to respond to new challenges may be institutionally important. But none of this is indicated in Bullinger's confessional statement. The church does not merely survive. The church lives, suffers, and dies following its Lord,

---

ful ecclesiology, to recover the biblical sense of the corporate as that which is fundamental to and gives rise to the personal.

61. The allusion is to Robert Grant's 1833 hymn, "O Worship the King, All Glorious Above!" The text of the hymn, of course, actually reads, "Frail children of dust, and feeble as frail."

whose entire life is summarized in the Apostles' Creed with those terse phrases "born of the virgin Mary, suffered under Pontius Pilate, was crucified, dead, and buried." The church bears its cross for the sake of Christ and his gospel over and over again in history. And God raises the church from the dead to new life in Christ repeatedly. This is what it means to say that the church will always exist. It is not a statement of confidence in the church's resources, because the church we can save, the church that survives, is not the *ecclesia crucis,* the church of the crucified Christ. Nor, even less, is it a statement of reliance on an inevitable, mechanical historical process. To say that the church will always exist is to confess (and to confess radically) our trust in God's faithfulness. This must be stated unambiguously in the face of an age in which some churches sink into the morose swamp of despondence and thrash about in despair over declining numbers and shrinking budgets, ready and willing to try *anything* if it will promise survival. This must also be said in the face of an age in which other churches thrive and grow but may be tempted to confuse their numerical and financial success with faithfulness or may altogether misplace their confidence in the shoddy idolatry of ecclesiastical triumphalism and the harlotry of the marketplace.

The church is not called to jealously guard its privileges or to greedily cling to its existence. Paradoxically, the church is always most winsome and attractive precisely when it runs the ultimate risk, when, unconcerned with institutional survival, it holds mere creaturely existence lightly enough to hold to the cross of Jesus more firmly and to entrust its life to the God and Father of our Lord Jesus Christ who alone has the power to raise even the church from the dead and to give it the risen life that is the only life worth having.

Part 4
Responses

8

Low-Church and Proud

PAUL F. M. ZAHL

As an evangelical and Protestant Episcopalian, I wonder about the attraction that high-church ecclesiologies have for many of my evangelical sisters and brothers on the free church side. It is a strange feeling to observe the magnetic attraction that sacramental catholicism has for many in the evangelical community in North America. It is especially strange when one has been fighting a defensive action for thirty years against a triumphant "liberal catholicism" in the Episcopal Church (ECUSA). By "liberal catholicism" I mean a version of Christianity that is catholic superficially—i.e., it *looks* catholic—but liberal ethically and theologically—i.e., long on modernity and pluriformity but short on the Bible.

It is disturbing, in other words, when Bible conservatives fall for chasubles, smells, and hierarchy. It seems like a reaction to something that was missing or kinked in childhood, a compensation to make up for an earlier loss. I am just a little too skeptical of forms and (endlessly revised) prayer books and bishops and words such as *unity* and *semper.* When the Canterbury Trail started being forged in the 1970s, I wanted to put my hand up and say, "Been there. Done that. It's not what you think. It's form without substance, *Schein* without *Sein.* All that glitters is not gold."

213

I used to say, in cautioning evangelical Christians who were compulsively attracted—or so it seemed—to high-church ecclesiology, "If this is what you really want, why not go all the way? Why not convert to the Church of Rome? Pull a Cardinal Newman. Be consistent. Go all the way." Many have done so, in fact. Many have "poped," as we used to say. Many, however, have not. Many are still standing on the brink, seeking to "force" Anglicanism and Lutheranism and even variants of Orthodoxy to be both evangelical *and* catholic.

For myself, both a systematic theologian by training and an Episcopal cathedral dean by day, I cannot be both. I cannot be Protestant *and* Catholic. I cannot be evangelical *and* ecclesiologically "high." A house divided cannot stand. It has to fall. It always does.

All this is to say that Roger E. Olson's essay is a breath of fresh air for all evangelicals who are thinking about "church." It is Olson's essay that I wish to affirm and perhaps even extend. Again, I write as an Episcopalian who is okay with labels: low-church, Protestant, and evangelical, with a pinch of charismatic.

Evangelical Christianity is by nature low-church. This is because, for evangelicals, "ecclesiology and especially polity are secondary to the gospel itself" (Olson). I don't see how this axiom can be denied. The gospel message of the forgiveness of sins and the new being in Christ is addressed, in every case at the start, to an individual. No one *hears* collectively. It just doesn't happen. As a parish minister for thirty years, I have never met a person who actually hears collectively. We hear individually, at least in the first instance. Of course, I observe that Christian people in their growing integration of heart, mind, and especially will often come to appreciate social and political notes in the sound. But given the pain and losses and crimes of the heart, people hear the Word as a word to them individually. So right off the bat, our approach to a listener cannot be ecclesiological.

Moreover, the sanctifying Word is, for Reformation Anglicans and Lutherans, at least, the justifying Word addressed to new areas of our sinfulness—the unevangelized dark continents of the human heart. The sanctifying Word is heard primarily as a word to inhering, continuing sin. Because we are always in this life both saved and sinner, loved and human, the conflicts within our character and temperament require a concrete, specific word.

In short, we are not addressed collectively by the gospel. Only people do that—people who are thinking abstractly or who see us in categories.

Olson understands what more and more evangelical Anglicans are beginning to wake up to. When our high-church brothers and sisters chastise us for having no ecclesiology, the right response is, "We have an ecclesiology, but it is not your ecclesiology. We have a low ecclesiology. We have a high Christology and a high soteriology but a *low* ecclesiology. Why should we feel defensive about that? Ecclesiology is important, yes. It is certainly interesting. But it is not saving. If you think ecclesiology is saving, then become a Roman Catholic. Don't become an Episcopalian. Don't become a high-church anything unless you wish to swallow the whole loaf: Become a Roman Catholic." The Canterbury Trail is a schizoid path to walk. I would be surprised if many of the free church evangelicals who have walked it will still be on it by 2020.

My axiom is: "Evangelical" has to be translated, among other things, as low-church. This is the core point of Olson's essay: "The free church tradition regards itself as *consistent Protestantism*" (Olson's emphasis).

The other essays in this book are all tied into this issue. Are evangelicals consistently free church in polity, or is the trend to ecclesiology a necessary correction?

Bruce Hindmarsh confirms Olson's view and argues that "early modern evangelicalism displayed an unprecedented transdenominational and international ecclesial consciousness that was characterized by an unparalleled subordination of church order to evangelical piety." How can the facts of history be interpreted otherwise? What Hindmarsh observes did actually happen. It happens today. *Christianity* breaks down the barriers and reduces all churchmanships to secondary status.

Howard A. Snyder's piece is interesting and narrative, but is it correct? Is it correct that the four classical marks of the church are *una, sancta, catholica,* and *apostolica?* Not according to the Reformation understanding, as also expressed in the Anglican Thirty-nine Articles. There we read that the marks of the church are its preaching of the pure Word of God and the faithful administration of the two sacraments. The Reformed add a third note: church discipline. But these are not the four so-called classics. They, the four Latin adjectives, only got the church into the apostate mess it was in. So Snyder's paradigm is flawed, at least to me.

George R. Hunsberger's pumping for missional ecclesiology is great. It may be "one note," but what a true and right note it is!

Edith M. Humphrey's and Kerry L. Dearborn's pieces hit a different note. I believe I understand where Humphrey is coming from and do wish that her sacramental aspirations for the Christian, and also the evangelical Christian, church could be achieved within Anglicanism. But I doubt it. Evangelical people who respond to the Episcopal Church's apparent objectivity and verticality are responding to something proper and biblical. But a closer look—and I know it well—discloses not consistent catholicism but rather liberal catholicism. And liberal catholicism rarely satisfies, because it is a construct for people to have their cake and eat it too. Liberal catholicism cannot stand. Liberal views of authority and Scripture and cultural rapprochement do not finally cohere with a historic, catholic view of the church. The Church of Rome's history renders this point beyond dispute. So Humphrey wants Anglicanism to be something it cannot be. Just spend some time, any amount of time, serving within a conventional Episcopal diocese, at least in North America. Bible-anchored evangelicals are bound to be disappointed. I can almost guarantee that.

While Humphrey writes with high hopes, which I admire, Dearborn's essay is a fully realized abstraction. Only this essay, of all the essays, seems to be coming from an unreal world. Celtic spirituality is a notorious wax nose! Why is that? Because no one really knows anything absolutely verifiable about it. The sources for Celtic Christianity are extremely limited. A great deal of what we think Celtic Christians felt and taught and prayed are figments of nineteenth-century imagination. Yes, there are some elements in the archaeological record that seem to bear comparison with New Age thinking, yin/yang, complementarity and "weavings," nonhierarchical views of women and men, and so on. But I know the Irish! St. Patrick himself was a wild man. He was a wonderful wild man. And he was also devastating, iconoclastic, and polemical. Dearborn is making much more of Celtic spirituality than the actual sources admit. I know this pattern. It has happened for almost a century now within the liturgical movement in respect to Hippolytus. Everyone cites Hippolytus. The fact is that the Hippolytus source is weak and thin and very possibly heretical. Please don't base an ecclesiology on the slim pickings of Celtic spirituality. A little *orange*, please!

I wish I could have been physically present at the Regent College ecclesiology conference. I wish I could have been there, even as a conflicted but more or less lifelong Episcopalian, to applaud Roger Olson. The point is, too much ecclesiology always turns to Christology-lite, soteriology-lite, gospel-lite. I wish to resist that.

9

Reimagining the Church

Evangelical Ecclesiology

RICHARD BEATON

The turn of the millennium has witnessed a renewed interest in ecclesiology. The collection of essays in this volume addresses the topic of an evangelical ecclesiology, if there is such a thing, and discusses many of the salient issues related to the history and popular notions of ecclesiology among evangelicals. This is a fascinating venture because it is becoming increasingly apparent that evangelicalism is in the throes of an identity crisis, and at the heart of this crisis is a lack of clarity concerning the nature and function of the church. It seems far from clear that a well-considered ecclesiology does indeed lie at the center of the movement and, even if it does, that this ecclesiology is robust enough to withstand the global forces that challenge it today.

Bruce Hindmarsh's fine essay, "Is Evangelical Ecclesiology an Oxymoron?" surveys the historical background and identifies several key ideas that provide a starting point for the discussion. Evangelicalism is an international, transdenominational movement unified by subordinating church order to piety. Not surprisingly, therefore, some within the movement have long maintained that evangelicals alone constitute the true church. Others are more generous in their understanding, holding that they comprise a segment of the mystical church or an *ecclesiola in ecclesia*. The separatist mind-set, which has been integral to evangelicalism almost from its inception, retains such a strong influence that one wonders how pervasively it shapes evangelical theological discussion. Furthermore, a personal testimony of one's conversion and an individual experience of grace have become hallmarks of the movement. Closely tied to a prominent pietistic element, such emphases lead to the frequently made assertion that the evangelical movement is as much an ethos as a commitment to various doctrines. Although this emphasis on personal responsibility in issues of faith continues to be a strength of the movement, the various individualistic influences of modernity and postmodernity threaten to push it in a direction away from historic Christianity.

It may be, then, that what are often considered essential characteristics and strengths of the evangelical ethos could become its Achilles' heel. While evangelicalism has certainly capitalized on its proximity to modern culture, the discussion of evangelical ecclesiology in this volume points to the difficulties this can create. The continued isolation of the autonomous individual witnessed by both modernity and postmodernity has had a particularly potent impact—both positive and negative—on the evangelical conception of the church. One example of this, which is lamented in almost all the essays in this volume, is the dilemma of division and even fragmentation. While division has posed a danger to the church (see in particular Paul's Corinthian correspondence), a culture that stresses the autonomy of the individual to the degree that Western culture currently does can only aggravate the problem. While the evangelical emphasis on personal testimony, experience of grace, and pietism may have tempered the predominantly corporate outlook of previous generations, its potential to contribute further to the fragmentation within postmodern culture must be addressed. The frequently commented on elevation of individual spirituality over institutional religion is just one symptom of a more serious illness.

One way into the problem is to appeal to the ancient creedal formulations of the church for help. The Nicene Creed's "one, holy, catholic, apostolic church" provides a straightedge by which to measure the alignment of our present notions about the church. This is the starting point for Edith M. Humphrey's challenge and trenchant critique of the current state of affairs in evangelicalism. Her nuanced discussions of unity, the corporate nature of the church, and hierarchy are particularly helpful, especially if, as Hindmarsh observes, piety has indeed subordinated church order. Humphrey points to what is the essential issue for evangelicals, namely, the nature of the church. We must answer the related questions What is the church? and Where is the church? Arriving at a conclusion is no simple task.

Marketing experts affirm that an advertisement's message ought to spring from the core identity of the organization being advertised. If one were to apply this strategy to the church today, one might come away somewhat confused. What, after all, is the church? Is it a loose fellowship of autonomous individuals? Is it missional, seeker sensitive, purpose driven, or worship driven? Is it an organization that is primarily concerned with issues of social justice or with the salvation of souls? Numerous models of a core identity and message face believers today. What is often left unconsidered is that these overarching models, or metaphors, have the power to shape and transform. They are not mere descriptors; rather, they articulate who we are and even have the power to shape identity. If this is the case, then it is imperative to select the right model. So how do we choose among the often competing models? Which is the most appropriate or accurate? It is perhaps at this point that a reconsideration of the primary metaphors used in the New Testament to describe the church is appropriate. These may be especially useful because each one presents us with an image that probes the nature and function of the church, and they may uniquely allow us to see beyond the present confines of our ecclesiological understanding.

The New Testament authors employed various metaphors in their attempts to describe what we now call the church. These would include, for example, the people of God, the household of God, the body of Christ, the bride of Christ, a holy nation, the saints, and a city of light. Unfortunately, for the twenty-first-century audience, these metaphors have often been reduced to clichés by vain repetition. Additionally, by treating these metaphors as mere images, some interpreters have robbed them of their power. Since research of the past half century has debunked the assumption that one can fully express the ideas latent in a metaphor through "plain speech," metaphors are now commonly understood as inherently complex entities that associate two apparently unrelated subjects. This novel association creates new possibilities of meaning and offers in a few words what would otherwise take many. Perhaps most importantly, metaphors have the power to transform the listener, much in the same way as parables do. A classic example is the phrase "Argument is war." After one considers this metaphor, it is difficult to conceive of argumentation in quite the same way as before. Likewise, biblical metaphors are more than mere images. They encapsulate a social and theological world, but it is a world that needs to be unpacked for a twenty-first-century audience if we seek to unleash their power to shape and transform. The image of "the people of God" is one that, due to its elasticity and breadth, may help the church as it undergoes today's cultural shifts and global expansion.

The metaphor of the people of God presents us with a conceptual world in continuity with Jewish conceptions of a people of God that challenges the individualism and temporal isolation of postmodernity and embraces the language of unity and catholicity found in the Nicene Creed. Of course, the people of God is a designation that derives from the Old Testament (Deut. 26:17–18; 32:9; Hosea 2:23) and expresses God's choice of a people to bear his name and be his own. To understand the metaphor, one must be aware of the narrative of this people, their interaction with God and the surrounding peoples. The narrative presents us with a metanarrative that shaped each person's individual narrative. The New Testament witness is to a God who seeks to redeem a people (Matt. 1:21). Like the Old Testament usage, it is a corporate image that is difficult to conceive of in an individualistic manner. First Peter 2:9–10 (NRSV) presents us with as much:

> But you are a chosen race, a royal priesthood, a holy nation, God's own people, in order that you may proclaim the mighty acts of him who called you out of darkness into his marvelous light. Once you were not a people, but now you are God's people; once you had not received mercy, but now you have received mercy.

This powerful passage identifies a people that is God's own, a people redeemed. Two points are worth making in the present context. First, the people are intimately related to God.[1] However else we choose to define our ecclesiology, this must remain at the forefront.[2] Second, in constructing his argument, the author of 1 Peter draws on the rich Old Testament themes that further define and clarify this people (Exod. 19:5–6; Isa. 43:20–21; Hosea 2:23). These passages emphasize the corporate, social aspects of belonging to this people. One thing is clear: The biblical text does not refer to a loose collection of autonomous individuals.[3] Instead, it implies that there is a distinct corporate aspect to

---

1. The metaphor of the bride of Christ, a subtle but key New Testament image, explores in greater depth the mystical intimacy of the corporate people with their God.

2. See, for example, Miroslav Volf, *After Our Likeness: The Church as the Image of the Trinity* (Grand Rapids: Eerdmans, 1998).

3. It is lamentable, for example, that the concept of the priesthood of all believers, which is in Luther a corporate notion, has been reduced and diminished in a highly individualized world. (I am grateful to my colleague John Thompson for pointing this out to me.)

the identity of this people, that in some profound way they differ from the nations surrounding them. In other words, this group of people is related not only to God; the members are also related to one another. This concept seems particularly difficult for highly individualized Westerners to comprehend. An imperfect analogy to the biblical idea might involve one of the many ethnic communities in Los Angeles in which one finds a distinct society of people with their own food, language, and social world. This differs from a stadium filled with fifty thousand people. The first involves a people with a unique identity and relationship; the latter consists of a grouping of individuals gathered to observe a specific event.

Essential to the New Testament metaphor of people of God is an eschatological framework that places the present in the context of the past and the future. As opposed to postmodernity, which rejects any sense of memory and historical continuity,[4] the concept of the people of God can be understood only in light of the past (both Israel's history and the work God accomplished through Christ) and the future (the final consummation of the ages and eternal life). It dares to offer and assume a metanarrative of God's actions in history. One might also add the important qualifier that, in this new age, the New Testament authors present the Spirit as the defining marker of the newly constituted people of God (Romans 8). Thus, this people is shaped by the narrative past of the people of God, the present experience of the Spirit, and the future expectations of God's redemptive purposes for creation.

A related point concerns the notion of entrance into the people of God. As George R. Hunsberger noted in his essay ("Evangelical Conversion toward a Missional Ecclesiology"), the problem with the current model lies in part with a facile understanding of the gospel and the personal psychological model of conversion prominent among evangelicals today. To this one might add that the personal narratives that mark an individual's momentary experience are also potentially isolating. When one becomes a member of the people of God, the emphasis is not so much on a personal narrative (or even the rehearsal of individual conversion narratives) as on the fact that an individual has been incorporated into God's people. Thus, an individual's narrative is but one element of the overarching narrative of this people. Hunsberger's argument that the whole people of God needs to live as a community with a purpose lies in continuity with both the Old and the New Testament presentations. To suggest otherwise would have seemed strange to the biblical world. This is a moment in which a rearticulation of the meta-

---

4. David Harvey, *The Condition of Postmodernity: An Enquiry into the Origins of Cultural Change* (Oxford: Blackwell, 1990), 39–65.

phor of the people of God could help the church realign its perspective not only on what it means to be a community with a purpose but also on the broader implications of conversion and salvation within God's purposes for his people (see the earlier volume in this series, *What Does It Mean to Be Saved?*)[5] and the relationship of this people to the surrounding culture.

An insight by the Canadian media studies doyen Marshall McLuhan is worth considering at this point. His well-known phrase "the medium is the message" opens up another vista when applied to the church. If the church is the *medium* through which God seeks in part to reveal himself to the world, the effects of the gospel on and within the church become part of the *message*. McLuhan's point is that the message is shaped in part by the medium, and thus the medium itself becomes the message. In this context, then, the discussion concerning the nature of the church becomes crucial, if only because how one conceives of the nature of the church permeates and shapes one's understanding of the functions of the church and, ultimately, the gospel itself. For example, if the church is viewed as a triumphant army in Christ, such a concept will inevitably influence the music, worship, prayers, architecture, art, attitude toward outsiders and the broader culture, and even polity and order. Furthermore, because it also influences the way in which the church presents itself and the gospel to the world, it cannot but influence the way the church is perceived by outsiders. Similarly, if the church is viewed as a community of justified and redeemed sinners, it will take on differing attributes. If we take McLuhan seriously, the church is the primary medium for God's message and purposes in the world. The message to the world (Hunsberger's missional church) cannot but be shaped by this medium. This is why Paul, for example, is so concerned about protecting the gospel. And we ought to be concerned about the overarching metaphors we use to describe ourselves. They have the power to shape and change the medium, which is indeed the message.

The evangelical movement has already had a profound impact on the history of Christianity and its self-understanding. Nevertheless, there is something odd about a discussion of ecclesiology from within what is very much a subset of broader Christendom. One might have thought that the horse belongs in front of the cart: A consideration of the essential elements of ecclesiology would precede reflection on the various commitments of evangelicalism. This seems an important distinction given the vigorous growth of the church in non-Western con-

5. John G. Stackhouse, Jr., ed., *What Does It Mean to Be Saved? Broadening Evangelical Horizons of Salvation* (Grand Rapids: Baker, 2002).

texts and the tectonic cultural shifts in the Western world. The challenge is to articulate an ecclesiology that seeks to be as catholic as possible while maintaining what it means to be truly evangelical. The essays in this volume certainly assist in that exercise and attest to the existence of an ecclesial consciousness. But if the church is to reimagine what an ecclesiology might look like in the twenty-first century, it seems that part of that exercise will require a return to the biblical metaphors that have contributed to the structuring of the identity of the church throughout its history.

Subject Index

Scripture Index

231